MAGIC
MONEY

MAGIC MONEY

THE RISE OF CRYPTO DEGENS, RUG PULLS, AND A DIGITAL REVOLUTION

ANDREW LUNARDI

First published in Australia in 2024

by Andrew Lunardi

Copyright © 2024 by Andrew Lunardi. All rights reserved.

Print ISBN: 978-1-7637015-0-2

Ebook ISBN: 978-1-7637015-1-9

Cover design: Josh Durham

Formatting: coeurdelion.com.au

A catalogue record for this book is available from the National Library of Australia

PRAISE FOR *MAGIC MONEY*

"Andrew Lunardi offers a damning portrayal of the greed of developers and naivety of investors partaking in fatally flawed cryptocurrency schemes that flourished during the pandemic years. He recalls the pump and dumps, rug pulls, and hard luck stories such as the Welshman who still can't access his $450m bitcoin fortune without its password. He recounts Dogecoin under Elon Musk, the multi-billion dollar wipeout of the stablecoin Terra, the dramatic fall of mercurial investor Sam Bankman-Fried, and explains how 2 percent of the Philippines population made a living by playing the crypto-fuelled game Axie Infinity. Yet Lunardi remains confident that cryptocurrencies and blockchain will work for mankind's betterment, despite the greed and scamming."

– Chris Griffith, Technology Journalist

ABOUT THE AUTHOR

Andrew Lunardi is the Head of Chain Adoption at Immutable (as at the time of publication), a crypto gaming platform based in Australia. He was previously a lawyer at Allens, specialising in Banking & Finance, and Mergers & Acquisitions. He also worked at Boston Consulting Group as a management consultant. He has an academic publication on cryptocurrency, titled "Finance v2.0 – An Analysis of the Impact of Blockchain, Smart Contracts and Extensible Markup Language on Debt Capital Markets in Australia." The publication appears in the *Journal of Banking and Finance Law and Practice* 30, no. 4, (Dec 2019): 297-317.

He holds a Bachelor of Commerce from the University of Melbourne, a Juris Doctor from the University of Melbourne, and a Master of Science in Law and Finance from the University of Oxford. He lives in Melbourne, Australia.

Keep in touch with Andrew on X: https://x.com/cryptonardez and through https://andrewlunardi.com/.

CONTENTS

INTRODUCTION

The Beginning

It's 2 am. I'm lying in bed with my laptop open, doom-scrolling Reddit about the news of yet another COVID-19 pandemic lockdown.

I open the website "Poocoin" (yes, that is an actual website) and scroll to the new listings section. As I trawl through the names of new cryptocurrencies, one piques my interest. "Morty" coin. A new season of the popular animated show *Rick and Morty* has been airing, meaning Morty coin may have some solid meme potential. In my lockdown boredom, I decide to buy $5,000 of Morty coins – exchanging my actual money for this new "Magic Money."

I switch back to reading about the latest lockdown news. My hometown of Melbourne, Australia, had just entered its fifth COVID-19 lockdown (receiving the dubious honor of being the most locked-down city in the world). Eventually, I turn back to the price charts of the Morty coin on Poocoin. My heart skips a beat. I see a stream of green on the screen. The price is pumping.

I'd doubled my money in less than five minutes. Should I sell? No, I think to myself – this could go to the moon – a repeat of Dogecoin, the original crypto "meme coin" that, with the help of the eccentric billionaire Elon Musk (CEO of Tesla, SpaceX, and owner of X), skyrocketed in value. Dogecoin was created in 2013 to make fun of cryptocurrency; satire that at one stage elevated it to the seventh most popular cryptocurrency.

Another ten minutes pass, and I'm up five times (or 5x, in crypto lingo) on my investment. I'm a genius. Just imagine what I can do with this money if Morty goes 10x from here. But why stop there? What happens if it goes 100x or 1,000x? This occurs in crypto markets all the time – the controversial crypto token with no purpose, SafeMoon, increased 20,000x from its initial price in under a few months in 2021.

My only regret now is that I didn't put more money in.

I start to think about what kind of car I would buy with all the money I was going to make. A Ferrari or Lamborghini would be nice, although I do really like Tesla. My thoughts are interrupted by a flash of red on the screen. The price has started to drop. Just a healthy dip, I think – a great opportunity to buy in before the price rises again.

More red on my screen.

I'm back to 2x my investment. No need to panic – still in the green.

Suddenly, it's a sea of red.

I frantically try to sell out. I put my sell order in, but it's too late. The price has crashed to zero. In the space of 30 minutes from the launch of Morty, it saw a meteoric pump followed by a savage dump. My entire investment is gone.

I've been "rugged," a type of scam in crypto markets where developers abandon their crypto project and run away with investors' money.

I'd need to stick with my 25-year-old Toyota Corolla for a while longer.

As my heart rate slows, I contemplate how exactly I'm going to explain to my girlfriend that I'd just lost $5,000 in the stupidest way possible. My defense is that what's just happened to me is a microcosm of the truly insane things happening daily in the crypto space. Crypto currencies are truly the Wild West and, on their frontiers, normal and abnormal are very, very different things. And yet, amid the self-justification, a further thought takes shape. Someone should write a book about this one day.

The world of crypto

The $5,000 investment lost on Morty coin formed just a small drop in the ocean of the estimated US$2.8 billion in funds lost to cryptocurrency "rug pulls" in 2021. In crypto markets, being "rugged" is another term for being scammed. So-called rug pulls can take many forms – from malicious code to project creators pumping up the value of their crypto before dumping it and disappearing with the money. While the methods can differ in crypto, it is nothing more than a good old-fashioned scam. In retrospect, the most absurd part of my investment was that I was certain that the Morty coin was a rug pull but still bought into it. In crypto, it is what we call a "shitcoin." The name speaks for itself.

The bet I was making (along with many traders at the time in the frothy, or inflated, crypto markets in 2020-2022) was that I could sell out at the top of the "pump" (when the price is high) before the rug pull happened and the price plummeted. In crypto communities, this is referred to as "degen" (short for degenerate) behavior. Far from being an insult, in crypto circles the term is almost used as a badge of honor. Stories abound of degens making ill-advised speculative investments in shitcoins only to literally make millions from their investments.

In the strange times of COVID-19 lockdowns and markets awash with cheap money, the allure of making millions overnight from the next meme or shitcoin was too much for many. Why sit your money in an index fund, returning 9% per year, when you could retire tomorrow if you bought the next biggest shitcoin? Of course, for everyone who made a million by buying shitcoins, there were thousands more who lost money. Shitcoins are akin to a casino – open 24-hours a day, seven days a week.

Shitcoins are indicative of the strange dichotomy of cryptocurrencies. There are egregious scams and rampant speculation, and yet they're simultaneously balanced by a technology that has the potential to revolutionize many aspects of our lives for the better. The technology used for rug pulls may yield a more fair and open financial system, enable actual ownership of digital items – from art to gaming items – and help create new organizational models centered around transparent and decentralized decision-making. While the benefits on our lives may seem esoteric, it can cut across many activities we do often – from faster and cheaper payments to greater options for our investments and savings.

It's fair to say that wasn't my first impression of cryptocurrencies. I initially saw them as a speculative bubble. In 2017, I watched markets rise rapidly only to crash – at the time confirming my skeptical view. In 2018, I started my career as a lawyer. The nerd in me decided to write an academic paper in my free time. Scoping out a range of topics, I eventually decided to write about the law and cryptocurrency, following the decision of the World Bank to partner with a local Australian bank to issue a bond using the new "blockchain" technology I had heard about. I published a paper in a legal journal on how blockchain and smart contracts could be used to revolutionize debt capital markets in Australia. While the article was legal-heavy, and functioned more as a cure for my insomnia than anything else, the research I did showed me that cryptocurrencies were much more than a speculative instrument. The technology could solve legitimate business problems.

The underlying technology is complicated, but you don't need to understand the intricacies of blockchain to realize its potential. Only some of us today understand how the internet *works*, but our daily interactions with it shows its value. I have a similar view of crypto more broadly, seeing its potential to help innovate across finance, create a more egalitarian world with transparent governance, and open up new, more creative fields. I have staked my career on this, leaving the certainty of a professional career to join a crypto-gaming company.

And yet, hand-in-hand with its future potential, goes the other side of crypto – the rampant speculation, the tales of incredible instant wealth, and even more sudden ruin. From the downfall of crypto billionaires Sam Bankman-Fried and Do Kwon, to tracing the rise and fall of shitcoins through the lens of the infamous crypto "SafeMoon", this book covers many of those stories. Amid the crazy, they also take us deep into the world of crypto and give us a full understanding of both its massive potential and its huge pitfalls. And they're also sometimes just very, very good stories.

CHAPTER 1: THE RISE OF SHITCOINS

"A cryptocurrency with little to no value or a digital currency that has no immediate discernible purpose." – Investopedia's definition of a shitcoin

Times Square is a living embodiment of American capitalism, plastered with advertisements from global brands like Coca-Cola, McDonald's, and Nike. However, if you walked through Times Square in March 2021 you would have seen a very different advertisement – a billboard displaying the word "SafeMoon" accompanied by a logo of a moon with a rocket in the center. The billboard reads: "SafeMoon the world's fastest growing cryptocurrency… sponsored by Reddit. com/r/SafeMoon."

Simultaneously, "SafeMoon" was trending on social media platform X, propelled by tweets from celebrities such as the Backstreet Boys member Nick Carter, rapper Lil Yachty and Youtuber Logan Paul. A "SafeMoon army" has formed, consisting of diehard SafeMoon investors. They stand ready to shut down anyone online who dares spread FUD (crypto slang short for "Fear, Uncertainty, and Doubt") about SafeMoon. A SafeMoon army fanatic gets a SafeMoon logo tattoo on his leg, and naturally posts it online for all to see. Their actions are reminiscent of rabid football fans supporting their beloved team. And yet the commotion is centered around the cryptocurrency SafeMoon, kick-starting one of the most insane periods in crypto market history.

The hype around SafeMoon was due to its explosive increase

in price in a short period. At its peak, SafeMoon reached a market capitalization of $5.75 billion in the space of just three months from launch. To put this into perspective, if you bought one dollar's worth of SafeMoon at launch (trading at the measly price of $0.0000000010) and sold at its peak, you would have made nearly $580,000. Was this staggering amount of value creation in such a short space of time the result of a new innovation in crypto? Or was it a unique revenue model, generating massive returns for holders?

The short answer is no.

SafeMoon's success boiled down to one thing: a catchy motto. Leveraging the crypto meme "going to the moon", SafeMoon augmented this in its now-famous motto: "Join us on our journey safely to the moon." Who could resist the promise of safe money? The journey, as it turned out, was not safe at all. Following its peak in May 2021, SafeMoon has crashed by 99.98% (at the time of writing).

Although possibly the most dramatic, SafeMoon was just one of many examples of shitcoins that characterized the so-called "shitcoin era" from 2020-2021. The shitcoin era gave birth to many crypto millionaires (a number of whom subsequently lost it all), an almost daily cadence of scams and rug pulls, and a legion of degens who swarmed onto the next shitcoin that they hoped would be the new SafeMoon.

How did this madness happen? And what actually is a shitcoin?

Crypto 101

Before diving into the world of shitcoins, it's essential to understand what exactly terms like "crypto" and "blockchain" mean. By now, most would have at least heard the terms, most likely from news stories featuring Bitcoin or infamous industry players like the disgraced Sam Bankman-Fried (covered in Chapter 9). However, when pressed, most of us would struggle to explain what the terms actually mean. Unsurprisingly, these concepts are often highly technical or rooted in jargon – much like the internet. Despite being used by billions of people each day, if you were to ask how the internet works, you would likely be met with a blank stare.

Cryptocurrency, or crypto, has become a catch-all term to relate to a broader industry that has developed around blockchain technology. There are many different definitions of what blockchain is, but I favor the definition as simply being a "fancy database." All innovations that flow from the technology center around the advantages and opportunities unlocked by having a fancier database.

Let's say, for example, you deposit $1,000 into your bank account today. You log into your online banking app and see that your bank balance has increased by $1,000. What you don't see are the operations behind the scenes for that $1,000 to be reflected in your app. At the back end, the bank has a large database (called a "ledger") that it continuously updates and reconciles. Every time a transaction is made, the bank will update its database to reflect it. The issue with this kind of database is that it is private, not transparent, costly, and clunky to maintain (with many bank databases using code from more than 30 years ago).

Blockchain technology, at its core, is just a new type of database, using a combination of complicated cryptography and mathematics to ensure its accuracy. The main benefit of blockchain technology is that it allows for a public, trustless system, and a decentralized database. It does not have to rely on a trusted party to maintain the accuracy of the database (e.g., a bank continually updating and reconciling its database). This is why blockchain technology has the potential to revolutionize finance, as it can replace many of the operations of financial institutions with something significantly better.

Blockchain is necessary for cryptocurrencies to exist. A cryptocurrency needs a blockchain to store it. For example, Bitcoin is stored on the Bitcoin blockchain. Every time a Bitcoin is transferred from one person to another, the Bitcoin blockchain is updated. Unlike banks, every single transaction on the Bitcoin blockchain is visible for everyone to see.

The key to understanding cryptocurrencies is to think of them as a combination of shares and currency. Like shares, they trade in public markets with prices constantly changing (often quite rapidly). However, unlike shares, they have characteristics of currency – they can be used to pay for things or perform specific actions. Each cryptocurrency will vary in what it can or cannot do, but the critical thing that binds them all together is that they are stored in a blockchain database. When referring to cryptocurrencies, the terms crypto, "token" and "coin" can all be used interchangeably. Purchasing crypto is straightforward as well. Many crypto exchanges as well as payment providers allow you to directly exchange currency (e.g., US dollars) for crypto, and vice versa.

Okay, so what is a shitcoin then? This is where the fun starts. Most of the largest cryptocurrencies have clear utility (e.g., can be used to pay for services) linked to the innovative potential of blockchain technology. Take, for example, Ripple Lab's cryptocurrency "Ripple" (trading under the ticker "XRP"). XRP is designed to enable secure, instant, and nearly free global financial transactions of any size. Overseas money transfers can be very time-consuming and costly, but Ripple Lab has designed a way to use the benefits of blockchain technology to radically improve this experience.

While companies like Ripple Labs are structured like a typical tech company (e.g., teams of engineers, designers, and product managers) trying to crack a complex business problem, others see the potential of blockchain technology in a different light. And it's a much easier path than putting in the effort to create a viable product. What these people see is an ability to exploit the powerful human desire to get rich. And get rich quickly.

This is how shitcoins were born. The term shitcoin dates back to the early 2010s, only a few years after Bitcoin was created. It was originally a derogatory term used to describe "altcoins" (i.e., alternative coins to Bitcoin), with the earliest mention coming from the poster "ribuck" on the forum Bitcoin Talk in November 2010. In an almost prescient post, ribuck wrote:

if bitcoin really takes off I can see lots of get-rich-quick-imitators coming on the scene: gitcoin, nitcoin, witcoin, titcoin, shitcoin… Some of them are sure to attract users with promises like "Why use bitcoin, where you can only generate 50 bitcoins every few months? Use shitcoin instead, and you'll get 51 shitcoins every 2 minutes". Of course the cheap imitators will disappear as quickly as those 1990s "internet currencies" like flooz and beenz, but lots of people will get burned along the way.

The term did not gather widespread usage until the 2020-21 bull market, at which point it entered the mainstream. During this period, shitcoins took on a life of their own, devolving into pump-and-dump schemes, straight-up scams, and rug pulls. While shitcoins are usually clearly a case of "you know it when you see it," they typically share the following three characteristics:

1. cryptocurrencies with no definable use cases or vague/illusory promises of future utility;
2. branding and marketing centered around a meme or gimmick (e.g., Trump Coin); and
3. underlying code that tends to be wholly recycled from other projects (with little to minor tweaks).

But the most striking thing about shitcoins is the absolutely crazy amount of money people can make from them – their investment often going from a value of $0 to millions in a matter of a few days. This, of course, is matched by the large number of investors who subsequently lose their money when the shitcoin's price collapses. The glory days of shitcoins can be traced to the COVID-19 era of 2020 to 2021, led from the front by SafeMoon.

Crypto bubbles – the genesis of shitcoins

Like other financial markets, crypto has seen many boom-and-bust cycles. In 2017, crypto prices exploded. Bitcoin was trading at around $1,000 at the start of the year but climbed to nearly $20,000 towards the end of the year. When Bitcoin's price increases, it typically coincides with the entire market rising with it. During this bull run, the previously mentioned XRP token led the way – increasing by around 36,000% (a $1,000 investment at the start of the year would be worth nearly $36 million by the end of it). And these types of returns were not simply on paper – one could quite easily sell this cryptocurrency (or any cryptocurrency for that matter) in minutes for US dollars, and get ready to retire on a beach in a tropical location.

While many legitimate cryptocurrencies saw explosive growth, an exuberant market can result in heavy speculation in more dubious cryptocurrencies. As more capital and awareness came to the market, speculators turned to more and more fringe projects. As the saying goes, "a rising tide lifts all boats", hence even shitcoins experienced price rises in these periods as well.

Asset bubbles are, of course, not a new phenomenon in markets. Rewind to the 1600s in the Netherlands: from 1634 to 1637, the price of tulips exploded. First introduced by the Ottoman Empire, tulips became a prized possession in the Netherlands, eventually leading to wild speculation. Labeled "Tulip Mania," a single tulip at its peak was sold for the price of a luxurious mansion. The bubble in many ways was very modern, seeing the use of sophisticated financial instruments that are commonplace today, such as futures trading. These futures contracts allowed people to trade on the price of tulips at a future date, without the need to actually hold the tulips themselves. This meant that speculators could leverage their investments up through these contracts, increasing their potential return but simultaneously increasing their risk. These innovations in part allowed for prices to run well above their "fundamental value." The bubble finally burst in early 1637, but it set a pattern for financial asset bubbles that we're still witnessing today.

A more recent example is the dotcom bubble from 1995 to 2000. In a similar arc to crypto markets, the dot-com bubble was driven by the revolutionary potential of the internet. Market participants quickly realized the revenue opportunities possible through the internet, and massively boosted investment into internet companies.

While investors' central thesis that the internet would radically change the world proved correct, the price paid for these investments became utterly divorced from their fundamental value. Internet companies at the time generally had little to no income or positive cash flows, meaning their entire valuation was based on forward-looking estimates. Investors could "choose your own adventure" on valuation, inputting whatever numbers they liked into their spreadsheets to justify their investment. As more investment capital piled into the market and speculation grew, prices rapidly increased in tandem.

During this period, the NASDAQ stock index rose around 800%. In a frenzy, seemingly any company that added a ".com" to their name saw the value of their shares rise dramatically. Perhaps the most famous example of exuberance was Pets.com. The company grabbed attention by using a dog sock puppet in advertisements (including during the 2000 Super Bowl). Its business model was simply selling pet supplies directly to retail customers online. The challenge for Pets.com was that it could not sell supplies for a profit, losing money on each sale due to high shipping costs for large items and intense competition with bricks-and-mortar pet stores. Undeterred, markets poured huge capital into the business – including $82.5 million during its NASDAQ Initial Public Offering in early 2000. The company went on to lose around $147 million for the next nine months post-listing before collapsing.

The dotcom bubble ended in 2000, with the NASDAQ falling more than 75% over the next two years – wiping out more than $5 trillion in market value. While the dotcom bubble led to money flowing into unsuccessful businesses, many modern-day behemoths, like eBay and Amazon, started around this period. In many ways, the dotcom bubble has parallels with crypto market bubbles. The base foundation is an innovative technology with genuine potential, leading to these capital inflows – but eventually turning a corner into wild speculation.

GameStop and the birth of shitcoins

Following the boom and bust of crypto markets in 2017, there was relative calm. Referred to as a "bear" market, these periods typically focus on legitimate projects continuing to build and refine their products and services. However, by late 2020, things started to turn. With the global economy in recession in the wake of the COVID-19 pandemic, governments and central banks coordinated to pump stimulus into the economy. Led by the Federal Reserve, the US Central Bank cut interest rates to zero and embarked on a "quantitative easing program" (banker jargon for printing money). With excessive capital circulating and many people staying inside and therefore online due to the pandemic, conditions were perfect for another crypto bull market.

Cryptocurrency prices started a significant upward trend from mid-2020. The northern hemisphere summer of 2021 kick-started the rise of shitcoins. The surge had an unlikely source: the bricks-and-mortar gaming store GameStop. The increase in digital distribution of games disrupted GameStop's business model. This resulted in a steadily decreasing share price hovering around $1 at the start of 2020. It still had an air of nostalgia around it, with people having fond memories of going into their local GameStop store to buy their favorite video game in their youth.

Momentum around GameStop's shares started to build on the subreddit forum (a sub-community on the social media platform, Reddit) "WallStreetBets". These posts focused on shares and options trading – but it was nothing like a traditional forum. WallStreetBets' users called themselves "degenerates" seeking "tendies" (i.e., profits), likening the share market to a casino. Users were infamous for posting so-called "loss porn" – typically consisting of a screenshot of the user's trading account down an enormous amount of money. Users tended to be surprisingly stoic and supportive of each other in the face of such losses.

WallStreetBets propelled GameStop to become the first-ever "meme share". Many institutional investors had a negative view of the long-term prospects of GameStop and tried to profit from this view by "short selling." Short selling, in essence, involves borrowing shares in a company and then selling them on the market. Short sellers are betting that the share price will fall, at which point they will buy back the shares at a lower price and return them to the lender. Cutting through the jargon: short sellers make money when the share price falls and lose when the price goes up.

Through a series of so-called "due diligence" posts on the positive prospects for GameStop, it became more popular amongst the more than 10 million WallStreetBets subscribers. The public face of WallStreetBets became Keith Gill, better known by his YouTube account name "Roaring Kitty" and Reddit username "DeepFuckingValue". Gill, a former financial analyst in the US, started his YouTube channel with videos and livestreams about his investment philosophy, research tools, and methods for assessing stocks. Gill's early videos were quite technical, covering complicated valuation metrics he used to research and compare stocks. Despite the subject matter often being quite dry, Gill's laid-back and charismatic personality shone through – enhanced by frequently appearing in a bright red bandana with assorted colorful t-shirts displaying cats. Gill could have easily been relegated to one of many semi-popular financial YouTubers, garnering a solid following posting videos about stocks. It was his posts on WallStreetBets that catapulted him to international fame and led him to testify in front of Congress.

Gill frequently posted on WallStreetBets about his GameStop "YOLO" investment (taken from the abbreviation for "you only live once," meaning a large extremely risky investment), first posting a screenshot of his call options (giving him the option to buy at an agreed price) on GameStop in 2019. Gill had purchased nearly $54,000 worth of shares and call options, which at the time were already at an almost $46,000 profit. Call options are a type of derivative, of which value is derived from the underlying value of the share (being GameStop in this instance). Gill purchased call options with a strike price of $8 (expiring in January 2021), meaning that if GameStop's share price did not go above $8 by January 2021, his call options would be worth $0. However, if the share price rose above this, he would return many multiples of his investment, as call options give the holders higher leverage than simply owning the shares. Given that call options can often result in a complete investment loss, they are risky. However, with high risk comes the chance of high returns.

With high conviction in GameStop (which trades under the ticker "GME"), Gill held onto his investment, making monthly update posts on WallStreetBets titled "GME YOLO month-end update". Gill's posts earned him rapport from other users, seeing him as a fellow degen. By July 2020, Gill increased his investment in GameStop call options and shares to nearly $150,000, but was sitting at a loss of around $40,000.

On July 28, 2020, Gill posted a now infamous video on GameStop titled "100%+ short interest in GameStop stock (GME) – fundamental & technical deep value analysis." Sporting a t-shirt with a cat wearing aviator sunglasses, Gill presented a detailed bull case for GameStop shares. In the nearly one-hour video, Gill addressed the major negative market commentary on GameStop and gave a detailed financial analysis, positing that it was massively undervalued at the $4 price it was trading at. In this video, Gill identified the chance that a "short squeeze" could occur for GameStop shares, stating, "I'm not betting on a short squeeze, but it seems like something that could take place." A short squeeze refers to a situation where short-sellers race to buy shares on the market to cover their position in the face of rising prices. Their purchases then lead to the share price rising (as demand increases), often resulting in a spike in price.

By September 2020, Gill's luck changed. Posting a screenshot in WallStreetBets, his GameStop position was now worth nearly $830,000. The top upvoted comment reflected the forum's unique humor, with user "Lesath213" posting:

> Now that people see your gains they're just going to FOMO it up to $15 a share, you will be the Game King or something stupid and then it will drop 20% and everyone will blame you

for ruining their lives. But you won't care, you'll be sitting on 2.5m in mattresses and buying lambo's for your boyfriend and his wife.

Over the next few months, Gill's investment continued to rise in value, with hype building around GameStop from WallStreetBets and retail investors more broadly. This reached a crescendo in January 2021. With retail investors buying large volumes of shares, GameStop's share price rose sharply. As foreshadowed by Gill, this led to a short-squeeze, with hedge funds that had shorted GameStop shares, like Melvin Capital, experiencing heavy losses. Melvin Capital was supported by other hedge funds, like Citadel Capital, which were able to (at least temporarily) backstop Melvin Capital. Citadel Capital's founder and billionaire Kenneth Griffin became a major antagonist in the drama and was famously portrayed by Nick Offerman in the movie *Dumb Money*. WallStreetBets viewed Melvin Capital's support by billionaires like Griffin as elites looking after other elites, while the retail traders were left to suffer their losses. This began to reposition the entire GameStop saga as a David vs Goliath battle of retail investors vs large and powerful financial institutions.

This resulted in the share price increasing from a low of $2.57 to a peak of $483 on January 29, 2021. Many initial investors became extremely wealthy, with Gill's investment sitting at $46 million. With posts flooding WallStreetBets of huge gains, the "meme share" era of the share market had begun. For the moment, large institutional investors like hedge funds didn't dictate share prices – it would be the retail investors moving the market.

On February 19, 2021, Gill was hauled before a House Committee to testify on the GameStop saga. Appearing in a suit and tie (with a picture of a cat in the background with the text "hang in there"), Gill defended his involvement in GameStop against allegations he solicited others to buy the stock for his own profit. He ended his testimony justifying his investment decision by stating, "in short, I like the stock." With his testimony complete, Gill disappeared from public view, posting a final update on WallStreetBets showing a screenshot of his GameStop position of $34 million.

With meme shares as front-page news, many retail investors turned their attention to cryptocurrencies. Crypto markets became fertile ground for memes and shitcoins, and had some inherent advantages over traditional equity markets for speculation. Firstly, a person can create a cryptocurrency in under 10 minutes. Boilerplate code is available online and can be easily used with minimal adjustments to launch a cryptocurrency. Even those without any coding skills can launch a cryptocurrency, with several code-free cryptocurrency launchpads available. This allowed almost instantaneously the creation of meme cryptocurrencies. Secondly, limited regulatory barriers to listing cryptocurrencies on exchanges enabled widespread access. Finally, given the relative anonymity that came with cryptocurrency creation, there was limited fear of repercussions for scams or rug pulls.

Taken together, crypto markets had perfect conditions to create a series of memes and shitcoins to rival GameStop and traditional equity markets. The fuse was first lit with the rise of the meme coin "Dogecoin" (covered in Chapter 4). Dogecoin had traded well under one cent in late 2020 but rapidly increased in value shortly after GameStop's price multiplied in January 2021. Crypto traders quickly realized a flood of capital was coming for meme coins, with SafeMoon to be one of the first recipients.

SafeMoon is born

Just a few months after the GameStop saga, SafeMoon was created. The creator of the project elected to remain anonymous, using only the name "Kyle". Kyle had previously launched a token called "Give Me Your Money (GMYM)", which unsurprisingly failed to get any traction. Kyle appointed Braden John Karony as the CEO of SafeMoon, with Karony acting as the public face of the company. Karony had limited experience in business, with his professional work experience solely consisting of six years as an analyst at the US Department of Defense.

The project itself had no utility or use-case when it was launched – only vague promises of some future utility. This did not transform the financial system or push the limits of blockchain technology. The very source code for SafeMoon was based on "Bee-Token" – itself a cryptocurrency that was a rug pull. The real purpose of the project itself is hinted at by its design. SafeMoon employed a mechanism that directly encouraged people to "HODL". HODL is a deliberate misspelling of "hold" – standing for "hold on for dear life." The logic is that if everyone HODLs the cryptocurrency and doesn't sell, then the price would rise, making everyone rich.

The mechanism SafeMoon used to encourage investors to HODL was a huge transaction fee for selling – sitting at 10%. Half of this fee was redistributed to SafeMoon holders, with the other half going to a crypto wallet in a different cryptocurrency (Binance Coin) that was used to provide liquidity for trading of SafeMoon. The intent is clear: you get rewarded for HODLing and penalized for selling. This would be essential to SafeMoon's rise after it launched, with a supply of 777 trillion tokens priced at $0.000000001 each.

While other shitcoins employed similar mechanisms, the marketing of SafeMoon set it apart. There was catchy branding, journeying "safely to the moon" – but a clever name and slogan are not always enough to become a successful shitcoin. You need to reach a wide audience. Who better to leverage than famous influencers?

SafeMoon engaged numerous celebrities to spread the word. With Dogecoin's rapid price rise, rapper Lil Yachty tweeted, "#safemoon is the new dogecoin." YouTuber and professional boxer Jake Paul tweeted a reply a day later saying, "factsss." Paul, who initially rose to fame on the now-defunct social media video platform Vine, is suspected to have been paid nearly $190,000 for his endorsement (based on blockchain analysis of a payment from SafeMoon to his personal wallet).

A few weeks later, Backstreet Boys member Nick Carter tweeted, "it's time for blast off [rocketemoji] #SAFEMOON." The combined impact of celebrity influencers, SafeMoon's marketing, and the meme potential of the coin, sent the price skyrocketing. Those who invested $1,000 near launch would be sitting on a million-dollar investment in little over a few months.

The growth trajectory and the number of investors with huge financial gains quickly made SafeMoon a crypto legend, further driving its value. On May 10, 2021, a billboard display in Times Square went live, promoting the token as the "World's Fastest Growing Cryptocurrency." Karony then announced SafeMoon was talking with the Government of the West African country, the Republic of Gambia, to use SafeMoon "for innovation and learning purposes." The vaguely-worded project also apparently purported to bring wind turbines to households in Africa.

SafeMoon was trending on X and occupied the front page of the sub-reddit SatoshiStreetBets. SatoshiStreetBets is a cryptocurrency-focused offshoot of WallStreetBets, named after the anonymous founder of Bitcoin, Satoshi Nakamoto. With more than 500,000 subscribers, SatoshiStreetBets was the go-to place on Reddit to discuss shitcoins and YOLO crypto investments – with SafeMoon featuring heavily. Posts flooded SatoshiStreetBets, in a bid to increase the price of SafeMoon, such as the following by user "GMEandAMCbroughtme":

> Consider this the official announcement of a community driven campaign to pop off the biggest squeeze of all time. This will be the crypto version of Gamestop and AMC but way bigger. We aim to take the power from the banks and transfer it to the people. Why Safemoon? Because it's fkn sexy, it has a cool name, and we like the fkn moon. It's time to make #SafeMoonSqueeze go viral. Start tweeting it. Let the world know.[1]

The post ended with (as per usual in crypto), "I'm not a financial adviser and this is not financial advice."

Speculation across X and SatoshiStreetBets was now about how high the price could go. The self-titled "SafeMoon Army", consisting of SafeMoon holders, was out in full force with a simple objective: pump up the price in whatever way possible and suppress any opposing viewpoints (i.e., FUD). This was a distinctive and unsavory aspect of the crypto community at the time – self-interested individuals seeking to suppress debate and legitimate critiques of projects for fear it could result in their investment declining in value.

Despite the SafeMoon Army's attempt to keep the price rising, inevitably, its bubble burst. With no utility for the token and its value solely the function of speculation, SafeMoon's price relied on new investors providing fresh capital to support it. Existing holders started to cash out their investments to shift to new shitcoins, causing the price to fall. As the hype subsided, the well of new investors began to run dry. Following its peak in April 2021, the price spiraled downwards (notwithstanding some occasional pumps) to sit more than 99% lower at the time of writing. This had a devastating impact on many investors, who bought in wholeheartedly to SafeMoon's narrative. In a Reddit thread, user "TNGsystems" posted a message from a former Reddit SafeMoon "maxi," who stated:

> For me, safemoon was my first crypto. I was working at a school board at that time and was completely burnout and hating my life, it gave me hope that I could exit the job and become financially free, and bought into the misinformation and blatant false project potential. I understand and sympathize with people that are still maxis as they are trying to protect their declining investment, regardless of the signs. As more people left the "company" and continual articles and videos were released about the fraud and money stolen from the LP I started to wake up. The fact that John [Karony] never came out and made a statement raised my suspicions and then I finally dug deeper, it was obvious the whole time. I feel like an idiot haha, all good though lesson learned.

The SafeMoon team itself faced a class action lawsuit alleging SafeMoon engaged in a pump and dump scheme, deliberately misleading investors so the project creators could sell their holdings at a profit. Fraud allegations surfaced, with prominent independent researcher and YouTuber Stephen Findeisen (better known by the name of his channel "Coffeezilla") first accusing them of misappropriating millions of dollars of funds. Coffeezilla has built a following of more than 3 million subscribers on YouTube through his detailed investigations of scammers across the internet and (more recently) in the crypto space. His videos feature him in front of a microphone with a white shirt and suspenders, reminiscent of a neo-noir private investigator. Inspired to shed light on scammers after his mother was sold "snake oil" following a cancer diagnosis, Coffeezilla's video on SafeMoon garnered over 4.5 million views. Based on blockchain transaction data research, Coffeezilla and his team concluded that SafeMoon's founder, Kyle, had transferred around $10 million worth of SafeMoon to his personal wallet.

The CEO, Karony, would go on to win Utah Business' CEO of the year in 2022, much to the ire of investors who lost money on their investment. As hype in SafeMoon subsided, the company attempted to market itself as more than a shitcoin, with Karony stating, "While memecoins might have a different purpose, SafeMoon isn't a memecoin. We have a real mission behind us for a tech company. And again, our plan is to bring the future to now."

SafeMoon's founders and executives, including Karony, face fraud charges by the US Securities and Exchange Commission (SEC). It alleges millions of dollars were misappropriated to buy extravagant items like McClaren cars and luxury homes. Despite the eventual collapse of SafeMoon, one thing stood out in the minds of crypto investors. If I can get into a shitcoin project like SafeMoon early and get out at the right time, I could make millions. If it can happen to SafeMoon, it can happen with other cryptocurrencies.

Other shitcoins rise

Imitators of SafeMoon quickly sprang up. A spiritual successor came in the form of "Safe Mars." Why simply go to the moon when you could go to Mars instead? In a similar arc to SafeMoon, SafeMars experienced a rapid appreciation in price. The value of the project went from $0 to a peak of $427 million. Unsurprisingly, the project is now back to being worth almost nothing.

During this period, I invested in "MoonJuice", a project which marketed itself as "the first ever crypto-powered energy drink." The precise intersection of blockchain technology and energy drinks was unclear then (and still is today). At the time, I was passively following a small telegram group discussing shitcoins. A prominent poster in the group (self-titled the "shitcoin whisperer") had posted about MoonJuice being the next big shitcoin. He had established his credentials in the group through a series of successful shitcoin investments netting him over $500,000. Having been laid off due to the COVID-19 pandemic, he had taken to shitcoin investing full-time, posting at all hours of the day and night. He would often brag about how much he had lost to rug pulls (over $100,000) and preface his investment recommendations to the group, saying, "90% chance this is a rug pull, but…".

As was the pattern with most shitcoins, the price of MoonJuice experienced a brief pump, followed by a savage dump, with the price of their token "MOJO" worth nearly nothing today. The project stopped all updates in mid-2021.

In a test of just how ridiculous names could get, the project "CumRocket" was launched with the token name "CUMMIES." This token caught the attention of Elon Musk, who tweeted a series of graphics translating to "CumRocket to the moon." This promptly sent the price of CUMMIES soaring more than 400% in the ten minutes following the tweet. The project intends to "bring web3 to the adult industry" and is still in operation despite the token dropping from a peak of $290 million to around $4 million at the time of writing.

Some shitcoins didn't pretend to be anything but a shitcoin. Such an example was the "Dogshit" token, with one of its catchy marketing tweets as follows: "Lost all your gains due to the market SHITTING the bed? Invest in DOGSHIT now to recoup these lost gains and realize your own financial freedom!" Others saw how ridiculous the whole situation was. This included the creator of the ironically titled "Safe Crypto And Money" cryptocurrency, giving it the acronym "SCAM". While the SCAM coin community on Reddit is no longer active, you can still get SCAM tokens for the bargain price of $0.007.

Money started to flow to other projects that were not even set up to be a meme. Take "Omicron coin", launched as a decentralized finance project (referring to crypto projects aiming to replace traditional financial services). The cryptocurrency garnered limited attention but when the World Health Organization named the latest COVID variant from South Africa "Omicron", the price of the token rose nearly 1,000%.

Rug pulls and scams begin

As money was cycled from one shitcoin to the next – opportunities abounded for scammers to enter the space and ruthlessly exploit the information asymmetry between parties.

Cryptocurrencies are governed and issued using smart contracts (simply lines of code that automate actions). Most investors do not have the technical expertise (or time) to properly understand smart contracts, which can allow scammers to include malicious code in them. Often referred to as a "hard rug pull", scammers can build different loopholes in the code to steal cryptocurrencies from investors. An example of this was AnubisDAO. The project was named after the Egyptian deity Anubis, typically depicted as a man with the head of a dog. Many investors immediately saw the meme potential of the coin, with dog-related cryptocurrencies at the time performing strongly (e.g., Dogecoin and Shiba Inu). In total, around $60 million of investor funds poured into the cryptocurrency only for the project to be rug pulled using an exploit in the code. The scammer (suspected to be a project development team member) absconded with the funds.

One such victim of a rug pull was Julian Mangione, an accountant in Australia. Mangione, through his commerce degree at the University of Melbourne, had long been taught a "traditional" approach to investing, mainly focused on a long-term buy-and-hold strategy in Australian equities. Over time, Mangione grew frustrated by his relatively low returns from this strategy, which were compounded when a close friend, Michael Cardamone, rang him with the news he had made $40,000 from a shitcoin in under a few weeks.

Cardamone, a HR worker, had seen a post for the shitcoin "POODL" trending on the front page of SatoshiStreetBets. POODL was one of the many dog-themed shitcoins that were popular following the success of Dogecoin. Cardamone decided to, as he described, YOLO (go all in) a $500 investment in POODL. Forgetting about his investment for a few weeks, he checked his account and was astonished to see that it was worth $40,000, nearly an 8,000% return. Cardamone cashed out half of his investment, which he almost immediately regretted, as POODL continued its price rise (his investment would have been worth more than $100,000 if he had held for just a few more weeks).

Entranced by the possibility of life-changing returns, Mangione dipped his toes into this strange world. Mangione was admittedly a novice to cryptocurrencies, at this point only holding some Bitcoin (which he had rather humorously attempted to transfer to an email address, not entirely understanding how addresses work in crypto – being a unique set of characters to send and receive crypto). These types of investors were prime targets for rug pulls and scams. Mangione recounted his initial sense of excitement in the risk and possibilities of shitcoins, which would be a temporary reprieve from the mundanity of COVID-19 lockdowns. Cardamone recommended he invest in a shitcoin called "Pablo", a name that immediately resonated with Mangione due to the notoriety around the Columbian drug lord Pablo Escobar. Needing no more convincing, he invested $8,000 into Pablo. His excitement would be short-lived.

Mangione went to sleep and awoke to check the price of Pablo. To his dismay, Pablo had been rug pulled, with the token now worthless and his entire investment erased. It was a devastating experience for Mangione. Money that he had spent months toiling at work to save, evaporated in an instant.

While tokens like Pablo took the form of a hard rug pull, other rug pulls took a more traditional route in the form of organized pump and dump schemes, which can often proliferate in penny stocks in equity markets (best illustrated in the 2013 film *The Wolf of Wall Street*). Pump and dump schemes are either led by the project team or an organized pump and dump group. This was typically the primary modus operandi for a large number of shitcoins. Normally, the project team took a large allocation of cryptocurrency when the shitcoin was created. It would then embark on aggressive marketing tactics, spamming the social media platforms X, Reddit, and Discord about the cryptocurrency. It often also paid influencers and celebrities to promote it.

This became the primary lever to increase the virality and, subsequently, the price of the shitcoin. The more people talk about how it will be the next SafeMoon, the more buyers there are, and the higher the price goes. Importantly, pump and dump schemes are intended to increase the liquidity (i.e., trading volume) of the cryptocurrency. The inflows of buying volume allow the project team to be able to sell a large number of tokens without crashing the price.

Shitcoin project teams often directly paid influencers to tweet and promote a shitcoin, meaning the influencers would be directly incentivized to increase the price. This, of course, is nothing new in the world of influencers, whose livelihoods are almost entirely made from promoting goods and services. However, it is one thing to promote skincare products and entirely another to promote a shitcoin.

There are some egregious examples, including the American YouTuber Tana Mongeau, famous for her "story time" videos involving exaggerated stories of her life as an influencer. Mongeau posted a video to Instagram to her more than five million followers, promoting the cryptocurrency "Titscoins". In the video, Mongeau stated, "Can you believe my ownership in Titscoin just bought me this beautiful Rolls Royce?" as the camera pans to show the car's interior, "Get yours now," she adds. Titscoin's price eventually plummeted, even with Mongeau's endorsement.

Kim Kardashian was paid $250,000 by the creators of EMAX for a post to her more than 250 million Instagram followers: "Are you guys into crypto????.. This is not financial advice, but sharing what my friends told me about the Ethereum Max token! A few minutes ago, Ethereum Max burned 400 trillion tokens – literally 50% of their admin wallet giving back to the entire E-Max community." The price of EMAX eventually plummeted by approximately 97%, and the SEC rewarded Kardashian with a fine of $1.26 million for not disclosing to her followers that she received money for the promotion.

Adin Ross, a Twitch streamer, went live promoting MILF token. MILF token was a project that aimed to create a vibrant "meme ecosystem" that tied together both tokens and NFTs (non-fungible tokens, essentially verifiable unique digital assets), which included launching an NFT project called "Cyber MILFs". In a live stream, Ross spent 15 minutes buying MILF tokens. It is estimated he was paid nearly $200,000 for the promotion (which he disclosed during the video, saying, "I'm getting paid for this shit").

Later, Ross said in a video, "By the way, that MILF Token shit I did a while back? I already told you guys don't buy that shit…. I got paid a bag to do that shit. Like, I don't give a fuck. I hope none of you guys actually bought." MILF coin would subsequently crash in price to be trading near $0 at the time of writing.

The rapper Soulja Boy, famous for his debut single "Crank That (Soulja Boy)," was paid to promote the shitcoin "SaferMars" (not to be confused with SafeMars). Soulja Boy was supposed to tweet to his more than five million followers: "Found an interesting project @safermars – looks moon worthy. $SFM Presale is now live on @

dxsale." However, he accidentally botched the tweet, including details of how much he would earn if the project successfully raised funding, stating: "They raising 240k, if they raise it after your tweet – will get you 24k."

Soulja Boy quickly realized his mistake and deleted the tweet.

Organized pump and dump groups

Organizing pump and dumps wasn't the sole domain of project teams. With shitcoin after shitcoin following a boom-and-bust cycle, it seemed like buying a shitcoin was like buying a lottery ticket. You would either win big or lose it all. But what if you could rig the game to buy the winning ticket?

This was the genesis of several large pump and dump groups that sprung up between 2020-2022. Typically organized through the Telegram messaging app, the group would function as follows: One of the group's administrators would select a shitcoin to invest in. The group would then accumulate a holding in the cryptocurrency and go out "shilling" the cryptocurrency across social media networks. Shilling would often involve the spread of false information about the cryptocurrency (e.g., the project is in negotiations for a deal with Microsoft) or low-effort tweets and posts like "this is going to the moon" with a few rocket emojis added for good effect.

The goal of the group was straightforward. Spread the word about the shitcoin and hope unsuspecting individuals invest in the cryptocurrency – raising the price and volume traded (the "pump"). Once the shitcoin had pumped, the group would collectively sell the token on the market, causing the price to collapse. This would leave the investors holding onto "a bag" – crypto parlance for holding tokens that have lost almost all their value. These groups could have a tremendous impact on price and volume. In a report to the Australian Securities Investment Commission, University of Technology Sydney crypto researcher Professor Talis Putnins gave an example where pump and dump groups increased the price of a token by 90% in less than a minute. These schemes distorted around 65% of price trends on average, with abnormal trading volumes and unfair wealth transfers across investors.

Pump and dump schemes are illegal, being a form of market manipulation. What is most interesting is how openly these groups operate, allowing anyone to enter and even calling themselves a "pump group". Those who join often think they are getting an edge on the market. However, the structure of the group can mean these joiners get scammed themselves.

Many pump and dump groups operate in a hierarchical structure – with an inner group and an outer group. The inner group typically consists of a small number of founding members, responsible for deciding which shitcoin the wider group will buy. What is not disclosed to the outer group is that the inner group will quietly acquire the shitcoin before publicly posting about it. The inner group, therefore, acquires the shitcoin at a lower price, and when the outer group starts purchasing the shitcoin, the inner group can start dumping on them. In effect, it's the creation of a pump-and-dump scheme within a pump-and-dump scheme.

Shitcoins morph into real-life squid games

In the smash hit Netflix series *Squid Game* released in 2021, a group of players accepts an invitation to compete in a series of children's games to win a large cash prize of $35 million. Unbeknownst to the contestants, the games are a life-and-death scenario. But for every death, another $80,000 is added to the prize pool. After the first game, the players narrowly vote in favor of sending all contestants back home without any prize money. However, after a short period, most of the contestants decide to return to the game. They know the odds are stacked against them but choose to roll the dice anyway.

Squid Game formed an interesting parallel to the shitcoin era. While many unsuspecting investors were convinced to purchase worthless cryptocurrency, a large contingent knew precisely what they were buying. The self-styled degens knew they were playing a form of squid game. Many would even openly brag about how much money they had lost (posting loss porn pics) or joking on Telegram how many rug pulls to which they had fallen victim. Losses and rug pulls became a badge of honor in the community. These degens treated shitcoins as a casino – you win some and lose some – all with the hope that the next shitcoin they purchased would be the next SafeMoon, and they could retire early.

The analogy to Squid Game was not lost on some. In late 2021, a cryptocurrency inspired by the show was launched, called "Squid." The project promised to create a crypto game at some point in the future. Of course, investors immediately rushed in, with the price rising from one cent to a touch under $3,000 in less than a week. To put that in perspective, if you had invested $100 in that coin on Monday, by Sunday, you could have quit your job and bought a penthouse in the Bahamas with a nearly $30 million return.

True to its inspiration, the shitcoin, of course, ended up being a rug pull. The project developers were able to make off with an estimated $3.38 million, crashing the price of the token in the process by 99.99%.

The end of the shitcoin era

Squid, in retrospect, became one of the closing chapters in the 2020-2021 shitcoin era. Shortly after the Squid rug pull, Bitcoin would hit approximately $64,000 – representing the top of the crypto market. As 2021 drew to a close, the era of cheap (mainstream) money that spurred on the shitcoin bubble was also ending. The central banks' rapid increase in money supply through quantitative easing in traditional money markets, and near-zero interest rates, combined with a range of pandemic-related supply constraints to unleash an inflationary storm around the world.

For years, the near-zero interest rates had encouraged a mad dash to speculative investments. With interest rates on savings accounts next to nothing, investors searched for yields in increasingly risky assets. With inflation starting to rise by the end of 2021, central banks inevitably had to respond by raising interest rates and ending quantitative easing programs.

This coalesced into a "risk off" mentality amongst investors, leading to falls in tech shares and crypto more broadly. With prices falling, the fear of missing out (FOMO) that had driven so much speculation in shitcoins started dissipating. Increasingly, investors were more concerned with the fundamentals of the project in which they were investing, reallocating capital to legitimate crypto projects. As investor Warren Buffett said, "Only when the tide goes out do you learn who has been swimming naked." Shitcoins had been swimming naked, and when the music stopped, all that was left of these projects was a worthless number of tokens sitting in investors' wallets.

The aftermath

In retrospect, it is easy to look back at the shitcoin era in 2020-2021 and conclude that the market was irrational. In many senses, this is a correct interpretation – when SafeMoon can reach a market capitalization of more than $5 billion, it's clearly not a sustainable market. The price of coins like SafeMoon are dictated by the marginal buyer. At some point this demand will dry up, and in the absence of any fundamental value, the price will inevitably fall from astronomical valuations.

Many investors lost money from scams and rug pulls, as well as investing in shitcoins at the peak of their valuation. However, a large number of these investors viewed their investments as completely rational. They were not content with a steady 8% return on the S&P 500 index fund – they wanted generational wealth. Instead of gambling at a casino, they gambled with shitcoins, rolling the dice and hoping their next investment would be the new SafeMoon. Viewed from this angle, what other investment could potentially return over 1,000% in the space of just a few days?

Notwithstanding this view, the shitcoin era can hardly be considered a high point for the crypto space. Shitcoins and rug pulls and the many investors who were burned during this period have left the nascent industry grappling with the perception that the entire technology is a scam. Nevertheless, the power of the "meme" in crypto would endure. As crypto market conditions improved in late 2023, investors would once again flock to meme coins. While not quite reaching the highs of the 2021, a new class of meme coins would appear.

On the Solana blockchain network, a class of political meme coins emerged, tracking the US election. Influenced by the "Doland Duck" meme, meme coins were created for US presidential candidates. This started with "Doland Tremp" and "Joe Boden" giving buyers a de facto bet on their preferred presidential candidate. The meme coins would move roughly in sync with their candidates' chances – with the Doland Tremp coin rising rapidly after Donald Trump survived an assassination attempt. Conversely, the Joe Boden coin collapsed once Joe Biden announced he would no longer be running. This then caused the "Kamala Horris" meme coin to spike when she became the Democratic nominee for president.

Other dog-themed meme coins also reaching staggering valuations, including the "dogwifhat" coin – a variant of the dog meme, this time equipped with a hat. Another dog-themed meme coin "Bonk" emerged, rising to a more than 1 billion valuation. With the price of Bonk rising, this created a strange arbitrage opportunity in the market. People could buy and sell in different markets to take advantage of price variations.

The aforementioned Solana chain released a crypto-focused smart phone called "Saga phone" which had a preinstalled crypto app and a specific crypto-related app store. The Saga phone had lackluster sales, only selling around 2,500 units up until early December 2023. Not even a price drop in August 2023 from $1,000 to $599 could boost sales. However, fortunes quickly turned. Saga phone holders were eligible to receive 30 million $BONK tokens by downloading an app on the phone. In June 2023, the 30 million $BONK tokens were worth roughly $10. As the price of $BONK started increasing in December, the value of the tokens surpassed $1,000. This meant in effect that you would make money if you purchased the phone. Savvy individuals quickly capitalized on this opportunity, with Saga quickly selling out (including nearly 15,000 units selling in just one day). The sold-out phones quickly appeared on eBay for almost 10 times their sale price. Phone buyers were also the recipients of other, free tokens and NFTs, equating to more than $30,000 in value.

While most investors might view these coins as a gamble, one cannot discount the community aspects that emerge from meme coins. People can directly participate in their preferred candidate's election bids, or the opportunity to own a piece of a new social trend, or simply to have a group of people to chat to on the meme coin's Discord or social media channel. For better or worse, shitcoins and meme coins appear to be a permanent part of the crypto landscape.

CHAPTER 2: THE MILLION DOLLAR PHOTO OF A ROCK: NFTS

"These virtual rocks serve NO PURPOSE beyond being able to be bought and sold…" – Ether Rock's official website.

On November 2, 2021, a user navigated Opensea, a popular trading marketplace. The user browsed some of the top NFT collections like CryptoPunks and Bored Apes Yacht Club (BAYC). Eventually, they settled on a different collection. They scrolled through this new collection, finally pausing on an item they liked. They put this item into the cart and completed the transaction. This sounds relatively mundane now, in the digital age, like browsing and buying something on Amazon. Except this transaction was different. It wasn't a $20 purchase on Amazon.

It was a $1.8 million purchase.

It wasn't for a house. It wasn't for a Lamborghini. It wasn't the most lavish holiday you could dream of.

It was for a picture of a rock. A cartoon JPEG of a grey rock.

The collection in question was Ether Rocks, one of the earliest incarnations of NFTs. From what initially started as a means for digital artists to earn a decent living from their art, NFTs morphed into one of the biggest speculative frenzies the world has even seen in 2021, as profile picture (PFP) NFTs exploded in price. As the name suggests, PFP NFTs could be readily displayed as a profile picture across social media sites like X, typically in the form of a cartoon character or avatar (e.g., an ape). In the world of NFTs, a simple JPEG can make you a millionaire overnight (or make a billionaire into a millionaire).

What is an NFT?

Non-fungible tokens, sometimes referred to as "digital collectables", are a relatively new type of token that function as a unique digital identifier that is recorded on a blockchain. NFTs are priced and traded in other cryptocurrencies (e.g., a NFT collection like DeGods can be purchased by exchanging a cryptocurrency called Solana). NFTs can be best understood by discerning between fungibility (which characterizes the cryptocurrencies discussed in Chapter 1) and non-fungibility.

Fungibility, put simply, means that a good or asset is interchangeable. An example of a fungible asset is the US dollar (or any national currency) – $100 is $100, whether in the form of a single $100 note or two $50 notes. Non-fungibility, conversely, refers to when a good or asset is unique and not interchangeable. A classic example of a non-fungible asset is real estate – with each piece of land distinct and unique.

In crypto, Bitcoin and other cryptocurrencies are fungible. Like the US dollar – 1 Bitcoin is equal in value to another Bitcoin. For the first few years in crypto, the only assets available were fungible. However, over time, many in the crypto space started to see the potential for creating non-fungible assets, using blockchain technology.

In 2012, the idea behind NFTs was described in a paper by Meni Rosenfeld[2] who described a concept known as "Colored Coins" for the Bitcoin Blockchain. The idea was to create a class of methods to represent and manage real-world assets – with an additional layer to signify their use. This layer would, in effect, make each of the assets unique and non-fungible, given that a "red" Bitcoin (which may represent the ownership of a car) would then be unique and separate from a "blue" Bitcoin (representing the ownership of a house, for example). Having separate and distinct coins could then facilitate the transfer of ownership, along with evidence of ownership between parties – in the same way conceptually that a land title can be transferred between parties.

This spurred the creation of the first-ever NFT. New York-based digital artists Jennifer and Kevin McCoy created the generative artwork called "Quantum." The McCoys are famous for using new technologies to create digital art and moving images aimed at questioning the impact of technology on the individual and society at large. Quantum contains five separately-colored images that hypnotically change color and pulsate in a manner reminiscent of an octopus. The artists describe their work as "code driven work [that] presents an ongoing, abstract, cycle of birth, death, and rebirth. It tells this story through color, line and movement."

At the time, there was no way to verify digital ownership of an image or piece of digital art – making pieces like Quantum difficult to sell. Undeterred, the McCoys joined forces with Anil Dash, a tech entrepreneur, to solve this problem. The team quickly recognized that blockchain technology could be a solution. Using the Namecoin blockchain, the McCoys minted (i.e., published) Quantum onto the blockchain. In a live demonstration at the "Seven on Seven Conference", Dash bought the Quantum NFT for $4 – the first recorded NFT sale in history.

From a purely technical perspective, there isn't anything particularly complicated about NFTs. They are simply tokens on a blockchain that have unique identifiers associated with them (e.g., "NFT#123456") that contains "metadata", which is online information about the item it represents (e.g., a link to an image or video file). The question logically follows: what benefit is there to store this information on a blockchain?

As digital artists like the McCoys know firsthand, any digital file (e.g., an image in JPEG format) is replicable. One could simply copy and paste Quantum from the internet onto their computer at home, making it extremely difficult to sell any digital art. However, by making Quantum an NFT, it now has a unique identifier. Through this identifier, one can directly verify the ownership and authenticity of the piece. Blockchain plays its part by storing this information publicly, making transparent to all the identity of the owner of the original work (as well as being able to identify the artist who created it). It is still, of course, possible to copy and paste Quantum even if it is an NFT. But, like buying a print of the Mona Lisa, the individual only has a copy – not the original.

This set the foundation for a paradigm shift for artists. Reflecting the increasing digitalization of the world, artists could now create and sell digital art that could be genuinely and verifiably owned. In effect, the critical innovation of NFTs is that one can now bring scarcity to the digital world. It also has the added benefit of enabling enforcement for artist royalties, making it easier to earn a living for their craft. In physical art markets, it is difficult to enforce artist royalties, relying on trusting art marketplaces to enforce them. This often means artists sell a painting for a small amount only for it to increase in price and be traded multiple times; all the while, the artist does not receive a penny from these secondary sales. The advantage of NFTs is that they can have enforceable royalties in code, meaning artists can receive income as the NFTs are traded.

The introduction of digital scarcity through NFTs is a revolutionary concept that has repercussions across many different mediums. While the first and most immediate application was art, NFTs could be applied to any form of scarce asset or be a tool to digitize information. Examples include having an NFT representing your ID, medical records, a land title, a concert ticket, or even representing ownership of physical assets. While Quantum was minted in 2014, it took until 2021 for NFTs to truly enter the mainstream, creating what could be viewed retrospectively as the PFP NFT bubble.

The early days of NFTs: CryptoPunks

One of the earliest, and perhaps the most famous PFP collections of NFTs in crypto is the series "CryptoPunks," referred to by the art auction house Christie's as "[the] alpha and omega of the CryptoArt movement." CryptoPunks is a collection of 10,000 pixelated cartoon JPEGs of male and female characters – some smoking cigarettes, wearing 3D glasses, or sporting a mohawk. The rarer CryptoPunks do not take human form; instead, they consist of aliens, zombies, and apes. CryptoPunks represent the quintessential PFP NFTs, easily used as one's X or Facebook profile picture.

CryptoPunks were the brainchild of John Watkinson and Matt Hall, a duo of Canadian software developers. Watkinson and Hall "met" while studying computer science at the University of Toronto – when Watkinson was chatting with some friends after class and noticed that Hall was still fast asleep in the classroom (evidently put to sleep by the math lecture they were in). Watkinson and Hall would have limited interactions throughout their time at university, with Hall a self-professed poor student who would only attend class when an exam or test was scheduled.

It was a serendipitous meeting on the streets of Toronto that led them to reconnect after university, go into business together, and found the company Larva Labs in 2005. Together, Watkinson and Hall had a penchant for innovation and creativity, experimenting with different technologies in their infancy. They started building products in the 1990s on the internet, moving to apps for mobile phones (starting in the pre-iPhone days), and eventually they got interested in Bitcoin and blockchain.

The duo wanted to do something creative in the space; more than simply buying some Bitcoin. They settled on trying to rekindle the joy they got as children in collecting sports cards (particularly hockey cards) but instead do it in the digital realm. They previously tried to do something like this using a conventional app, but it didn't produce quite the same feeling they were aiming for. They reasoned that with digital ownership now possible, NFTs may be able to replicate the feeling of collecting physical items.

Inspired by the cyberpunk vibe and countercultural ethos of the crypto community, Hall and Watkinson settled on the name of their collection as "CryptoPunks." They set up CryptoPunks to be given away for free, keeping 1,000 of them for Larva Labs. At launch, uptake was slow – with only a dozen or so CryptoPunks claimed initially. Watkinson and Hall were dismayed by the uptake, recalling "because the first week was really slow…. we were like, that [idea] was dumb."

They tried to get the word out through Reddit, posting on the Ethereum subreddit, and emailing journalists. It wasn't until a Mashable article published by Jason Abbruzzese – which discussed how CryptoPunks could change the way people think about digital art – that all of the 9,000 CryptoPunks were claimed (known as "minting" an NFT). This snowballed into a wider discussion of the value of NFTs, with the idea resonating particularly amongst digital artists. The impact was more than what the duo expected, who summarized the experience as follows: "Two nerds make new website, try to get people to go to website, and accidentally become artists."

Looking at CryptoPunks, you may think they are fun little images a child created using Microsoft Paint while bored at school. However, they used AI to algorithmically generate each CryptoPunk. Known as "generative art", the artist defines the process (e.g., colors, numbers, geometry, etc.) and inputs this into an AI algorithm. The AI then produces a series of images with an element of randomness. This leads to some "traits" associated with the project of particularly rarity (e.g., only 0.09% or nine of the CryptoPunks have the alien trait), creating ultra-rare CryptoPunks that fetch a substantial premium to other CryptoPunks. Some CryptoPunks sport a face mask – which prompted conspiracy theories to circulate that somehow Watkinson and Hall knew about the COVID-19 pandemic ahead of time (the truth is less engaging, with Watkinson getting the idea from photos of punks in Japan, who were often photographed wearing face masks).

Watkinson and Hall created CryptoPunks at the height of the 2017 crypto bubble, watching interest in the crypto market wane through the subsequent bear market. From 2017 to mid-2020, the price of CryptoPunks remained relatively steady, with the floor selling price ranging from $50-200. In 2021, CryptoPunks prices started to rise dramatically. With hype in NFTs booming, investors turned to

CryptoPunks as one of the first and, therefore, "blue chip" NFT collections. Prices grew exponentially in 2021, starting at ~$4,000 before rising to an incredible floor price of $500,000, at its peak in October 2021. Watkinson and Hall watched in amazement amid a rising buzz around the project, with Hall stating, "something crazy would happen every day…. Some big sale, some person said that, or this person bought one or said this. This is part of what's crazy about having something decentralized. It's just happening out there. It's not under our control."

Punks became the hot commodity in the NFT space – having a Punk was the ultimate flex in the crypto world. Celebrities bought into the hype as well. Snoop Dogg – an avid NFT collector (trading under the pseudonym "Cozomo de' Medici") – owns nine CryptoPunks, with two clocking in at $2 million each. Jay Z purchased a CryptoPunk in early 2021 for around $130,000. The "Wolf of Wall Street" Jordan Belfort – the former stockbroker who spent time in prison for fraud (famously depicted in the 2013 film of the same name by Leonardo DiCaprio) – purchased a Punk for nearly $420,000 in 2021.

The most expensive CryptoPunk sold for an astounding $11.75 million at Sotheby's, which in the auction also received an $87 million dollar bid (that was subsequently withdrawn). That particular CryptoPunk had the ultra-rare combination of being both an alien punk and wearing a face mask – no doubt reflecting the anxiety of the COVID-19 pandemic. While an exorbitant sum to pay, the CryptoPunk was purchased by Shalom Meckenzie – an Israeli entrepreneur and largest shareholder in the fantasy sports and gambling company Draft Kings. The sum is chump change for Shalom, who had an estimated net worth of $1.1 billion at the time of writing.

All-time sales of CryptoPunks (both initial sales and secondary sales) are north of $3 billion, making it one of the most successful NFT projects of all time.

While people may scoff at spending so much money on a JPEG, there is a core human element at play. CryptoPunks represent one of the most significant status symbols in crypto. Changing your X display picture to your newly acquired Punk brings immediate credibility in crypto, and, usually, an increase in followers as well. It doubles as a wealth flex, showcasing that the buyer can afford to drop millions on an NFT. Others see CryptoPunks in the same way as baseball or Pokémon cards – tapping into the desire to collect rare or historical items – just as Watkinson and Hall intended.

As the CryptoPunk community and brand grew, Watkinson and Hall increasingly found themselves out of their depth. Creative and experimental developers at heart, the duo was not cut out for the level of community and brand management typically required for an NFT project of this size. This led the duo to sell the rights to CryptoPunks (along with 400 CryptoPunks) to Yuga Labs, the company behind another hugely successful NFT project, Bored Ape Yacht Club, launched in April 2021. Like CryptoPunks, Bored Ape Yacht Club consists of a collection of 10,000 JPEGs of cartoon apes. The collection counts celebrities such as Snoop Dog, Gwyneth Paltrow, Paris Hilton, Jimmy Fallon, and Justin Bieber amongst its owners.

The PFP NFT bubble from 2021 to 2022

As Watkinson and Hall experienced with the CryptoPunks price moving from under $100 to sales fetching more than $11 million in 2021, the NFT market – like the broader cryptocurrency market – experienced an incredible bull run starting in 2021. The same macroeconomic forces at play in the rise of shitcoins and meme shares would touch NFTs as well. This was aided by the additional enthusiasm generated from the market coming to grips with a new application of blockchain technology. No longer would the crypto markets be solely dominated by just cryptocurrencies.

The growth in the size of the NFT market was staggering. A report by nonfungible.com estimated that the market for NFTs increased from $86 million in 2020 to $17.6 billion in 2021, a nearly 21,000% increase. NFTs became part of the cultural zeitgeist, with Collins Dictionary crowning "NFTs" as the word of the year in 2021.

South Park, too, joined in the action, parodying NFTs through an adult Butters brainwashing the residents of South Park to invest their entire life savings in NFTs (with devastating results).

Large global brands like Nike, Gucci, Dolce & Gabbana, and Tiffany all launched or licensed NFT collections. Nike launched its own NFT collection of digital shoes, earning over $180 million, further increasing hype around NFTs. The NBA launched a collection called "NBA Top Shots," which allows users to buy, sell, and collect NFTs of important "moments" in NBA history. Users can buy a pack of NFTs online, with the chance of receiving a "legendary" moment in NBA history (coming in the form of a short video). Top Shots was a major success, with over $1 billion in lifetime sales. The most expensive NFT sale thus far is a dunk by Lebron James in the 2020 NBA finals, which sold for $230,000.

I was unfortunately late to the NFT party. Having followed the rise of NFTs in early 2021, I was more interested in their legal implications rather than buying them. I initially set out to publish another academic paper examining what (if any) Intellectual Property rights would attach to NFTs (e.g., is the image copyrighted? Could you sue someone who downloads a copy of the image of your NFT?). I subsequently abandoned writing the article and now shudder at the investing opportunity I missed, particularly as I was considering buying a CryptoPunk at the time. While NFTs started from foundations to help digital artists, like many things in crypto, the idea gave way to rampant speculation. No better example of this is the NFT collection "Ether Rocks."

Ether Rocks was one of the very first NFT collections ever launched, dating back to December 2017, only six months after the creation of CryptoPunks. Created by an anonymous group (or individual), the entire collection consists of 100 different colors of the same JPEG of a rock, spanning from your run-of-the-mill grey rock to more exotic red and blue rocks. Evidently, the project was designed to mimic the "Pet Rock" craze in 1975, whereby advertising executive Gary Dahl proved you could sell anything with the proper marketing around it. Dahl's idea was to sell rocks in cardboard boxes, fitted out with a straw and breathing hole with the tagline: "This box contains one genuine pedigreed Pet Rock."

The Pet Rock came with an instruction pamphlet giving a rundown of how to care for your rock, along with a description of the lineage of your rock (some exclusive rocks had apparently come from the Great Pyramid of Giza of all places). Dahl had developed the idea while at a bar with his friends discussing get-rich-quick schemes. And get rich, he did. Pet Rocks sold over one million units, making Dahl a multi-millionaire.

Ether Rocks did not initially follow the wild success of Pet Rocks. The first rock sold for around $300. Between 2017 and 2020, only 30 of the 100 rocks were sold. That all changed in 2021. Like the experience of CryptoPunks, NFTs everywhere started to increase in price. As the NFT craze gained steam, so did the price of Ether Rocks, aided by famous entrepreneur Gary Vaynerchuk (commonly known as Gary Vee) tweeting in response to an Ether Rock – causing a massive spike in price with multiple sales in excess of $1 million, a peak price of $1.8 million, and the lowest price of an Ether Rock at $300,000. This was particularly crazy as Ether Rock's website was explicit in what the project was about: "These virtual rocks serve NO PURPOSE beyond being able to be bought and sold, and giving you a strong sense of pride in being an owner of 1 of the only 100 collectible rocks :)"

While many early buyers of Ether Rocks benefited greatly from the price increase, a trader going by the name of Dino Dealer on X mistakenly listed his $1 million Ether Rock for less than a cent. Before he realized his mistake, an NFT trading bot snapped up the bargain. Dino Dealer despondently tweeted about his mistake, asking "Am I GMI [Going to Make It]?" before sending a message to NFT trading bots' wallet address, in an attempt to recover the NFT (to no avail).[3] Another X user, rather mockingly replied to Dino Dealer's tweet, saying, "the silver lining is that your entire net worth is no longer in a rock jpeg?"

Why Ether Rocks became so expensive is a matter of heated debate. Some speculate that nobody would be that stupid to pay an exorbitant sum for a JPEG of rock, arguing it's clearly a means to launder money. Others point to its historical significance of being an early NFT project, like CryptoPunks. I favor the simplest explanation: good old-fashioned speculation.

Early NFT projects like Ether Rocks were not alone in benefitting from the bull market in 2021 – new NFT projects emerged. In an attempt to bring drug trafficking into the Metaverse, a Columbian artist based in Medellin (home to the infamous Medellin Cartel founded by Pablo Escobar), Camilo Restrepo, created an NFT collection called "a ToN of coke." True to its name, the collection contains 1,000 NFTs of one-kilo (2.2 pounds) crypto cocaine packages. Each NFT is identical – a white rectangle with a gray background – save for the serial number inscribed in the bottom right corner. As per the description in the Opensea listing, the artist notes, "For the first time, since the War on Drugs started, a ToN oF cocaine floating on the open sea can be legally owned and its ownership officially verified." The NFTs were initially priced according to the serial number, with the first kilo costing 0.001 ETH (short for ether, being the native cryptocurrency of the Ethereum network), working its way up to 1 ETH for the 1,000 kilo.

Restrepo intended the project to be a critique of Colombia's drug war, along with a social commentary on life in Colombia. Restrepo noted, "I also know that if this project goes viral… I could live off [sales of] a ton of NFT coke as effectively a drug dealer who can live a lifetime off moving a single ton of cocaine." The cheapest NFT in the collection will now set you back ~$400 – a hefty price for a big night out in the Metaverse.

Artists were not the only ones to launch their own NFT collection. Ever the opportunist, Donald Trump dived headlong into the NFT scene, launching his own collection. While some initially considered the collection to be a joke, it was indeed backed by the former president, labeled as "Trump Cards." He announced his NFT collection with a post: "Collect all of your favorite Trump Digital Trading Cards, very much like a baseball card, but hopefully much more exciting…Only $99 each!"

The collection contains multiple different variants of Donald Trump in digital form. These include him in a wide array of costumes, from holding a shotgun in military gear, dressed as a version of Superman (with Superman's famous "S" replaced with "T", presumably called "TrumpMan"), and as an astronaut. There is also Trump in the middle of a boxing ring with boxing gloves on, Trump in a fighter pilot outfit standing on the top of the globe, and Trump giving the double thumbs up while gold bars float around labeled "Trump."

In a post on his Truth social media platform, he said he was offering, "limited edition cards feature[ing] ART of my Life & Career." It appears that some of the images may be fictionalized (unless Trump had time during his presidency to become an astronaut). While there was a heavy dose of skepticism about the NFTs, Trump's supporters came out in force when the collection dropped. The 45,000 NFTs sold out in less than a day, netting the project a cool $4.5 million in sales.

Key to the project's success was the additional utility of the NFTs. A criticism often leveled at NFTs is that they offer nothing more to the owner than a digital image. Notwithstanding that digital art projects have aesthetic value, many NFT projects try to provide some utility to their owners (e.g., IP rights, access to a community, physical items). Trump's NFT collection did precisely that. His collection markets itself on the "Sweepstakes Bonus," with every NFT purchased given an entry into the "Trump Sweepstakes." The prizes on offer included:

- A dinner with Trump in Miami
- Mar-A-Lago Group cocktail hour
- One-on-one meeting with Trump
- Golf match with Trump and your friends
- Hand-signed memorabilia

If the prizes on offer didn't appeal to you, they would, at a minimum, represent a pretty good investment. Priced at $99 each, post the initial sale, the price of the NFTs subsequently skyrocketed on the secondary market. The lowest-priced NFTs on offer were sitting at a cool 700% return on the original purchase price, at the time of writing.

As the NFT market grew throughout 2021, the scope of what would be minted on the blockchain as an NFT expanded. Early PFP NFT projects typically followed the blueprint of CryptoPunks, having a collection of around 10,000 NFTs, each procedurally generated by AI. However, nothing could stop other images or items from also being NFTs. One such example was an NFT sold by Jack Dorsey, the co-founder and former CEO of X, who is no stranger to the crypto world. X is a hotbed of crypto activity, from keeping up-to-date with crypto news to influencers shilling the newest shitcoin.

It was, therefore, no surprise when Dorsey dipped his toes into the world of NFTs. Dorsey put an image of the very first tweet on X up for auction as an NFT, with proceeds given to a charity (GiveDirectly's Africa Response fund). The tweet, written by Dorsey himself, states: "just setting up my twttr." The tweet, from March 21, 2006, forms an important piece of internet history. It also illustrates how digital ownership in the form of NFTs opens up a whole new world of items to be bought, sold, and collected. No longer are collectors constrained to physical items. Worried about a first edition print of a famous book getting damaged? No worries – you can now buy an NFT of its first digital print. There are other opportunities to tokenize physical items as NFTs – such as Pokémon cards –which give the owner the ability to redeem the NFT for the physical item. This makes buying and selling the item much easier, as ownership can transfer via the NFT (preventing the physical transfer of the item, which is both costly and risks damaging the item). As the auction for the first tweet drew near, the question became: how much is a little piece of internet history worth?

The answer: $2.6 million.

Sina Estavi, an Iranian businessman, bid aggressively in the auction to snare his prize. Estavi is a crypto entrepreneur and CEO of the crypto exchange Bridge Oracle (along with the CryptoLand exchange), which issued the "BRG" token. In May 2021, a few months after the auction, Iranian authorities arrested Estavi, charging him with "disrupting the economic system" in relation to his crypto activities after suspecting that he was attempting to flee the country on his private jet. This caused his CryptoLand exchange to fold, resulting in the value of the BRG token crashing from 35 cents to nearly zero. Estavi would spend the next nine months in prison before being released.

Even before his arrest, many were critical of his decision to acquire the NFT, leading Estavi to later tweet in defense of his purchase: "This is not just a tweet! I think years later people will realize the true value of this tweet, like the Mona Lisa painting." It remains to be seen if Estavi will be vindicated – but the best offer from 2022 of a mere $6,200 (a near 99% loss on investment) may mean he will have to wait a while longer.

Beeple's 69M NFT

An example of the peak of the NFT bubble was the sale of "Everydays" by Michael Winkelmann. Winkelmann, better known by the name "Beeple", enjoyed huge success as a digital artist. Embracing the new medium, Beeple produced a mixture of images and videos evoking abstract style, sci-fi elements, and biting social commentary. Some of his stranger pieces include a naked Joe Biden urinating on a giant Donald Trump, Hilary Clinton with a golden teeth grill titled "Senator Clinton makes a last ditch effort to reach black voters," and an image of Tom Hanks physically beating up a humanoid coronavirus.

In 2007, he started a project that would eventually transform into his magnum opus titled "Everydays". Beeple promised to create a new piece of digital art every day under the "Beeple Crap" moniker. Come rain, hail, or shine, Beeple made a piece of digital art every day – including on the day his first daughter was born (he asked his wife for a few minutes to whip up a new piece before driving her to the hospital). The project is ongoing, with the creation of more than 5,000 pieces of digital art. Prior to the rise in popularity of NFTs, digital artists such as Beeple struggled to fully monetize their art. This was reflected in Beeple's art sales – the highest sale price being less than $100.

It was all about to change.

Capitalizing on the growing market, Beeple sold an NFT called "Crossroad", a short 10-second video that would change based on the outcome of the 2020 US presidential election (with the defeat of Trump, the video showed an apparently dead giant version of Trump tarnished with graffiti, prominently displaying the word "loser"). The NFT was sold by Beeple for ~$66,000 and later resold for $6.7 million.

Beeple wasn't done yet. Through the art auction house Christie's, Beeple pieced together the first 5,000 pieces of digital art from his "Everydays" series. The enormous collage was put to auction, starting at $100. The bidding culminated in a frenzy, eventually selling for an incredible $69.3 million (42,329 Ether). This crazy price was the highest sale price for an NFT in history, along with being one of the most expensive art sales ever. The price prompted even Beeple to acknowledge how crazy it was, calling the NFT art boom at the time an "irrational exuberance bubble." He was careful to note that "if you look at art historically, blue chip stuff does pretty well over time. But most of it goes to zero. That's just how it is. And I believe NFTs will be no different."

The PFP NFT bubble bursts

NFT markets would reach their peak around April 2022. Projects like BAYC, which initially sold NFTs for around $200, traded at a floor price of approximately $430,000. Simultaneously, there was a tremendous surge in the number of NFT collections available, totaling in excess of 50,000. The supply increase coincided with the initial novelty of NFTs starting to subside. Investors' expectations of NFT projects would start rising – they were unsatisfied with purchasing a PFP NFT that offered nothing more than ownership of a JPEG.

Investors expected utility for their NFTs, whether in the form of giveaways, a profit-sharing mechanism, or access to exclusive events.

Simultaneously, many investors became deterred by the markets' proliferation of hackers. The highest profile example was when hackers tweeted a malicious phishing link on Ethereum Founder Vitalik Buterin's X account in 2023. Upon clicking on the link and accepting the transaction, victims would have their entire accounts drained. Blockchain analyst ZachXBT estimated nearly $691,000 was stolen from this incident alone, with almost 75% in the form of NFTs.

While these undercurrents contributed to the PFP NFT bubble popping, the combination of broader market conditions and crypto shocks ultimately ended the bull market. With inflation and interest rates rising in 2022, investors shifted capital away from "riskier" assets like cryptocurrencies and NFTs. Two major shocks in crypto markets compounded this; the first occurring in May 2022 with the collapse of Terra Luna (a major cryptocurrency), and then FTX in November 2022 (both covered in later chapters).

PFP NFT projects were particularly sensitive to these shocks – many projects had limited fundamental value or utility, with value derived either purely from speculation or some aesthetic value or social status attached to the project. A report by the website dappGambl estimated that of around 73,000 NFT projects it studied, nearly 70,000 are now worthless.[4] This equates to roughly 95% of all NFT investments held, worth nothing. Even blue-chip PFP NFT projects were not immune from the carnage, with BAYC NFT floor prices falling by nearly 90%. This has undoubtedly created a stigma around NFTs, with many seeing them as scams or Ponzi schemes. While this is certainly the case in some NFT projects, it obscures some important nuances around NFTs.

The community aspects, particularly for large and popular NFT collections, cannot be understated in crypto. Having an NFT from a large NFT collection, like DeGods, Mad Lads, CryptoPunks and BAYC, as your profile picture on X or Discord, still provide an important signal in the world in crypto. They preserve anonymity through not publicly displaying one's face or name, while also signaling that you are part of the broader community. They introduce a form of blindness into crypto – your ethnicity, country and gender are unknown. The only criteria for getting entry and acceptance within the community is holding an NFT. I can personally attest to this, proudly displaying my DeGods NFT (which graces the cover of this book) across my social media channels, and continually interacting with other DeGods NFT holders on Telegram.

Furthermore, the market bubble was mainly centered around PFP NFTs, which were particularly prone to rampant speculation. These are, however, just one type of NFT. We are already seeing a greater range of NFTs emerge, with clear utility. Tickets to sporting and musical events are slowly being replaced by NFTs. In the gaming space, in-game items are being traded as NFTs (covered in a later chapter). Asset titles, such as land and car titles, are being "tokenized" on blockchains as NFTs (known as "Real World Assets") with Boston Consulting Group estimating that this market will reach $16 trillion by 2030. Redbelly, a purpose-built asset tokenization blockchain, has already tokenized more than $70 billion of carbon credits, facilitating efficient trading of credits globally. These use cases demonstrate an evolution in the use of the technology and point toward a future where NFTs may underpin a broad range of industries, redefining how we own, trade, and interact with assets in our increasingly digital world.

CHAPTER 3: THE $450 MILLION DOLLAR LOST PASSWORD

"I tried everything. I would stay up all night trying different ideas for how to recover it, or just, like, staring at the ceiling for hours." – Stefan Thomas on his attempts to recover his $200 million of Bitcoin

A truly staggering amount of wealth has been created in a short period of time from cryptocurrencies, starting with the invention of Bitcoin in 2009. The collective market capitalization of cryptocurrencies now sits around the $1 trillion mark, on par with the world's biggest multinational companies like Apple, Amazon, and Microsoft. For early adopters, there was a lot of money to be made. Take the Winklevoss twins, famous for their depiction in the movie *The Social Network* (detailing the creation of Facebook). After reaching a reported $65 million settlement in a lawsuit against Facebook, the twins parlayed their earnings into crypto investments. *Forbes* now estimates each twin has a cryptocurrency holding of $1.4 billion each (including 70,000 Bitcoins).

In the early days of cryptocurrencies, not even the most devout believers would have predicted just how large the industry would become. Many viewed their Bitcoin holdings as a fun little experiment. And who could blame them – the notion that some digital currency created out of thin air could eventually reach a price of nearly $70,000 would have been laughable in those early days. This is particularly true as, for the first years after the creation of Bitcoin, the price remained near zero. This attitude led to some fateful decisions from early Bitcoin adopters. Through a combination of circumstance and just plain bad luck, there are those who should have become multi-millionaires from cryptocurrencies, just like the Winklevoss twins. Instead, they are left ruing what could have been.

A unique feature of crypto markets is that cryptocurrencies can often be acquired for next to no cost. For example, projects often give out their cryptocurrency via an "airdrop" (covered in Chapter 10). An airdrop is a form of marketing, a user acquisition tool whereby the project will send out an amount of its cryptocurrency to active users in its community (e.g., those interacting with the project on Discord/X or using services offered by the project) for free. These airdrops can be worth a serious amount of money. For example, Blur, an NFT marketplace, completed an airdrop of its token in early 2023 to frequent NFT traders. One lucky trader snared 3.2 million Blur tokens – valued at around $1.93 million at the time.

Or take the example of Gavin Andresen, a US-based software developer who became interested in Bitcoin back in 2010. Andresen created a website called "Bitcoin Faucet" which gave away free Bitcoins to anyone with a Bitcoin address. If you were fortunate enough to claim from the website, you would have received five free Bitcoins – worth more than $300,000 at the time of writing.

Other early adopters could have made millions from mining Bitcoin. Mining refers to the process in which new transactions on the Bitcoin blockchain are validated and recorded accurately. It is a core measure to ensure transactions are not fraudulent (e.g., to stop an individual from adding 1 million Bitcoins to their wallet). What it means in practice is downloading a program that runs on a computer (or typically specialized hardware), which attempts to solve complex cryptographic puzzles using a brute force method to be the first to verify a block of transactions on the Bitcoin blockchain. The first program to solve the cryptographic puzzle receives an amount of Bitcoin as a reward. These rewards can be extremely lucrative. For example, an early supporter of Bitcoin, Hal Finney, downloaded Bitcoin mining software and received ten Bitcoins (worth more than

$600,000 today) for validating the first Bitcoin transaction on January 12, 2009.

Bitcoin mining has become a serious business, with dedicated organizations constructing warehouses of specialized Bitcoin mining rigs. Daily revenue from Bitcoin mining sits in excess of $20 million per day. As Bitcoin originally had no private or public sale (in contrast to how most cryptocurrencies are initially distributed) at the onset, you could only obtain Bitcoin by running mining software. As time progressed and interest increased in Bitcoin, people wanted to buy Bitcoin without having to run through the process of mining. Initially, the only way to purchase Bitcoin was the clunky process of organizing a direct peer-to-peer trade via a Bitcoin forum (such as Bitcoin Talk). Eventually, organized exchanges were founded, with the express intention to offer a streamlined way to buy and sell Bitcoin for the masses.

One of the first such exchanges was Mt. Gox, based in Tokyo. Launched in 2010, Mt. Gox rose to be the undisputed king of exchanges, handling more than 70% of Bitcoin transactions at the start of 2014. Mt. Gox was initially intended to be a trading site for the popular "Magic: The Gathering" game cards but was repurposed by American entrepreneur Jed McCaleb as a Bitcoin exchange. In 2011, the exchange was acquired by Mark Karpelès, a French software developer who took the position of CEO. It was through Mt. Gox that many got their first taste of cryptocurrencies. If you had bought a mere $400 of Bitcoin on Mt. Gox back in 2013, your investment would be worth in excess of $1 million today. However, that is under the assumption you withdrew your Bitcoin from Mt. Gox. In one of the most devastating hacks in crypto history, Mt. Gox had almost 750,000 of its customers' Bitcoins stolen, along with around 100,000 of the exchange's own Bitcoins as well (worth around $473 million at the time). This equated to nearly 7% of the Bitcoins in existence at the time. As it turned out, hackers had been taking Bitcoin from the exchange for years, using stolen credentials to systematically drain the exchange. Blockchain analysis subsequently confirmed that by mid-2013, Mt. Gox had already had its

Bitcoin stolen – around eight months before the exchange admitted so publicly. A recent US Department of Justice indictment alleges that the hack was perpetrated by two Russian nationals, Aleksandr Verner and Alexey Bilyuchenko (along with additional unnamed co-conspirators).[5] The hackers gained access to Mt. Gox's users' data and transactions (including the private keys), slowly siphoning away Bitcoins from the exchange over the course of three years.

The incident made Karpelès one of crypto's first genuine bad guys, earning him the title of "Bitcoin's Biggest Villain." When the exchange halted customer withdrawals and declared bankruptcy on February 28, 2014, Karpelès spent the next few days frenetically checking through Mt. Gox's digital wallets – finding each one empty. Karpelès was surprised to stumble across a wallet containing 200,000 Bitcoins, which had been untouched for three years. This "discovery" heaped additional suspicion on the CEO, with customers blaming him for their losses and suspecting him of stealing their Bitcoins. While Karpelès was not involved with the hackers, his hands were not clean. In March 2019, the Tokyo District Court found Karpelès guilty of falsifying data to inflate Mt. Gox's Bitcoin holdings (in an attempt to hide the Bitcoin losses from customers) and gave him a suspended sentence of 30 months.

The event was a devastating blow for the broader crypto community at the time but was acutely felt by those who had their Bitcoin stolen. One example was Kolin Burges, a British developer and early Bitcoin adopter. Upon news of Mt. Gox filing for bankruptcy, he immediately boarded a plane from London to Tokyo and started a protest outside Mt. Gox's headquarters. For two weeks, Burges protested, holding a sign reading "MTGOX WHERE IS OUR MONEY." Burges got an opportunity to confront Karpelès directly, brandishing his sign as Karpelès attempted to enter Mt. Gox's headquarters. Karpelès simply ignored Burges' protests. Despite the Mt. Gox hack, the fact remains that if you got into crypto early (and avoided the hacks), you could be sitting on a pile of cash today. That is, if you didn't lose your Bitcoin along the way.

The $520 million of Bitcoin in a landfill

Owning cryptocurrencies involves having two distinct "keys". Keys are like passwords, comprised of a combination of letters and numbers. There are two types of keys: public and private. Public keys function like your bank account number – they can be shared publicly and used as an address for cryptocurrency to be sent. Conversely, private keys are not to be shared with anyone. They function like the password to your bank account. As long as your private key is safe, so too will your cryptocurrency.

However, given that private and public keys are long and difficult to remember, many people opt to store their cryptocurrencies on exchanges (e.g., Binance and Coinbase) or in online wallets (like MetaMask). Both solutions come with a degree of risk. Crypto exchanges can be hacked or become insolvent, resulting in the complete loss of your cryptocurrencies. Holding cryptocurrencies in online wallets can also be dangerous. For example, if you approve a malicious transaction, hackers can drain your account.

To protect against this, many people store their private keys in "cold storage", either writing them on a piece of paper or storing them on a laptop/hard drive not connected to the internet. While great for protecting against digital theft, it means that if you lose the laptop/hard drive (with the private key), you can never again access your cryptocurrency. Crypto data firm Chainalysis estimates that as of 2021, about 20% of Bitcoin has been lost or stored in wallets that can no longer be retrieved.[6]

This is precisely what happened to James Howells, a Welshman with around 8,000 Bitcoins (worth approximately $520 million as of the time of writing) sitting at the bottom of a landfill site. Howells, a former IT systems engineer and project manager, obtained these Bitcoins back in 2009 through mining – one of the first five people in the world to do so. After stripping his laptop for parts, Howell put the laptop hard drive containing the private key into his desk drawer. A few years later in 2013, as part of a routine cleanup of his desk, Howell mistakenly threw out the hard drive with Bitcoin stored instead of an identical blank hard drive. Howell recalled at the time, "As soon as I put it [the hard drive] into the bin at home I had a second thought in the back of my mind, you have never thrown a hard drive out before, why start now, you shouldn't do this sort of thing." Howells forgot this incident until he started to hear news about Bitcoin's price rising, including stories of people making millions from their holdings. Upon checking the hard drive that should have contained his Bitcoins, he realized he had thrown the wrong drive out.

He described the feeling as "absolute devastation," wishing he could "go back in time and not throw that drive away." Years later, Howells continues to speak agonizingly about this mistake, able to precisely quantify the impact of his error in dollar terms: "Seeing the value of my coins going from 700,000 to 1 million, 2 million, 9 million and I'm like [Howells puts his hands over his face in agony]." This fateful mistake set up one of history's most interesting scavenger hunts. After some frantic research, Howell identified the precise location of his hard drive – a local council landfill. Howells hatched a plan to get it back, involving searching through 110,000 tons (232 million pounds) of rubbish, using AI and robot dogs.

The plan

Finding a 6cm (2.5 inches) large hard drive, about the size of an iPhone, in the middle of a landfill, is no easy feat. To accomplish this task, Howells assembled a crack team of eight experts to try to do it. They come from various fields: from landfill excavation to AI, and even includes an advisor who recovered the data from the black box of the 2003 fatal Space Shuttle Columbia disaster (which took the lives of all seven astronauts on board).

The plan first involves progressively excavating the landfill, with the rubbish then placed onto a conveyor belt for sorting. Humans would sort through the rubbish, assisted by an AI-trained algorithm created by Max-AI. The algorithm would be trained to identify hard drives that fit the description, using a mechanical arm to pick and retrieve any matches. Once the project is underway, there is a material risk that fortune hunters will converge on the landfill to retrieve the hard drive for themselves. To counter this, a series of CCTV cameras will be placed around the facility. Not only that, two robotic "dogs" from the robotics company Boston Dynamics (famous for their robots doing dances on YouTube videos) would also patrol the area at night.

The plan has some heavy Venture Capital backing, with Karl Wendeborn and Hanspeter Jaberg agreeing to fund the venture – committing funding up to $11 million. However, even if the hard drive is found, it's possible that it's too damaged to retrieve the data. The hard drive was disposed of in a sealed plastic bag, so the team hopes it remains preserved. Phil Bridge, a data-recovery advisor for the project, indicated that if the platter (an internal component in the hard drive) isn't cracked, there is around an 80-90% chance the data can be recovered.

While the project itself is a large challenge, the greater difficulty for Howells has been getting approval from the Newport City Council to commence the project. The council is concerned about the significant environmental impact on the surrounding excavation area, with the cost of digging, storing, and treating the waste costing millions of dollars. To sweeten the deal, Howells has offered to give each of Newport's residents 50 pounds worth of Bitcoin and create a crypto investment hub in the area. He would keep around 30% of the value of the Bitcoin, with the rest flowing to the team and his financial backers.

At the time of writing, the Newport City Council had not yet agreed to the plan.

Howells at least can see some humor in the situation, with his LinkedIn profile stating that he "Might know a thing or two about landfills" along with his profile banner displaying the words "Never Give Up". Despite Howell's determination, undoubtedly, the search has taken its toll on him, with his friend Liam Screen describing him as "obsessed" and the search having "taken over his life".

The $450M lost password

Stefan Thomas, a programmer based in San Francisco, was an early adopter of Bitcoin. Thomas has an impressive career in crypto, serving as the Chief Technology Officer of Ripple Inc., the company behind one of the largest cryptocurrencies, "Ripple". An extremely talented developer, Thomas has now co-founded Interledger Foundation, which aims to create a web-based payments infrastructure that will allow greater global financial inclusion.

In 2011, Thomas was approached to create a video explaining Bitcoin. He eagerly accepted and received 7,002 Bitcoins – worth around $6,000 for his services. At that time, Thomas was obsessed with Bitcoin and blockchain technology; it started to consume his entire life. Thomas described falling asleep on his keyboard from exhaustion and waking up with keys imprinted on his face. Knowing the risks of holding so much Bitcoin on an exchange or storing it online, Thomas opted to store the private key on an IronKey USB device. IronKey devices are renowned for their encryption, providing a secure solution for protecting sensitive data. The device is encrypted by a password, and the user has only ten incorrect guesses before the device digitally "nukes" the information on it – deleting it forever.

Thomas wrote the password to the IronKey device on a piece of paper. Impaired by his lack of sleep, he subsequently lost the piece of paper and forgot the password altogether. He then watched on helplessly as Bitcoin went on an almighty bull run, knowing the value of the Bitcoins stored on his device was sitting at around $450 million as of the time of writing. Thomas described being devasted watching the price of Bitcoin rising, with his entire world changing.

With the original password lost, Thomas had ten shots to get the password correct, or else the Bitcoin will be lost forever. He has made eight failed attempts at the password so far, trying different variants with no success. The hope of remembering the password makes this situation all the more difficult for Thomas, as he told the *Today Show*, "it's easier if you can let it be in the past and forget about it." Thomas described sleepless nights lying in bed, thinking of different ways to recover the Bitcoins, but each attempt has failed. He has turned to other methods, offering 700 Bitcoin to anyone who can help recover the data using a backdoor method. However, IronKey has stated it is impossible to hack its system, and no one has been able to offer Thomas any help.[7]

Unfortunately, there is no "forgot your password" link to reset your private key on the Bitcoin blockchain. Thomas became stoic about his predicament, stating that "time heals all wounds" and he's "at peace" with his situation. However, hope remains with his two final password attempts still in play.

The $650 million pizza order

On May 18, 2010 – nearly 1.5 years after the launch of Bitcoin – Laszlo Hanyecz posted a peculiar request on the Bitcoin Talk Forum. Hanyecz, a Florida-based programmer, got interested in Bitcoin in college and was one of the early active contributors to the community. At the time of his first post on Bitcoin Talk in 2010, the community numbered less than 100, compared to more than three million today. Hanyecz is credited with creating one of the first graphics processing unit (GPU) miners (which he freely shared with the Bitcoin community). GPU miners were more efficient than central processing units (CPUs), giving Hanyecz a competitive advantage in mining. From this innovation, Hanyecz was able to mine a large number of Bitcoins in the days when mining was not the competitive multi-billion-dollar industry it is today. Interestingly, Bitcoin's founder Satoshi Nakamoto (covered in a later chapter) had mixed feelings about Hanyecz innovation, correctly predicting that using GPUs would limit mining to only those using high-end, expensive GPUs (compared to mining on a CPU that anyone with a computer can use).[8] This would have the impact of centralizing Bitcoins into the hands of a few who could afford the expensive GPUs – directly against the philosophy of decentralization at the core of Bitcoin's creation.

Hanyecz's post on the Bitcoin Forum was titled "Pizza for bitcoins?" In essence he wanted a couple of pizzas (two large ones, in fact, so there would be leftovers for the next day) in exchange for some Bitcoins. Hanyecz – being a man of taste – specified that the pizza should have "just standard stuff, no weird fish toppings or anything like that." Jeremy Sturdivant (posting under the username of "jercos") answered Hanyecz's call. A 19-year-old student in California at the time, Sturdivant had become interested in Bitcoin on philosophical grounds, attracted to its design that ensured open access to all. Sturdivant organized the delivery of two Supreme pizzas from the popular pizza franchise Papa Johns, to Hanyecz. At the time, Sturdivant was concerned that Papa Johns would not accept his out-of-state debit card, but fortunately, the transaction went smoothly. A happy Hanyecz posted a picture of himself with the two pizzas, thanking Sturdivant for the trade. At the time, Hanyecz thought it was incredibly cool to have been involved in the transaction, stating, "Hey, I just traded this, you know, open source internet money for a real world good."

This would, however, prove to be a seminal moment in both of their lives.

At the time, the Bitcoins exchanged were valued at a measly $41. Sturdivant had already made some money on the trade, with the pizzas purchased for $25. The $16 profit margin would start to expand rapidly, coalescing into potentially the most lopsided transaction in history. This is because Hanyecz didn't pay one or two Bitcoins for the pizzas. Rather, he paid 10,000 Bitcoins.

The 10,000 Bitcoins are now worth $650 million.

Just to rub it in further, the value paid for the pizzas is tracked live on the website "Bitcoin Pizza Index," serving as a constant reminder to Hanyecz of the transaction. The website breaks down the cost of the pizzas:

- $312 million per pizza
- $39 million per slice
- $5.9 million per piece of bacon
- $5.3 million per piece of salami

- $2.8 million per piece of pepperoni
- $2.7 million per piece of sausage
- $1.8 million per tomato slice
- $1.5 million per piece of green pepper
- $1.3 million per olive

The solace for Hanyecz is that the transaction has now become folklore in the crypto community. At the time, Bitcoin was solely the domain of tech enthusiasts. The Bitcoin pizza transaction represented the first recorded time in history that Bitcoin was exchanged for a good or service. This pre-empted the eventual adoption and proliferation of Bitcoin as a currency/medium of exchange. Today, an estimated 36% of small to medium businesses in the US accept Bitcoin, including large companies such as Microsoft, AT&T, and Wikipedia. Bitcoin ATMs are now available, allowing people to buy Bitcoin directly, using fiat currency (i.e. a national currency such as the US dollar).

Even El Salvador, the Central American country home to an estimated 6.6 million people, decided to join the party. In 2021, El Salvador's President Nayib Bukele announced that his country would be the first in the world to accept Bitcoin as legal tender, meaning it could be used to buy groceries or pay taxes. The decision was intended to reduce the country's reliance on the US dollar, along with giving access to a digital payment method for nearly 70% of people in El Salvador without a bank account.[9]

The Bitcoin pizza transaction has since been commemorated as "Bitcoin Pizza Day," celebrating the anniversary of the transaction on May 22. The crypto community is encouraged to commemorate this day by buying two pizzas (using Bitcoin, of course), with pizza shops often offering special discounts.

More important than the celebrations are what became of the 10,000 Bitcoins Sturdivant received in the deal. Unfortunately for Sturdivant, he is not enjoying a life of luxury on a private island with a yacht. Instead, he sold the Bitcoins to "cover expenses" while on holiday with his girlfriend travelling around the US. At that time, the 10,000 Bitcoins were worth around $400.

Hanyecz himself has no regrets about the transaction. He told the *New York Times*, "it wasn't like Bitcoins had any value back then, so the idea of trading them for a pizza was incredibly cool." He subsequently spent a further 90,000 Bitcoins on pizzas that summer – equating to nearly $5.8 billion worth of Bitcoin spent on pizza. Yikes.

CHAPTER 4: HOW A DOG MEME BECAME WORTH MORE THAN THE GDP OF SRI LANKA

"Doge to the moon." – Elon Musk

Browsing through the top 10 highest-value crypto tokens gives you a quick sense of the Who's Who in the crypto landscape. There is the ubiquitous Bitcoin, which has held the title as the number one cryptocurrency by value since its inception – despite many so-far failed predictions of its downfall (including nearly 500 proclamations, and counting, in news outlets that "Bitcoin is dead").[10] A second is Ethereum, a ground-breaking use of blockchain technology conceived by one of the most influential figures in crypto – Vitalik Buterin. Ethereum pushed the potential of blockchain technology from simply sending and receiving a crypto token (i.e., the function of the Bitcoin protocol) to allowing developers to create, deploy and execute smart contracts (essentially opening a whole new world of possibilities for blockchain technology).

Then there is "Binance Coin", created by the world's largest crypto exchange Binance, with an estimated 30 million users.[11] There are also "stablecoins" like Tether or USD Coin (USDC), intended to trade at one to one with a currency (e.g., 1 Tether trades at 1 dollar). Stablecoins are heavily used across the crypto space, designed to hold crypto at a stable value instead of being exposed to price volatility. Although, when a stablecoin is no longer "stable," it can have devastating consequences, as will be explored in the chapter on the collapse of

Terra Luna. There is, however, one token that sticks out like a sore thumb in the top ten. Amid a series of tokens with significant user adoption and utility, there is a token that is based on a dog meme.

That token is Dogecoin. And it is worth an eye-watering amount.

It's named in reference to the "Doge" meme, centered around a photo of a Shiba inu, a Japanese breed of dog. The meme is typically presented with the dog surrounded by words in broken English, rendered in different colored text using Comic Sans font. Dogecoin was made as a joke by its creators, with an unlimited supply of tokens on offer (around an additional 14.4 million created each day).[12]

How, then, did this token not only survive, but go on to be valued at $81 billion at its peak (more than the GDPs of Sri Lanka, Kenya, or Bulgaria) and consistently rank in the top ten of crypto overall? And how the hell did Elon Musk become its biggest supporter?

Dogecoin's beginning

Dogecoin was created in the nascent stage of crypto markets. Its genesis was from the mind of Jackson Palmer, an Australian based in Sydney working as a product marketer at Adobe. A University of Newcastle graduate, Palmer would spend the day at work honing his marketing skills and spend his nights coding. The combination of his coding prowess and working at a tech company afforded Palmer exposure to blockchain technology and cryptocurrency. His interest growing, Palmer put his skillset to use by making the Dogecoin website, containing the iconic comical font and imagery associated with the meme. At the time, Palmer made the website purely for fun, riding on the viral sensation that the Doge meme was at the time. On November 28, 2013, Palmer fatefully tweeted (as a joke): "Investing in Dogecoin, pretty sure it's the next big thing." This attracted the attention of American IBM software engineer Billy Markus, also known by his X username "Shibetoshi Nakamoto" (a combination of Shiba Inu and Satoshi Nakamoto, Bitcoin creator). Finding the tweet hilarious, he wanted to take the joke one step further and create

Dogecoin. He contacted Jackson with his pitch, and both agreed to make Dogecoin a reality.

Markus subsequently designed Dogecoin's protocol (based on a combination of existing cryptocurrencies Luckycoin and Litecoin, both being forks/copies of Bitcoin's code). Given the code for Dogecoin was essentially a copy and paste of two different cryptocurrencies, the whole exercise only took Markus around three hours. Such was the simplicity of the code; the bulk of those three hours was spent making alterations to the client to make the text comic sans, to match the font in the Doge meme. Just ten days after Palmer's tweet, Dogecoin was born.[13]

Dogecoin's genesis was unlike most other crypto projects at the time. Following the success of Bitcoin, a raft of altcoins had been created. Altcoins varied in quality with many just being lazy clones of existing projects intended by their creators to make some quick cash. As valuations of altcoins continued to rise, Palmer grew increasingly frustrated at the money being thrown at these projects. The Doge meme went viral that year – and with that, Palmer saw an opportunity to make a pointed critique of crypto markets. By creating such an absurd token, markets would surely recognize the low quality of many of these projects. Palmer's critique foreshadowed the eventual rise of shitcoins a mere seven years later, with shitcoins being like altcoins on steroids. To make the satire obvious, both Palmer and Markus set out to make Dogecoin "as ridiculous as possible," intending to "not make this something that people actually care about" and to make it as "undesirable as a cryptocurrency so it doesn't become serious."

Safe to say, this is not what happened! The internet didn't take long to fall in love with it. Shortly after Dogecoin's launch on December 6, 2013, the price rose 300%. In a clear example of the modern-day power of a meme, the Dogecoin website went viral through the assistance of Reddit – with more than one million hits within 30 days of launch. The Doge meme was already extremely popular on Reddit and pairing it with a cryptocurrency saw it spread like wildfire across the website. Reddit would continue to be closely associated with Dogecoin, forming the base of the community.

The rise of Dogecoin

Despite every attempt by its founders to consciously design the most ridiculously unappealing token, Dogecoin proved resilient. Driven by its popularity on Reddit, it gained traction as a "tipping coin" with people sending Dogecoin as a reward for good deeds. One week after launching, it became the second-most tipped cryptocurrency.[14] Tipping was powered by the "Dogetipbot" which allowed users to easily tip and receive Dogecoin through Reddit's API (application programming interface). In a three-month period in 2013, there were over 262,000 individual tips of Dogecoin (averaging 26 cents), with the largest tip of nearly $1,000. This dwarfed the tipping of Bitcoin, which only managed 9,000 individual tips of Bitcoin across a one-year period. Tipping of Dogecoin became popular as a comedic way to reward other users, illustrated by the spike in tipping on days like April Fools'. This was aided by the tiny price of a Dogecoin, sitting at around $0.0005, meaning you could tip 100,000 Dogecoin, and it would only set you back $50.

Dogecoin's rise is indicative of the heavy focus on community in crypto, with Dogecoin's community known as the "Doge Army." A large part of the general ethos of crypto is that of decentralization – the idea that decisions and decision-making power be diffused across many actors (in contrast with the centralized decision-making structure of traditional companies). Crypto projects often explicitly try to build a community to help in this mold while also creating a reliable base of customers for their tokens/NFTs/other products. Communities are often involved in the project's technical and commercial decisions, with founders/employees directly speaking to them in spaces like X and Discord. An engaged and loyal community can be a powerful way to bring more people into crypto and into the project.

With Dogecoin's community growing rapidly, this prompted a shift in the founders' attitude towards the project. Dogecoin had started to symbolize unexpected generosity on the internet – a way to show appreciation to a stranger. It represented a change from the typical hostile and belligerent discourse permeating most corners of the internet. No longer would Dogecoin just be a joke – it would be a force for good. The centerpiece of this was the creation of the Dogecoin Foundation, a not-for-profit organization created by the founders. It was through this foundation that Dogecoin's community was harnessed in some incredibly wholesome activities. The Dogecoin Foundation's manifesto stated its purpose simply as to "Do Only Good Everyday." In 2014, the Dogecoin Foundation raised $50,000 (around 40 million Dogecoin at the time) for the community to fund the creation of two drought-relieving water wells in Kenya.

In January 2014, news broke that the Jamaican bobsleigh team had qualified for the Winter Olympics to be held in Sochi later that year (the last time they qualified was 2002). The excitement about qualification was muted by the fact that the team didn't have enough money to cover the cost of attending. The Jamaican bobsleigh team had entered into the realm of pop culture through the 1990s classic film *Cool Runnings*. Starring John Candy and Leon Robinson, the film was loosely based on the first-ever appearance of the Jamaican national bobsleigh team in the 1988 Calgary Olympics. The movie was a feel-good story of the team overcoming a series of adversities to compete in an event, with all odds stacked against them.

Wanting to recapture some nineties nostalgia and do a good deed in the process, the Dogecoin Foundation stepped in. The Foundation launched a fundraiser called "Dogesled" aiming to raise enough money to fund the team's attendance. The community rallied quickly around the cause, with a flood of donations of Dogecoin coming in. So quick was the pace of donations, the price of Dogecoin itself started to rise. The initiative successfully collected the $30,000 worth of Dogecoin required to send the team to Sochi. Although the fundraising was a success, the Jamaican Bobsleigh team, unfortunately, did not match this, and finished last at Sochi.

Following the success of the Dogesled project, the Dogecoin

community rallied around another cause: NASCAR racing. On the Dogecoin subreddit, a Reddit user going by the unfortunate username "unicorn_butt_sex" posted:

> I realized that the driver of the number 98 Chevrolet SS, Josh Wise was sponsorless. He was racing the wheels off the car. He was fighting his underfunded teams car like he stole it. Sadly the car was just black with no sponsors. I know its not the Chevy but it's the same. Now there are millions of people watching NASCAR every week. There are two major races that are very exciting and people are digging to watch. The track name? Talladega. It is known for its big one and it's exciting. Now imagine a Doge. A Doge that is going 200 MPH into victory lane. Anyone can win Dega. Underfunded or not, for example last years race where David Regan and the underfunded team brought home the win. Now imagine on TV. DOGE DOGE DOGE DOGE DOGE every time he talks about his car. "This Doge Ford Fusion is fast today." Every time they talk about the car....

The post exploded in popularity. A fundraising campaign was quickly set up to get donations for the cause. Within a week, the community raised the required $55,000 (67 million Dogecoins at the time). This was off the back of around 1,200 donations, averaging about $40 each. With the Dogecoin sponsorship secured, Josh Wise was ready to hit the NASCAR circuit. The Dogecoin-branded car debuted in the Aaron's 499 race finishing in 20th place – Josh's second-best finish at that point in his racing career.

The community mindedness of the Dogecoin community was even evident in a hacking event. Back in December 2013, Dogecoin was rocked by its first major hack. Dogewallet was a popular online wallet service to hold Dogecoins. The hackers successfully gained access to the wallet's systems, allowing them to send Dogecoins to the hacker's wallet. Around 30 million Dogecoins were stolen in the attack. Although only $12,000 at the time (now worth more than $3.5 million), it had a more devastating impact on the community. Saddened by the hack occurring so close to Christmas, the Dogecoin community rallied around the victims. A "Save Dogemas" campaign was launched on Reddit by user "NeutralityMentality", aiming to collect donations of Dogecoins to reimburse those hacked. The campaign raised a large amount of Dogecoin, with a significant portion of the 30 million Dogecoins stolen able to be refunded to victims of the hack.

Billy Markus leaves the project for a Honda Civic

Despite the rise in popularity and a slate of positive community-backed projects, there was trouble brewing behind the scenes. Billy Markus had continued to be actively involved in the project since its inception but was finding it increasingly difficult to continue. At the time, Markus was a victim of numerous online attacks and negativity. Dogecoin's price at this time was a mere fraction of the highs it would eventually reach, hovering around $0.001 to $0.003. Nevertheless it was, like most cryptocurrencies, highly volatile with the price changing without any apparent reason. This resulted in Markus being subject to multiple death threats and lawsuits with people holding him responsible for losing money when the price of Dogecoin dropped.

In 2015 Markus decided to leave the project, stating on Reddit: "[the Dogecoin] community started to strongly shift from the one I was comfortable with." Along with leaving the project, Markus decided to dispose of his Dogecoin holdings after losing his regular job, stating, "I gave away and/or sold all the crypto I had back in 2015 after being laid off and scared about my dwindling savings at the time, for about enough in total to buy a used Honda Civic." This would prove a fateful decision for Markus, as by the 2021 Dogecoin bull run, those Dogecoins would have been able to purchase thousands of Honda Civics.

In an open letter to the Dogecoin community on Reddit in 2020, Markus lamented the state of some sections of the Dogecoin community and crypto more broadly:

> Pump and dumping, rampant greed, scamming, bad faith actors, demanding from others, hype without research, taking advantage of others – those are all worthless. Worse than worthless, honestly, bringing more negativity to an already difficult world. As the creator, some have called me the "doge mother" so I say this with that mask – when I see things like that –and I've seen plenty of it through the last 7 years –I'm not mad, just disappointed.

Markus also reiterated his hope for the future of the community, stating, "Joy, kindness, learning, giving, empathy, fun, community, inspiration, creativity, generosity, silliness, absurdity. These types of things are what makes Dogecoin worthwhile to me. If the community embodies these things, that's True Value."

Palmer, too, was becoming increasingly unsettled with the direction of Dogecoin. The irony of Dogecoin was not lost on Palmer, with the project morphing into the very thing it had been created to critique. While the wholesomeness of the community had kept Palmer contributing since its inception, like Markus, he was uncomfortable with the changes he saw around him.

This culminated in Palmer also leaving the project in 2015, citing the Dogecoin project and the crypto community more generally as "toxic." Palmer had long been critical of the demographics in crypto, calling out the industry for not doing enough to make the space inclusive to all. "All in all, the cryptocurrency space increasingly feels like a bunch of white libertarian bros sitting around hoping to get rich and coming up with half-baked, buzzword-filled business ideas which often fail in an effort to try and do so."[15] Palmer continued to be deeply critical of the excesses in crypto markets, launching a short-lived podcast called "Griftonomics" The podcast focused on modern-day scams and Ponzi schemes, with crypto having a particular focus.

With both founders leaving the project, the future of Dogecoin was uncertain.

Elon Musk, the "Dogefather"

After the founders left the project, Dogecoin could have easily faded into obscurity. This looked to be the case in 2020 when Dogecoin's price plummeted to a mere 0.003 cents (with a total valuation of $250 million) following the market downturn due to the COVID-19 pandemic.

As fate would have it, Elon Musk stepped in. The intervention of Elon Musk would prove to be the catalyst that brought Dogecoin from a small tipping coin to the global name it is today. The link between Musk and Dogecoin is so strong that entire algorithmic trading strategies (i.e. automated trading by computers in response to data) are built around Musk's comments about Dogecoin. And for good reason. In April 2023, Musk changed X's logo to an image of Doge – causing Dogecoin's price to spike by almost 25%. Research by Decrypt shows that Dogecoin searches from 2019 through 2020 would spike significantly every time Musk tweeted about the coin.[16] Clearly, there is money in following Musk's tweets.

Engrossed in internet meme culture, Musk seemed to be destined to drive Dogecoin forward. From creating a meme of himself smoking a joint on the Joe Rogan podcast in 2018 to challenging Vladimir Putin to "single combat", Musk has a penchant for the unusual. This perhaps explains why Dogecoin became his cryptocurrency of choice. Before Dogecoin, Musk appeared to have had limited interactions or interest in cryptocurrencies, stating he owned zero (aside from 0.25 Bitcoin a friend had sent him). This would all change in 2019, with Musk tweeting: "Dogecoin might be my fav cryptocurrency. It's pretty cool."

From this tweet, his public love affair with Doge would begin. A few months later, on December 20, 2020, Musk tweeted: "One word:

Doge."

At the time, Musk had more than 50 million Twitter followers, with this count subsequently exploding to more than 100 million after his 2022 Twitter acquisition (later renaming it X in 2023). This gave him tremendous reach and potential to influence. More importantly, Musk's follower base was disproportionately made up of those who would potentially invest in cryptocurrency. Cryptocurrency ownership demographics skew to younger males (aged 34 or below), with bachelor's degrees or above.[17] While Musk's follower demographics are not publicly available, X users, more generally, are majority male (70.4%), with around 60% of users aged under 34.[18] Furthermore, his profile as a tech billionaire who espouses libertarian views perfectly fits the ethos of many sections of the crypto community.[19]

Put together, Musk was perfectly placed to publicly amplify a cryptocurrency while also reaching the exact demographic that would invest in it. With interest rates near zero, and massive monetary and fiscal stimulus pumped into the economy, people were itching for a high investment return asset – creating the "Goldilocks" (just right) conditions for Dogecoin.

Following his tweet in December 2020, equity markets would be rocked by the explosive rise of "meme shares" manifested in the WallStreetBets meme share rally. As described earlier, this saw the poster child GameStop jumping from $2.75 to a high of $483 in January 2021. Those same traders started to take notice of Dogecoin, with the price beginning an upward trend in January on the back of Musk's interest. On Feb 4, 2021, Musk tweeted: "Dogecoin is the people's crypto… no need to be a gigachad to own."

That tweet sent Dogecoin's price soaring more than 60%.[20] Traders at this time had started to take notice of Musk's tweets, eagerly anticipating any public appearance or statement from him as a catalyst to move crypto markets. Given Musk's association with Dogecoin at the time, the community gave him the nickname "Dogefather" with many tweets and Reddit posts stating the Dogefather would take them to "the moon." The moon was more precisely defined as

Dogecoin hitting one dollar – a steep rise given that Dogecoin had traded largely below one cent from its inception to 2020.[21]

However, as Dogecoin's price started to rise almost exponentially in 2021, it seemed the dream of one dollar could become a reality. And it was making early investors extremely wealthy.

Reddit trader Glauber Contessoto became a Dogecoin millionaire on April 15, 2021. Contessoto had discovered Dogecoin through Reddit merely a month earlier. He invested an enormous $188,000 into Dogecoin at 4.5 cents, using a combination of his savings, selling his shares, maxing out two credit cards, and taking out a margin loan.[22] He directly credited his investment in Dogecoin to Musk, stating, "I think the guy is a genius." In typical Reddit fashion, Contessoto shared his success in a post stating, "hey guys I just became a Dogecoin millionaire" accompanied by a screenshot of his trading account showing a balance of $1,081,441.[23] Commentators on the post praised Contessoto for holding, with one user "T-Fishdix" posting, "Soon you'll be a billionaire." Contessoto's story was one of many, with *Finbold*, a financial news outlet, estimating the number of Dogecoin millionaires sitting at around 1,000 by November 2022.[24]

As an aside, I invested in Dogecoin in January 2021. Keeping a close eye on US equity markets at the time, I anticipated that retail funds would soon be deployed into crypto meme tokens in a similar way as had happened with GameStop. After buying around $3,000 worth, I initially saw my investment rise by 30-40%. But in the volatile nature of investing in meme coins, these gains quickly evaporated, with my investment falling to around a 25% loss in the course of just over a week. Feeling tremendously stupid for losing money on a dog meme, tail between my legs, I quietly sold out of my holdings. At the time, I thought I had saved myself from a complete capital loss. Over the next few months, I sat and watched in absolute agony as Dogecoin's price skyrocketed. Painful as it is to admit, if I had held Dogecoin for a mere two more months, the value of my holdings would have been more than $100,000.

But the biggest beneficiary of Dogecoin's rise was the largest holder of Dogecoin. The wallet ("DH5ya") was held by an anonymous investor who had been steadily accumulating Dogecoin since 2019. The "whale" (in crypto parlance referring to an individual or entity holding a large amount of crypto) had accumulated 36.7 billion Dogecoins. This represented around 28% of Dogecoin's total supply in mid-2021, hitting a value of more than $10 billion during Dogecoin's rise in that period.[25] The whale's identity has been heavily speculated in the Dogecoin community – with many suggesting it is the Dogefather himself, Elon Musk.

Supporting this are three separate transactions that added 28.061971 Dogecoins to the whale's wallet. Separated, this is 28 06 1971 – Musk's birthday. In May 2021, 420.69 was added to the wallet. "420" and "69" are so-called "meme numbers". "420" is slang for smoking marijuana, typically around 4:20 pm. The number "69" does not need an explanation. Musk has been known to reference these numbers, with a 2021 tweet stating: "Due to inflation, 420 has gone up by 69."

Beginning in April 2021 and over the following months, the price of Dogecoin would explode, making the possibility of one dollar a reality. On April 1, Musk tweeted: "SpaceX is going to put a literal Dogecoin on the literal moon." Initially his tweet was written off as an April Fools' joke – an example of Musk humor. However, it actually proved to be true, with the "DOGE-1 Mission to the Moon" slated to send a small satellite to the moon. Dogecoin will fully fund the mission using a SpaceX Falcon 9 rocket.

On April 28, Musk tweeted ahead of his hosting of *Saturday Night Live (SNL)*: "The Dogefather SNL May 8." This tweet sent the DogeArmy into a frenzy and with it, the price of Dogecoin went to new heights. There was rampant speculation on what Musk would say on *SNL*. Would he announce himself as the Dogecoin whale? Would there be a big announcement about the project?

Investors bought the rumor, with Dogecoin more than doubling from 32 cents to its all-time high of around 70 cents in the period between his tweet on April 28 and his appearance hosting *SNL* on

May 8. The event was eagerly anticipated by Dogecoin faithful, with live streams on YouTube that tracked both the show and Dogecoin's price movements.

Along with the hype around Dogecoin, Musk's appearance on *SNL* was always going be controversial. Musk had recently shifted his political allegiances to the more conservative side of American politics, and thus opened the door to the polarization of both US politics and media. Some media outlets described his appearance as "awkward" and "bumbling" and as one of the "worst *SNL* episodes ever." This is particularly critical given that Musk revealed that he was the first host of *SNL* to have Asperger's syndrome, an autism spectrum disorder.[26]

Dogecoin holders cared little about Musk's politics or even about the show itself. All eyes and ears were focused on what Musk would say about Dogecoin. In the customary *SNL* opening monologue, Elon covered a range of topics, from his vision for humanity (as a multi-planetary spacefaring civilization) and a dialogue with his mother, who appeared along with him on stage. Most importantly for Dogecoin fans, his mother mentioned the token right at the end of the monologue, saying, "I'm excited for my Mother's Day gift. I just hope it's not Dogecoin." Musk replied, "It is" to laughs from the audience.

Musk would reference Dogecoin again in a subsequent skit, calling himself the "Dogefather" and howled at one point "to the moooon." Given the size of the *SNL* audience, this may have been one of the first times many of them had heard of Dogecoin, but the references did not appear to satisfy the expectations of Dogecoin investors. The level of hype and speculation around what Musk might do on *SNL* meant that, short of Musk appearing in a Shiba Inu costume and dedicating the entire show to Dogecoin, many investors would be disappointed. In what is a classic case of the investing maxim "buy the rumor, sell the news" the price of Dogecoin plummeted 30% during the show. Such was the ferocity of selling, popular share and crypto trading platform Robinhood saw a temporary trading outage.

Musk's *SNL* performance would mark the high point for

Dogecoin's price. With limited "fundamental value," Dogecoin's value would always be subject to heavy speculation. As the explosive narrative of the *SNL* performance faded, Dogecoin began a steady decline. It experienced some more Musk-inspired rallies, such as when Musk ran a poll asking if Tesla should accept payments in Dogecoin. 78.2% of respondents voted yes, with nearly four million votes. Musk followed through on his promise, allowing some Tesla merchandise to be purchased with Dogecoin (causing Dogecoin's price to spike 9%).[27]

While many investors had the foresight to sell out of Dogecoin towards its peak, others were not so lucky. Glauber Contessoto saw his investment in Dogecoin rise to nearly $3 million but made the fateful mistake that many in the crypto space make. Lacking a clear exit strategy, he did not sell a single Dogecoin, believing the value would continue to rise. His investment was still in the black as at the time of writing, sitting at around $220,000 (from an initial investment of $188,000), despite no longer being a Dogecoin millionaire.

Unfortunately, there was a large opportunity cost to his investment. Contessoto had sold his Tesla shares to invest in Dogecoin. Tesla shares then saw a remarkable rise in price on the back of the growth of the popularity of electric vehicles. Contessoto's investment in Tesla would now be worth around $3 million, if he hadn't sold them.[28] But Contessoto hasn't been deterred by the drop in Dogecoin's price. He believes that in the next crypto bull market, Dogecoin will hit $1 and Bitcoin $100,000.

The decline in Dogecoin's price may also have some direct repercussions for Musk. A lawsuit filed in New York claims that Musk, Tesla, SpaceX, and the Boring Company intentionally inflated the price of Dogecoin by more than 36,000% and then let it crash. The plaintiffs allege that Musk (and his companies) "profited tens of billions of dollars" directly at the expense of other Dogecoin investors.[29] Wrapped into the claim is the assertion that Musk owns the Dogecoin whale wallet.[30] The plaintiffs allege that Musk opened the Dogecoin wallet in 2019, supporting this with evidence that a transaction from the wallet spelled out "Hi Elon."[31] Musk has publicly denied claims that the wallet belongs to him, stating that it instead is held by Robinhood.

Robinhood was a popular share trading platform at this time, particularly amongst retail traders, as it offered trading commission-free. Robinhood also expanded in cryptocurrency, allowing trading in several popular cryptocurrencies (including Dogecoin). Robinhood does not operate like a typical exchange, which facilitates the buying and selling of cryptocurrencies between parties. Instead, Robinhood buys the cryptocurrency and sells it directly to users. This means that Robinhood needs to have a pool of Dogecoin to sell to users directly, hence the need to hold a large number of Dogecoin. Robinhood has not publicly commented on this claim.

The lawsuit is seeking an astounding $258 billion in damages.

Dogecoin's success spurned several copycat coins and was the catalyst for the rise of shitcoins (as outlined in a previous chapter). Dogecoin and Musk collectively can claim the credit for inspiring the creation of Dogelon Mars coin (approximately $150 million market capitalization), Baby DogeCoin (approximately $500 million market capitalization), and Floki (approximately $1.6 billion market capitalization). However, the largest impact was spurring the creation of the "Shiba Inu token" (SHIB). The Shiba Inu token was created in August 2020 with the clear and sole intention to be the Dogecoin killer.[32] Like Dogecoin, the Shiba Inu token features a logo of the Shiba Inu. The token was created by an anonymous individual (or group) using the pseudonym "Ryoshi."

The project could certainly have been classed as just another shitcoin. It may have been fortunate enough to experience a temporary spike in price, riding the meme wave of Dogecoin, only to fade into obscurity. However, as often is the case for meme coins – luck can be a fortune.

On March 14, 2021, Musk tweeted: "I'm getting a Shiba Inu #resistanceisfutile." While Musk's intention was to promote Dogecoin, this resulted in attention for Shiba Inu, causing holders of the Shiba Inu token to double to nearly 23,000 a month later. On

April 14, Jordan Belfort, the "Wolf of Wall Street", tweeted: "SHOW ME THE SHIBA INU."

These tweets formed the catalyst for the Shiba Inu token to explode in value, sitting at nearly $12 billion in May 2021. To put this in perspective, if you had invested $100 at inception, the value of your holding would be around $800,000 today. The token's early buyers were made incredibly wealthy, once again demonstrating that sometimes it is better to be lucky than skilled in crypto.

The rise in the value of Shiba Inu also created a strange conundrum based on an early decision in the project by the founder. When the token was created, Ryoshi sent 50% of all tokens to Ethereum co-founder Vitalik Buterin. Ryoshi didn't know Vitalik, nor did Vitalik agree to receive the tokens. So how did it happen?

This is a strange quirk of crypto, centered around the pseudo-anonymous nature of blockchain technology. Every crypto wallet has a public address: a string of letters and numbers (e.g., 1A1zP1eP5Qgefi2DMPTfTL5SLmv7DivfNa). The address functions identically to a bank account number. Therefore, if you know the number, you can send crypto to that address (even without the user's consent). This is also the case for bank account numbers – but in practice, these numbers are essentially private, only disclosed to third parties as needed.

This marks a clear distinction with blockchain technology. At its core, the technology is public and permanently recorded, meaning you can track every single transaction in and out of a wallet (typically through websites like Etherscan). It is akin to being able to see every single transaction in one's bank account. Why would anyone want a wallet then, if every transaction is public? An individual's privacy is still protected as the wallet address is not linked to an individual's identity. It is simply a string of meaningless letters and numbers. However, that does not mean working out who owns the wallet is impossible. People may choose to publicly identify their wallet address, or often savvy individuals can work out who owns the address.

As an aside, this feature of blockchain technology can be very useful for law enforcement. For example, if a criminal uses their crypto wallet to receive payments for drug trafficking, a permanent and public record of their activities is available for everyone to see. The catch, of course, is linking an individual or organization to the wallet (which can often happen when law enforcement seizes an offender's computer).

In the case of Buterin, his wallet address is public knowledge. Ryoshi, like many project creators, leverages this as a marketing tactic. They send their tokens to famous crypto figures, like Buterin, and then claim that the figure is an investor in the project. This can be used to bring legitimacy and trust to the project. It has the flip side of resulting in strange situations where figures like Buterin will look at their wallet and find all manner of obscure tokens they received for free. Typically, these are shitcoins that are valued at almost zero. But the Shiba Inu tokens were different. The 50% of tokens Ryoshi sent rose to a staggering $6 billion. This undoubtedly would be one of the largest gifts in human history.

So, what did Buterin do with them?

Buterin, one of the most principled and benevolent people in crypto (and possibly the world), did not use the assets for personal gain. Rather, he donated 10% of the tokens to charity. He then "burned" the remainder of the 90% of Shiba Inu tokens he held. "Burning" is the digital equivalent of destroying crypto tokens, analogous to physically burning actual currency. Burning has the effect of pro-rata distributing wealth back to holders (similar to a share buyback in equities markets), helping to support the price (given a decrease in supply should, all things being equal, increase the price).

Buterin's choice to burn the tokens rather than sell them was significant for the future of the Shiba Inu token. Holding such a large proportion of tokens gave him the power to "rug" the entire project. If Buterin had decided to sell the tokens on the market, the value of Shiba Inu would have plummeted to near zero and destroyed the project. His decision to destroy such a huge volume of tokens allowed Shiba Inu not only to survive, but continue to grow.

Unwilling to be tarred as another meme or shitcoin, the project decided to pivot. The Shiba Inu token is now a decentralized community with various utilities for the token. The Shiba Inu ecosystem now includes a decentralized swap (allowing you to swap tokens for other tokens) and plans to continue growing this community further.[33] This, in part, has enabled the Shiba Inu token to retain a high market capitalization (over $10 billion) and consistently rank in the top 30 cryptocurrencies. With projects like Shiba Inu, there is now a collection of dog-inspired tokens trading. These tokens tend to be highly correlated with each other, representing an almost "risk on" style of asset (i.e., they tend to see rapid price rises when market conditions are strong). They also are heavily sensitive to tweets by Musk. As an homage to Dogecoin/the Doge meme, Musk bought his own Shiba Inu dog and named it Floki.[34] In February 2023, Musk tweeted a series of photos of his dog Floki posing as the CEO of X, stating: "The new CEO of X is amazing. So much better than the other guy! He's great with numbers."

As you would now come to expect, his tweet sent the prices of Dogecoin and other dog-themed coins rising.

The future of Dogecoin

Dogecoin has proven remarkably resilient for a token intended as a satire of cryptocurrency. The project has survived its founders leaving, hacks, widespread criticism from the media, and spectacular rises and crashes over its 10-year history. Its survival is a testament to the strong and wholesome community that has formed around the coin, helping it navigate these challenges.

But what is next for Dogecoin?

Musk might have the answer. As he stated about Dogecoin, "Fate loves irony. The most ironic outcome is that the currency that was invented as a joke, in fact becomes the real currency." While Bitcoin was created as an alternative digital currency, Dogecoin has some technical advantages over Bitcoin as a currency (for example, processing much higher transactions per second).[35] With the popularity and widespread awareness of Dogecoin, it's not entirely ridiculous to think that one day many people will be using it in their daily lives, perhaps following its original use case as a currency for tips.

In the future, the Dogecoin community holds out hope that the coin will figuratively "go to the moon" and hit its prized one dollar per token valuation. And even if it doesn't hit that value, Dogecoin itself will literally go to the moon if the DOGE-1 mission succeeds.

CHAPTER 5: THE $65-BILLION-DOLLAR QUESTION: WHO IS SATOSHI NAKAMOTO?

"Satoshi is either a team of people or a genius" – Security researcher Dan Kaminsky

The single largest mystery in crypto is the identity of the person who started it all. The original creator of Bitcoin continues to be shrouded in mystery; the subject of wild speculation throughout the entire history of crypto. And for good reason – the person who started the crypto revolution would stand on par with other tech giants like Steve Jobs, Mark Zuckerberg, Jeff Bezos and Bill Gates. From its beginnings as a decentralized currency, Bitcoin has seen an explosive rise in usage and value since the network went live in 2009. The unparalleled success likely exceeded even the wildest dreams of its creator.

Despite this, we know tantalizingly little about them.

The creator went by the online name "Satoshi Nakamoto", a name of Japanese origin that is almost certainly a pseudonym designed to keep their actual identity private. [36] This name first appeared on October 31, 2008, as the author of the paper "Bitcoin: A Peer-to-Peer Electronic Cash System." [37] The nine-page whitepaper outlines both the conceptual and technical details of Bitcoin, [38] along with describing the foundations for what would later be called blockchain technology. The creator of Bitcoin would continue to use the name Satoshi Nakamoto as their username, communicating to the then-nascent Bitcoin community through Bitcoin Forum – making their first post on February 11, 2009. Despite their more than 500 public posts on Bitcoin Forum, nobody communicated with Nakamoto face-to-face or even over the phone. All interactions were done either via email or posts on a forum.

Nakamoto continued to contribute to the development of Bitcoin for a few years after the publication of the 2008 paper. But to add even more mystery to the situation, Nakamoto suddenly and unexpectedly withdrew from the project in 2011. This was immediately after Gavin Andresen – an early collaborator on Bitcoin who interacted directly with Nakamoto over email and on Bitcoin Forum – announced he had accepted an invitation to speak at CIA headquarters about Bitcoin. Was Nakamoto worried about what may come from this interaction with the US Government? Or perhaps they had something to hide?

While this story has all the ingredients of a mystery thriller book, it still begs the question: why does the identity of the creator of Bitcoin even matter?

At a micro level, if revealed, the creator of Bitcoin would have tremendous influence over the crypto industry today. Similar to how Ethereum's founder Buterin is perceived today, the creator's opinions would heavily influence the future development of Bitcoin and the development of cryptocurrency markets as a whole. While interesting, this is not the main reason the true identity of Nakamoto is so enticing. There is a more practical question at stake: who controls Nakamoto's Bitcoin wallets?

This is not an academic question – it is a multi-billion dollar one.

Nakamoto's wallets[39] are estimated to include between 600,000 to 1 million Bitcoins.[40] At the upper estimate, this represents around 5% of the maximum total supply of Bitcoin and equates to nearly $65 billion worth of Bitcoin. This puts Nakamoto's wealth on par with the founder of Facebook, Mark Zuckerberg,[41] and makes Nakamoto one of the richest people in the world.

This begs the question: Who is Satoshi Nakamoto?

The origins of Bitcoin

Satoshi Nakamoto began work on the Bitcoin code and concept in 2007, with the Bitcoin.org domain registered on August 18, 2008. The Bitcoin whitepaper was published a few months later, in October 2008. The idea behind Bitcoin built on several technological, mathematical, and cryptographic advancements that had developed since the 1980s. It was a combination of advancements across these fields that Nakamoto applied to solve a critical problem in commerce that arose with the development of the internet and e-commerce.

E-commerce is reliant on the processing of electronic payments, which is exclusively reliant on financial institutions (mainly large banks). Banks act as a trusted centralized third party that can receive and send funds between buyers and sellers. While banks have been essential in developing the sophisticated financial system we have become accustomed to, moments of crises in the last 20 years have revealed their vulnerability.

Bitcoin intended to change all of this. As stated in the Bitcoin whitepaper: "A purely peer-to-peer version of electronic cash would allow online payments to be sent directly from one party to another without going through a financial institution."[42] Bitcoin was envisaged to be the first widely-used digital decentralized currency. This would therefore involve Bitcoin directly competing with fiat currencies – centralized currencies issued by governments. While initially hard to grasp how a digital currency created out of thin air would be superior to the US dollar, Bitcoin has some structural advantages. In particular, Bitcoin's design mitigates a flaw in centralized currencies: the debasement of the currency over time.

Governments have a long history of debasing their currency, which has typically taken the form of reducing the coin's previous metal content (usually gold or silver). Typically, this is done to fund expenditure, allowing a given amount of silver or gold in the treasury to create more currency. The net impact of debasement over time is to reduce the value of currency. Debasement of currency goes back all the way to Ancient Rome. In 69AD, Roman Emperor Vespasian began debasing the denarius by reducing the silver content of the coins to 90% to fund construction projects like the Colosseum. Over the next 200 years, the currency would continue to be debased until the silver was reduced to 5%. While modern day currencies are no longer backed by precious metals as in Roman times, central banks and governments can instead simply increase the supply of the currency over time (leading to the same debasement effect). This typically occurs in times of economic downturns or crises, as was seen in the US when the money supply grew an astounding 40% during the COVID-19 pandemic. Increases in money supply at rates faster than economic growth can lead to inflation, which was the case across most Western economies from late 2021. Extreme examples of increases in money supply can result in hyperinflation, as famously happened in Zimbabwe where, in November 2008 on the back of enormous increases in the money supply of the Zimbabwe dollar, inflation peaked at an estimated 79,600,000,000%.

This problem is avoided in the design of Bitcoin, which has a hard cap on the number of Bitcoins created. Bitcoin's embedded source code means that the supply of Bitcoin will never exceed 21 million. In this way, Bitcoin can become a superior "store of value" compared to fiat currency, earning it the often-used label "digital gold".

The additional benefit of a decentralized currency is no single organization is a gatekeeper for usage and adoption. In traditional finance, centralized bodies such as banks and financial institutions hold a tremendous amount of power. Banks can decide whether or not they will lend to you, let you open a bank account, or even whether they will process a payment/transaction from your account. This ability can result in substantial unfairness and discrimination against individuals. Most notably in the US, this has resulted in minority groups not receiving loans that would have been provided to white people under identical circumstances.[43] This issue is particularly pronounced in developing countries without sophisticated financial systems with many individuals prevented from even opening a bank account. Across the world, an estimated 1.4 billion adults are "unbanked" (i.e., do not have a bank account),[44] with around two-thirds of them having a mobile phone.[45] For this segment, Bitcoin and other cryptocurrencies offer an opportunity to pay and receive money without having to rely on banks – requiring only an internet connection to participate.

This drives to one of the most revolutionary aspects of Bitcoin. The first transfer of Bitcoin was an historic event, as it was the first time a digital currency had been transferred to another party without a third-party intermediary (e.g., a bank) to facilitate. Bitcoin's permissionless and open system, and its decentralization, makes it a more robust means of exchange. There is no single point of failure in transferring or holding Bitcoin, so it can eliminate the ever-present risk of contagion in the financial system. In the banking sector, financial contagion refers to the spread of a financial crisis from one institution to another. Crises begin when one bank/financial institution fails to pay its debts, either due to mismanagement, fraud or adverse economic conditions. Given the interconnected nature of today's financial system, this debt is typically owed to another financial institution. A large default can leave the lending financial institution unable to service their own debts – leading to more defaults. Contagion can then spread across the entire global financial system, creating a banking crisis. The end result: individuals can have their entire life savings held in these financial institutions wiped out.

The most recent example of financial contagion was the Global Financial Crisis (GFC), beginning in 2007. The crisis came with the collapse of the global financial services firm Lehman Brothers, which filed for bankruptcy on the back of losses from holding subprime mortgage-backed securities. This triggered defaults across the entire American banking system, which spread across the globe. Inevitably, facing a financial crisis means governments step in to halt its spread. The US Government did exactly that with the $700 billion bailout of banks under the "Troubled Asset Relief Program" in 2008, while the UK Government had a £137 billion bailout.

It was precisely this experience that led to the creation of Bitcoin. In 2009, the first version of Bitcoin software was released, and the first "block" in the Bitcoin blockchain (called the "genesis block") was mined. Embedded in the transaction of the block was the text quoting a headline in the London newspaper *The Times*, inserted by Satoshi Nakamoto: "The Times 03/Jan/2009 Chancellor on brink of second bailout for banks."

The original article appeared on the front page of the paper, with the "Chancellor of the Exchequer" (roughly equivalent to the United States Secretary of the Treasury), then Alistair Darling, considering another cash bailout of the UK banking system following a £37 billion part nationalization of the banking system just a year earlier. The uncertainty at the time was palpable, with fears the entire banking system would collapse causing an unprecedented economic crisis. While government actions managed to stabilize the financial system, risks of further crises remained.

In this environment, it is clear that the choice of including this text as raw data in the first of block of the Bitcoin network points to the core rationale and benefits of Bitcoin. As a decentralized, self-custodial currency, there is no risk of financial contagion destroying Bitcoin. If Bitcoin participants were to fail like banks did in the GFC, your Bitcoin would still remain. To be clear, as anti-fragile as the Bitcoin network itself is, financial contagion can still occur in crypto markets. For example, if you were to deposit your Bitcoin with a "Bitcoin bank" that held custody of your assets, you could still lose your holdings if the bank collapsed. This of course is a risk whenever another party holds your assets, but it is eliminated if you hold your Bitcoin in a self-custodial wallet.

It wasn't just Nakamoto who saw this potential – other early contributors to Bitcoin quickly bought in as well. In early 2009, Hal Finney – a developer and contributor to the project – estimated in a post that if Bitcoin was to become the dominant payment system in the world, one Bitcoin would be worth around $10 million. Finney quickly pointed it out as a tough road ahead but noted that obtaining some Bitcoin would be "quite a good bet" with the enormous payoff available.[46] Nakamoto agreed with Finney in reply to his post, stating, "it might make sense just to get some in case it catches on."

With supporters like Finney onboard, the Bitcoin community continued to grow with the locus of conversation centered around the forum Bitcoin Talk. Created by Nakamoto, the forum attracted people interested in the technical details and development of Bitcoin. Nakamoto made a total of 575 posts on the forum starting in late 2009, all of which are still visible today.[47] The vast majority are technical posts about Bitcoin code and educating the growing community. Nakamoto last posted on Bitcoin Talk on December 12, 2010, a little over a year after their first post, regarding some technical details on a new version of the Bitcoin network.[48] Their contribution to Bitcoin would then end abruptly in 2011.

Andresen, the creator of Bitcoin Faucet discussed in an earlier chapter, received a private email from Nakamoto on the same day. It read: "I wish you wouldn't keep talking about me as a mysterious shadowy figure, the press just turns that into a pirate currency angle. Maybe instead make it about the open source project and give more credit to your dev contributors; it helps motivate them." In Andresen's reply, he noted that he was contacted by IQT – a government funded "strategic investment company". IQT was holding a conference for US intelligence agencies (such as the CIA) on emerging technologies, with Andresen invited to give a 50-minute presentation on Bitcoin.

Nakamoto didn't reply to the email.

This would be the last verified correspondence from Nakamoto, with Andresen stating he had no further contact with Nakamoto following that email. The timing of Nakamoto disappearing right after finding out that Bitcoin would be presented to intelligence agencies fueled more intense speculation. Was Nakamoto hiding something? Was Nakamoto afraid that the CIA would uncover their identity? Or did Nakamoto simply not want to be put into the limelight?

Nakamoto's disappearance right after this email may have just been a coincidence. Only a few days earlier, Nakamoto sent an email to Mike Hearn. Hearn, a former engineer at Google, was an early Bitcoin contributor working on the project in his spare time until 2014 when he left Google to focus his efforts on Bitcoin full-time. Hearn had numerous exchanges with Nakamoto in Bitcoin's early days, and received this from Nakamoto on April 23, 2011 (three days before the Andresen exchange): "I've moved on to other things. It's in good hands with Gavin [Andresen] and everyone."[49] Clearly Nakamoto wanted to withdraw from leading development of Bitcoin. Nevertheless, to disappear completely only further adds to the mystery.

More curious is the fact that Nakamoto appears to have not spent any of the Bitcoin mined from the network's creation. There has been debate about exactly how many Bitcoins are held in Nakamoto's wallets. We know for certain that Nakamoto controls the "genesis block address" (containing over 50 Bitcoin, worth over $1 million). Sergio Demián Lerner, the chief scientist of RSK Labs, completed an analysis suggesting that Nakamoto owns more than 1 million Bitcoin (based on being the dominant miner at the beginning of the Bitcoin network).[50] Subsequent research by the BitMEX crypto trading platform estimated that a dominant miner collected around 600,000 to 700,000 Bitcoin at the beginning of the network and cast doubt on whether all the Bitcoins could be attributed to Nakamoto.[51] Nevertheless, Nakamoto would likely hold a fortune in Bitcoin. Perhaps Nakamoto is not spending any of the Bitcoin amid concern it could be used to uncover Nakamoto's identity, or perhaps Nakamoto is simply not interested in material riches.

What then would drive Nakamoto to invest years in building Bitcoin with no motivation for material rewards?

Clearly there are ideological and philosophical underpinnings in Bitcoin's creation. This provides clues as to Nakamoto's identity. Bitcoin's design focuses on promoting financial freedom (for those underbanked or excluded from the financial system), privacy, and decentralization. In particular, the choice of quote on the genesis block referencing the "second bailout for banks" implies an aversion both to the traditional centralized banking system and associated government markets intervention. This points to a libertarian ideology, emphasizing individual autonomy, free markets, and limited government intervention. This viewpoint is supported by Andresen, who stated, in *Newsweek* that "I got the impression that Satoshi was really doing it for political reasons."

This is also supported by an interesting theory on Nakamoto's date of birth. Nakamoto listed April 5, 1975 as their date of birth on Bitcoin Talk. While entirely possible that this is Nakamoto's actual birthday, many theorize this date was chosen for a different reason. April 5 was the date that President Franklin D Roosevelt made Executive Order 6102. This outlawed the private ownership of gold in the United States, an example many libertarians suggested was government overreach. Such an action is simply not possible for Bitcoin, giving individuals the freedom to preserve their wealth away from the hands of the government. The executive order was eventually reversed by President Gerald Ford. The year of the reversal?

1975.

This could very well be a random coincidence – but it more likely points to Nakamoto having a deep understanding of monetary history and an expression of the political motivations behind Bitcoin. Besides Nakamoto's political ideology, there are other clues we can glean about Nakamoto that point towards their real identity.

First, the text embedded in the genesis block gives a clue to where Nakamoto lived or grew up. It quotes the headline of *The Times*, not an American newspaper. That decision is intriguing. Next, the GFC in the US was triggered by the failure of sub-prime mortgages created by large US financial institutions. These sub-prime mortgages were packaged up as "mortgage-backed securities," which were then sold and traded across the globe (the author recommends watching the 2015 film *The Big Short*, which tells this story in a digestible and entertaining way). Finally, the largest and highest-profile bank bailout was in the US – with the Troubled Asset Relief program used to inject capital into US financial institutions to buy toxic assets. This program was funded with $700 billion of taxpayer money. Why not reference a US newspaper article on this program?

The most logical answer is that Nakamoto was not living in the United States at the time (unlike Andresen, Hearn and other early Bitcoin contributors). Rather, it points to someone who grew up or lives in the United Kingdom –supported by the fact that Nakamoto would often reply to comments after business hours in the United Kingdom.[52]

Equally, it could be someone who grew up in or lives in a Commonwealth country. Commonwealth countries are former British colonies, with news and culture still closely linked to the United Kingdom. This means that they would give more weight to decisions in the United Kingdom than the US. This is further supported by an analysis of Nakamoto's language, which Benjamin Wallace argued in an article in *Wired*: "His [Satoshi's] English had the flawless, idiomatic ring of a native speaker." Nakamoto wrote around 80,000 words in public posts, with only a few typos. Further, Nakamoto used traditional British spelling (e.g., using "favour" instead of "favor," "grey" instead of "gray" and "modernised" instead of "modernized") and British idioms (such as referring to an "apartment" as a "flat").

Another clue to Nakamoto's identity is the technical knowledge that would be required to create Bitcoin. The tremendous vision required to come up with the idea of Bitcoin cannot be underestimated. Moreover, Bitcoin represented a profound technological shift, requiring expert knowledge of math and cryptography (where "crypto" got its name from) along with a detailed knowledge of computer programming. Also sprinkled is an understanding of economics and game theory principles. Together, this implies Nakamoto likely had an educational or work background in math and programming – and was undoubtedly a genius. In all likelihood, Nakamoto would have studied engineering, mathematics or physics at a prestigious university. Furthermore, analysis of Nakamoto's code indicates that they were likely not working as programmer; Nakamoto's code had many quirks, including using outdated code practices. X user @ Narodism concluded based on an analysis of Nakamoto's code:

He made big use of locks when it was out of fashion. He
used Hungarian notation which was no longer used. He
made spaghetti function recursion and never used objects to
encapsulate processes. He also targeted Windows. All of this
indicate an older person, possibly not a software dev but from
a close domain like engineering or physics. His whitepaper
hinted at a background with a practical focus but not a
mathematician.

Supporting the conclusion that Nakamoto was not a programmer was
the decision to write a whitepaper, which was not standard practice
for tech workers. Whitepapers are more common in the academic
world.[53]

Finally, there is the choice of the name Satoshi Nakamoto.
Satoshi, a Japanese name, may indicate a few things. Firstly,
Nakamoto may be ethnically Japanese and either grew up or moved
to a Commonwealth country. Conversely, Nakamoto may have grown
up in a Commonwealth country and later moved to Japan. Finally, it
may be a misdirection entirely and the name was chosen as they had
some interest in Japan or Japanese culture (e.g., through consuming
Japanese entertainment like anime). In summary, the evidence points
to Nakamoto as being someone who:

- holds a libertarian political philosophy;
- is a genius with an educational or work background in
  mathematics, physics or engineering;
- has some work history in academia;
- has no (or extremely limited) experience as a programmer;
- grew up or lived in the United Kingdom or a
  Commonwealth country; and
- has some connection to Japan, whether ethnically or from a
  cultural perspective.

There has been speculation that Satoshi Nakamoto is not an
individual but a group of people. While possible, it seems unlikely,
given Nakamoto's communications appear consistent (i.e., not the

product of different writers using the account). Further, Nakamoto never mentions that multiple people are contributing under the name. Finally, Andresen, who was actively reviewing Nakamoto's code, stated, "everyone who looked at his code has pretty much concluded it was a single person."[54] This conclusion was drawn on the basis that it was not written neatly (which, if working as a team, would have been cleaned up).[55]

Over the years there have been numerous individuals suspected of being Nakamoto. One of the first and highest-profiled is Dorian Nakamoto.

Dorian Nakamoto was one of the earliest candidates suspected to be the mysterious creator of Bitcoin. In 2014, *Newsweek* published "The Face Behind Bitcoin" by Leah Goodman, alleging that Dorian was the creator of Bitcoin. Dorian is a Japanese American who, at the time of the article, was a 64-year-old retired physicist and engineer. He had a career working on "defensive electronics and communications for the military," including classified projects.

The article claims Dorian tacitly acknowledged his role in the project. Goodman went to Dorian's house in California along with two police officers and described the interactions with Dorian in reference to his involvement in Bitcoin as follows: "'I am no longer involved in that, and I cannot discuss it,' he says, dismissing all further queries with a swat of his left hand. 'It's been turned over to other people. They are in charge of it now. I no longer have any connection.'"[56]

Other pieces of the puzzle appeared to fall into place. Arthur Nakamoto (Dorian's brother) stated the following in Newsweek about his brother: "He's a brilliant man. I'm just a humble engineer. He's very focused and eclectic in his way of thinking. Smart, intelligent, mathematics, engineering, computers. You name it, he can do it." Dorian's daughter added, "He was very wary of the government, taxes and people in charge."

There was even an explanation as to why Dorian would write using British spelling. When Dorian was a teenager learning English, he simultaneously had a keen interest in collecting model trains. These trains were imported mainly from England – meaning he would have spent these years absorbing British vocabulary and spelling through reading the manuals and instructions on the model trains. Dorian also coincidentally lived only a few blocks from one of the earliest Bitcoin contributors – Hal Finney (a potential Nakamoto candidate covered later) – who was the recipient of the first Bitcoin transaction from Nakamoto.

And to what many labeled the "silver bullet" – it was discovered that Dorian's birth name was none other than Satoshi. At the age of 23, Dorian changed his birth name from "Satoshi Nakamoto" to "Dorian Prentice Satoshi Nakamoto."[57] After the name change, Dorian now signs with "Dorian S. Nakamoto."

Taken collectively, there is compelling evidence to suggest that Dorian is the creator of Bitcoin. However, shortly after the Newsweek story broke, cracks started to emerge in the theory. Dorian came out publicly to deny he created Bitcoin. In a 2014 statement to Newsweek, he stated:

> I did not create, invent or otherwise work on Bitcoin. I unconditionally deny the Newsweek report. The first time I heard the term "bitcoin" was from my son in mid-February 2014… I have no knowledge of nor have I ever worked on cryptography, peer to peer systems, or alternative currencies.

Dorian claims he misunderstood Goodman's questions, thinking she was asking about a classified project he had worked on at Citibank. His reply to Goodman, stating "I am no longer involved" was not in reference to Bitcoin, but rather to Dorian no longer working in engineering. At the time Goodman visited his house, Dorian was recovering from a stroke he had only a few months earlier, potentially explaining his confusion around the questioning.

Forbes commissioned Juola & Associates to conduct a linguistic analysis on Dorian's and Nakamoto's writing in an effort to validate the theory.[58] Juola & Associates has a stellar reputation in forensic text analysis, with Patrick Juola being one of the first individuals who identified J.K. Rowling as the real author of The Cuckoo's Calling. Initially published under the pseudonym "Robert Galbraith," the author of the Harry Potter series was identified using Juola's mathematical analysis program to determine authorship.

John Noecker Jr. (chief scientific officer at Juola & Associates) forensically analyzed Dorian's and Nakamoto's writing and found with a fair degree of confidence that Dorian is not Nakamoto.[59] This, however, is not definitive, given analysis of this type is not 100% accurate (nor is it marketed to be). Barbara Matthews, a forensic expert who worked with Newsweek on its article, argued that the methodology for the analysis was flawed, given that the sample of Dorian's writings was too small and informal to be used as a legitimate comparison to Nakamoto's writing.[60]

Following the Newsweek article, Dorian was hounded by the media (including a comical low-speed car chase where a journalist tried to outrun other reporters in pursuit of the story). The Bitcoin community rallied around Dorian following the Newsweek story, focusing on the fact that he was living modestly (being unemployed for more than a decade) and certainly not living with the Bitcoin riches you may expect from Nakamoto. A GoFundMe page was created entitled "newsweeklied.com" alleging that the article contained "misstatements of fact and invented and altered quotes from Dorian and his family members." In a demonstration of the generosity of the Bitcoin community, more than 48 Bitcoins were donated (~$23,400 at the time) to support Dorian.

Regardless of whether or not Dorian is Nakamoto, his likeness has been immortalized in the crypto community. An NFT was minted, combining the face of Dorian with the Pepe the Frog meme (a popular meme in crypto) in trading card form. The trading card reads: "The creator of Bitcoin. One of the rarest Pepes in existence… Rareness Score 97."

In 2021, this NFT traded hands for an astounding $500,000.[61]

Another individual suspected of being Nakamoto is the brilliant American computer scientist Hal Finney, who has a direct connection to Dorian Nakamoto. Finney completed his bachelor's degree in engineering at the California Institute of Technology. After graduation, Finney worked for PGP Corporation, where he was instrumental in developing the Pretty Good Privacy (PGP) encryption program in 1991. The PGP system is used to send encrypted emails and encrypting sensitive files and has become the standard for email security. Most importantly, the PGP program utilizes public-key cryptography. Simply put, it is a type of encryption using two keys – a public key (e.g., your bank account number) and a private key (e.g., your bank password) to securely transmit data between two parties.

This is important as Bitcoin uses public-key cryptography as a fundamental design building block. Both Bitcoin and PGP use a public key to encrypt data – only the corresponding private key can be used to decrypt the data. While PGP uses public-key cryptography to ensure both the authenticity and integrity of communication, Bitcoin uses it as a basis for its security model (helping to secure the transfer of Bitcoin between users).

Is it possible that this work on PGP inspired him to apply what he learned to create a decentralized digital currency?

Finney would develop another technical building block for Bitcoin, being a "proof-of-work" system which required system participants to solve complex computer problems. This closely resembles the same proof-of-work system used to secure the Bitcoin network. Further supporting this theory is Finney's involvement as an early member of the cypherpunks movement. Not to be confused with the science fiction genre cyberpunk (focused on dystopian futures in which governments use technology to control or oppress the population), cypherpunk is a social and political movement centered around cryptography. The basis of the movement is to use cryptography to protect individuals' privacy and rights. Its technical roots have been credited to David Chaum, who wrote a 1983 paper describing a method for secure digital cash.[62] Chaum, also known as the "Godfather of crypto", developed the first digital currency called eCash, dreaming of a world of a decentralized and anonymous currency. Finney referenced Chaum on the Cypherpunks mailing list in 1992:

> It seemed so obvious to me…Here we are faced with the problems of loss of privacy, creeping computerization, massive databases, and more centralization – and [David] Chaum offers a completely different direction to go in, one which puts power into the hands of individuals rather than governments and corporations. The computer can be used as a tool to liberate and protect people, rather than to control them.

Finney, who was noted to carry around a large copy of the libertarian bible *Atlas Shrugged* by Ayn Rand, fits the bill for holding the philosophical underpinning for Bitcoin's creator. Additional evidence points towards Finney, who was the first Bitcoin transaction recipient, receiving 50 Bitcoins from Nakamoto's wallet on January 12, 2009.[63] Finney also lived in the small town of Temple City, with a population of 36,000. This, of course, was the same town as Dorian Nakamoto, fueling speculation Finney may have used his name to inspire the pseudonym.[64]

Finney directly denied being Nakamoto, stating in an email to Forbes writer Andy Greenberg:

> As for your suspicion that I either am or at least helped Satoshi, I'm flattered but I deny categorically these allegations. I don't know what more I can say. You have records of how I reacted to the announcement of Bitcoin, and I struggled to understand it. I suppose you could retort that I was able to fake it, but I don't know what I can say to that. I've done some changes to the Bitcoin code, and my style is completely different from Satoshi's. I program in C, which is compatible with C++, but I don't understand the tricks that Satoshi used.

Supporting Finney's denial is that Nakamoto was a Windows user. While not particularly strange given Windows operating system dominance, this is an anomaly in the coding world (where MacOS and Unix systems are the most common). Nakamoto even asked another Bitcoin contributor – Laszlo Hanyecz (yes, the pizza guy) – to code Bitcoin on MacOS as he did not own a Mac. Finney was a Mac user and could code proficiently on Mac systems.

Finally, Finney had numerous direct communications with Nakamoto, which included disagreements. These occurred both in public settings as well as in direct private email correspondences. Finney would have had to have a serious commitment to misdirection if he intended to obscure his involvement by arguing against himself in public forums. Greenberg (who interviewed Finney) concluded:

> A week earlier, I was following clues that seemed to point to either Finney's involvement in the creation of Bitcoin or one of the most improbable coincidences I'd ever encountered. Today, I believe those connections were, in fact, random, that Finney is telling the truth when he denies helping to invent Bitcoin and that I am only the most recent of a long string of journalists to succumb to the mirage of a Satoshi Nakamoto-shaped pattern in a collection of meaningless facts.

Finney was diagnosed with Amyotrophic Lateral Sclerosis (ALS) in August 2009. ALS (commonly known as Lou Gehrig's disease) would slowly paralyze Finney over the following five years until his death in 2014. After his death, his body was transferred to a cryonics firm (Alcor Life Extension Foundation) to be cryogenically frozen. The hope is that as technology progresses, he may get another shot at life and continue his enormous contributions to cryptography and privacy.

In the theme of brilliant tech leaders, in April 2013, speculation was rife that the legendary founder of Apple, Steve Jobs, may be Nakamoto. Fueling the speculation was the discovery of something intriguing in MacOS, the default operating system for all Apple desktop and laptop computers. Savvy users discovered a file path included in every Mac computer running MacOS. The hidden file path leads to a copy of Nakamoto's original Bitcoin whitepaper.[65] This "Easter egg" immediately set X ablaze with discussion on whether Jobs was Nakamoto. Jobs was widely considered a visionary genius, seeing new social and economic trends well before others. Could he have seen the utility and potential of a decentralized currency well before others?

While Jobs was notorious for publicly commenting on his political views, he did embody the counter-cultural narrative that defines Silicon Valley and a large segment of the crypto community. It would make sense for Jobs to therefore make his identity anonymous to divorce the political message that Bitcoin represented. The timelines for Jobs and Nakamoto also stack up. The last known contact of Nakamoto was emails sent to his fellow developers on April 26, 2011.[66] Jobs died only a few months after this date, of pancreatic cancer, in October 2011. This may explain both why Nakamoto stopped contributing to Bitcoin and why we have not heard anything since then.

While Steve Jobs as Nakamoto is a tantalizing theory, there are a few counterpoints. First and foremost, Jobs wasn't a programmer or engineer – and famously did not know how to code. The technical knowledge required to create Bitcoin was enormous – requiring expert cryptographic and mathematical knowledge. Unless Jobs was the ideas man behind the project, with others doing the technical lifting, it's highly unlikely that Jobs would have had the technical knowledge to pull the project off. Furthermore, the Bitcoin whitepaper was only added to MacOS in 2018 – well after the death of Steve Jobs. It's entirely likely this was merely a fun Easter egg that a Bitcoin aficionado working as a programmer at Apple decided to leave behind.

A more plausible candidate than Steve Jobs has been speculated as Nicholas Szabo, an American computer scientist, lawyer, and cryptographer. Szabo had an intriguing history before the creation of Bitcoin. Szabo was the creator of the concept of a "smart contract", a code that directly executes contract terms. Szabo described smart contracts in 1996 and envisaged their use in asset trading, property, and online payments. This idea would become a reality a little under 20 years later with the development of the Ethereum network, which took the underlying blockchain technology and integrated the use of smart contracts.

The most significant evidence of Szabo being Nakamoto is the development of Bit Gold. Bit Gold was conceived by Szabo in 1998 as a digital money system. The idea was to remove third parties that made the gold system inefficient and to replace it with a secure cryptographic process. Bit Gold is evidently a precursor to Bitcoin (the name makes this point quite obvious), using a similar proof-of-work system as Bitcoin and sharing many other technical features. The significant difference is that Bitcoin was intended to be a currency. At the same time, Bit Gold was envisaged to act as physical reserves (harking back to the era before fiat currency, whereby currency was backed by gold). Unlike Bitcoin, Bit Gold was not implemented as a protocol.[67]

Given that Szabo had the vision and technical expertise to create Bit Gold, it is no stretch of the imagination to suggest he would have the expertise to create Bitcoin. Further, Szabo may have seen greater potential in a digital currency, combining his legal and economic knowledge (see, for example, an article published in 2002 called "Shelling Out: The Origins of Money"). In 2008, before the Bitcoin whitepaper was published, Szabo authored a comment on his blog that said he was creating a live version of his hypothetical currency. A group of linguistics researchers from Aston University in Birmingham, England, analyzed the Bitcoin whitepaper and compared it against several individuals (including Dorian Nakamoto and Hal Finney). Of these individuals, they concluded that Szabo was the closest match.

The researchers noted: "The number of linguistic similarities between Szabo's writing and the Bitcoin whitepaper is uncanny; none of the other possible authors were anywhere near as good of a match."[68] They narrowed in on Szabo by comparing the whitepaper with several of Szabo's blogs and other publications, finding distinct similarities in expressions and grammar.

A more fun, speculative piece of evidence is the erection of a bronze hoodie-wearing Nakamoto statute in Budapest, Hungary. This has been speculated as an insider nod to Nick Szabo being Nakamoto, given that he is of Hungarian descent. Szabo has repeatedly denied being Nakamoto, including a tweet stating: "Not Satoshi, but thank you." Denial is a common theme amongst individuals suspected of being Nakamoto. However, there is one individual who openly claimed to be the infamous Nakamoto – Craig Wright.

Wright, an Australian computer scientist, came to prominence after a December 2015 *Wired* article by Andy Greenberg made the case. The article "Bitcoin's Creator Satoshi Nakamoto Is Probably This Unknown Australian Genius" presented a compelling argument at the time, including the discovery of blog posts related to cryptocurrency before the 2008 whitepaper.[69] Wright also fits the technical profile – holding teaching and lecturing positions in computer science at Charles Sturt University in Australia. Wright is described as a libertarian with a keen interest in Japanese culture (explaining his choice of the Nakamoto pseudonym). After the *Wired* article was released, Wright quickly confirmed he was indeed Nakamoto and updated his biography on his website to reflect this. To seal the deal, Wright posted a cryptographic signature in a blog post. That signature was associated with the private key that controls the address linked to block nine of the Bitcoin blockchain, being the private key held by none other than Nakamoto.

Case closed, then?

Not so fast. Wright's supposed air-tight case started to quickly fall apart. Security researcher Kaminsky investigated Wright's cryptographic signature and alleged it was an elaborate scam – with the signature publicly available. In a 2016 tweet, Kaminsky stated: "Satoshi signed a transaction in 2009. Wright copied that specific signature and tried to pass it off as new." This was supported by Bitcoin developer Peter Todd, who *Vice* quoted as saying, "It would be like if I was trying to prove that I was George Washington and, to do that provided a photocopy of the constitution and said, look, I have George Washington's signature."

There is a definitive way to prove that you are indeed Nakamoto. Only Nakamoto would hold the private keys to block 0 of the Bitcoin blockchain (i.e., the Genesis block). If Wright was indeed Nakamoto, he could publicly announce he would be doing a transaction from the account and then execute it. This would be available for all to see as a transaction on the Bitcoin blockchain, providing definitive proof that he is Nakamoto.

In 2020, Wright's attorneys said he did not have the private keys but expected to receive them at a later date (without specifying who would give them or why he did not have them). No update has since emerged. *Wired* subsequently amended its article, adding an editorial note stating: "This piece has been updated to clarify Wright's claims, and the headline has been changed to make clear that WIRED no longer believes Wright is likely to be the creator of Bitcoin."

Wright remained steadfast he is Nakamoto, entering into a series of defamation litigations against individuals disputing this fact. This would all come to a head in a judgment from the High Court of England and Wales. The Crypto Open Patent Alliance (COPA), commenced proceedings against Wright in 2021 to prevent him from asserting intellectual property rights over Bitcoin's open-source technology.[70] In the month-long trial, Judge James Mellor found: "I am entirely satisfied that Dr Wright lied to the Court extensively and repeatedly. Most of his lies related to the documents he had forged which purported to support his claim. All his lies and forged documents were in support of his biggest lie: his claim to be Satoshi Nakamoto."

With Wright now out of the race for being Nakamoto, hope was reignited that Nakamoto's identity would finally be revealed prior to release of the 2024 HBO documentary "Money Electric: The Bitcoin Mystery." The announcement of the documentary sent X ablaze when the director, Cullen Hoback, confirmed in a tweet that the documentary would reveal the identity of Nakamoto. Immediately, a market was opened on the extremely popular crypto prediction market "Polymarket".

Polymarket, built on the Polygon blockchain, had become one of the first truly mainstream crypto applications, largely on the back of the US presidential election. Polymarket functions as a prediction market for events, which allows users to buy and sell the probabilities of events occurring. The most popular market has been the 2024 US presidential election market (recording over $1 billion of volume), with the odds of candidates winning surfaced as a probability. For example, if a user thinks that Trump has a 90% chance of winning the election, but the prediction market has Trump at a 50% chance, they can "buy" Trump at a 50% chance. Conversely, if a user thinks Trump only has a 10% chance of winning, they can "sell" Trump at a 50% chance.

The net impact is to give individuals "skin in the game" for their predictions – instead of posting their predictions on X, they can put their money where their mouth is. Polymarket, founded by Shayne Coplan, is now a go-to source for understanding the world with markets spanning for the chances of conflict in the Middle East to what words Trump will say in a speech.

I will admit that in the presidential debate between Trump and Harris I had wagered that Trump would say "crypto or bitcoin" in the debate at 18% odds. While I lost this wager, many made money from their wager that Trump would say "cat" which he promptly did in reference to claims that Haitian immigrants had been eating cats and dogs in Ohio.

The market for Nakamoto on Polymarket proved to be accurate, following more than $44 million in bets. Just prior to the release of the documentary, the highest probability bet (>70%) was that the documentary would name "Other/Multiple", a catch-all category encompassing individuals not directly named in the market (which included Craig Wright, Nick Szabo, Hal Finney and Dorian Nakamoto amongst others). Despite the hype, the documentary did not match expectations. While initially providing a compelling narrative of

Bitcoin, it failed to provide conclusive proof of the identity of Nakamoto.

The documentary named Peter Todd, a Canadian graduate of the Ontario College of Art and Design, as Nakamoto. Todd was an early Bitcoin developer who had been involved in some key technical developments in the history of Bitcoin. This finding was largely based on two pieces of evidence.

The first was based on a post from Todd on Bitcoin Talk in 2010. On December 9, Nakamoto made a technical post on the forum about Bitcoin. The documentary asserted that Todd then "completed" Nakamoto's thought in a separate post under Todd's own account on Bitcoin Talk. The inference was that Todd had accidentally logged into his own account to do the post, instead of logging into the Nakamoto account. The documentary omitted the detail that Todd's post occurred 13 hours after Nakamoto's post – hardly indicative of one finishing their thought.

The second major piece of evidence, was a message that Todd sent, stating: "I'm probably the world leading expert on how to sacrifice your Bitcoins (a rather dubious honor…) and I've done exactly one such sacrifice, and I did it by hand." The documentary asserted that this was evidence that Todd had destroyed the private key to access all of Nakamoto's Bitcoin, and therefore represented a tacit admission that he was Nakamoto. In isolation this is a valid interpretation, however looking at the entire context of the messaging chain, it is clear that this was a joke by Todd and in fact a reference to proving blockchain integrity.

Todd immediately denied that he was Nakamoto and was forced to leave his home in fear that he may be targeted by criminals. Todd had been featured heavily in the documentary and it appears highly likely that Hoback wanted to end the documentary with a satisfying conclusion (with the added benefit of creating some buzz prior to the release). However, the evidence was circumstantial and flimsy at best – leading to criticism of the documentary and no widespread acceptance of Todd as Nakamoto.

The mystery continues

Multiple other candidates have been speculated to be Nakamoto, including cypherpunk Len Sassaman,[71] James McDonald – who made the first reply to Nakamoto's whitepaper – and Adam Back, one of the core Bitcoin developers. The quest remains to uncover the true identity of Nakamoto. In my research, at a point I was convinced that each candidate was indeed Nakamoto only to find a piece of conflicting evidence that threw the theory into doubt. Notably, no candidate ticked every criteria box to be Nakamoto, based on the profile I outlined earlier. It is possible that this points to a collection of different contributors, obscuring Nakamoto's identity.

While there is a desire to lift the veil of the Nakamoto mask, there is a part of the mystique that may be better left uncovered. Bitcoin was designed to always be bigger than any one individual.

The unsolved mystery of Nakamoto allows Bitcoin to continue on its journey to be the decentralized and autonomous currency the original creator dreamed it would be.

CHAPTER 6: HOW A GROUP OF INTERNET STRANGERS NEARLY BOUGHT THE US CONSTITUTION – THE STORY OF DAOS

"We are going to buy the US Constitution." – ConstitutionDAO

In the 2004 action-adventure film *National Treasure*, the protagonist Benjamin Franklin Gates, played by Nicholas Cage, goes on a wild adventure to find a legendary treasure. Triggered by a series of secrets and clues left by the Knights Templar, Founding Fathers, and the Freemasons, the treasure hunt leads Gates to hatch a plan to steal the US Declaration of Independence. This popcorn flick – in particular, an image of Cage holding a torch and bound book – would serve as one of the most unlikely inspirations for a crypto experiment. What started as a meme about Cage's theft of the Declaration quickly morphed into one of history's largest and most successful crowdfunding campaigns.

The campaign's target: the US Constitution.

Unlike most crowdfunding campaigns, it was not organized by a large group or corporation or even a crowdfunding platform like Kickstarter. Instead, it was organized by a group of strangers on the internet using a new kind of organizational structure developed in crypto known as a Decentralized Autonomous Organization (DAO).

DAOs are completely decentralized, relying on proposals and voting by their members to organize, operate and make decisions.

DAOs are run using code – an innovation enabled by blockchain technology. Often using NFTs or tokens for voting, DAOs can allow for collective action using smart contracts to vote and enforce decisions. The first major experiment in DAOs started after the launch of the Ethereum network. "The DAO" was the first decentralized and transparent investment fund aimed at collectively allocating capital across crypto. The ambitious project would eventually end in disaster, with a bug in its code resulting in ~$50M of cryptocurrency being stolen, almost destroying the Ethereum network.

Despite this setback, the concept of DAOs would persist. It would eventually culminate in an audacious attempt to acquire one of the most important documents in American history.

A DAO is a new form of organizational structure pioneered in the crypto space. Reflecting the broader egalitarian and libertarian ethos of crypto, DAOs are an alternative to the traditional centralized corporate structure that dominates finance and commerce today. While the idea of decentralized decision-making is not novel, it is blockchain technology that enables such an organization to function. DAOs can use the transparency and functionality of blockchain – smart contracts that operate by predefined rules. For example, a DAO could, at its onset, create a smart contract that allows for one token owned by the DAO to confer one vote in decisions. The advantage of using blockchain is that the technical design is such that "code is law" meaning members in the DAO can be certain the rules embedded in the smart contract will be followed. It removes the need for trust in the organization. One can verify the "one token is one vote" rule by looking at the source code of the (publicly deployed) smart contract.

DAOs offer an alternative to corporations where shareholders have limited influence over decisions and lack transparency in the companies' operations. The opaqueness in decisions and operations can create conditions for corporate malfeasance, illustrated best by the Enron scandal, which leveraged deliberately complex accounting practices to commit one of the largest frauds in corporate history. Such an occurrence would be difficult under DAOs, whose treasuries are displayed publicly on the blockchain allowing for corporate governance rules to be embedded directly in code.

One of the first experiments in a decentralized organizational structure was the creation of The DAO in April 2016. Created by Christoph Jentzsch, the DAO would disrupt the traditional investment fund model. Jentzcsh, a German theoretical physicist, had been a lead tester for Ethereum since 2014. Entranced by new possibilities enabled by smart contract functionality on Ethereum, he co-founded the company Stock.it. It was an early incarnation of the "Internet of Things" and involved created "Slocks" (short for smart locks), controlled through transactions on the Ethereum network. In 2015, Jentzsch demonstrated this functionality live at devcon one (a developer conference for Ethereum). Live on stage, he used his computer to make a Ethereum transaction, unlocking a smart lock for a kettle. The kettle then boiled water, with a colleague coming on stage to make two cups of tea (to the amusement of the audience).

Slock.it was looking for funding to continue its operations. Initially, it considered doing an Initial Coin Offering, but this idea slowly morphed into creating the DAO.[72] While not initially intended to be an investment vehicle, the DAO slowly morphed into a decentralized, open, and transparent investment fund.

Investment funds in traditional finance are typically open only to accredited (and typically wealthy) investors, who contribute capital, which is then used to invest in various ventures/equities. This structure inherently excludes a large portion of the population from investing, depriving them of the potential upside. Those investors who are fortunate enough to participate typically have little to no say in what the fund invests in, with an investment manager usually calling all the shots.

The DAO turned this entire model on its head.

The DAO was open to anyone – rich or poor, anywhere around the world – with an internet connection and some Ether (the cryptocurrency of the Ethereum network) to invest. DAO investors had a direct vote on how the capital was allocated. Investors could directly propose an investment (e.g., let's invest in this exciting new crypto project), and the DAO would vote for or against it. As described by Simon Jentzsch, Christoph Jentzsch's brother, who was also involved in the project, this structure sought to build on the "wisdom of the crowds," leveraging the group's collective knowledge to improve decision-making.[73] Ownership and voting rights in the DAO came with a token (being ERC-20 tokens on the Ethereum blockchain) instead of shares. These could also be traded on secondary markets meaning investors could speculate on the direction of the price (and, therefore, on the performance of the DAO).[74]

The DAO was built on the Ethereum blockchain and used smart contracts to govern the organization's rules. This had the benefit of making every decision made by the DAO transparent and auditable (given that every transaction is recorded on the blockchain). It also reduced the risk of bad actors in the DAO, given that the smart contracts were designed only to release investment funds when the DAO had voted in favor – giving strong oversight over the use of funds compared to traditional companies. The smart contracts were innovative and designed such that once the investment made a profit, the funds would automatically go to token holders. The DAO could be entirely automated, with the only human intervention based on a group of volunteers (known as "curators") who did an identity check of those submitting investment proposals (to make sure they were legal/not a scam). Such was the level of autonomy of the DAO, Jentzsch refused to give it a proper name arguing that it was something the members should vote on.

People in crypto at the time quickly saw the revolutionary potential of the idea. Some saw this as a sound investment choice by getting upside exposure to investing in a growing industry. Others were attracted to the ethos around the DAO: a merit-based, open-access organization to challenge traditional hierarchical corporate structures.

The DAO launched via a sale of tokens, giving the holders the right to vote on investment proposals. The token holders would also have the right to receive dividends from the DAO for a successful investment (making it an equity investment). The sale was a stunning success, quickly becoming one of history's most successful crowdfunding campaigns, raising over 150 million of ether in under a month. Such was the volume of token purchases that the price of ether itself started to rise. The nearly 11,000 investors in the DAO put in around 14% of circulating Ethereum at the time.[75] To put that in perspective, at the time of writing, this would be the equivalent of $33.6 billion. The rapid success of the DAO shocked even Jentzsch, who described feeling "uncomfortable" about the amount raised, thinking the DAO would raise a maximum of $5-6 million.[76]

Despite the hype and promise around the project, everything crumbled only two months later.

While the Ethereum blockchain is regarded as one of (if not the most) secure blockchains in the market, it allows developers to deploy any smart contract they choose (which is inherent in permissionless, decentralized blockchains). While the developers inherit the underlying security of Ethereum, smart contracts are still vulnerable to good old fashioned human mistakes. If there is an error in the code that is not picked up, hackers can exploit it.

On June 17, 2016, a crisis engulfed the DAO. The DAO's treasury (holding all its assets) started draining to an unknown wallet. Hackers exploited multiple flaws in the DAO's smart contract code to drain the treasury. Investors watched helplessly in real time as hackers stole the DAO's funds. Chemical engineering graduate Griff Green, an American-based community manager who worked for free for the DAO, was not content to see hackers escape with the entirety of the DAO's assets. He posted in a Slack channel:

> The DAO is being attacked. It has been going on for 3-4 hours, it is draining Ethereum at a rapid rate. This is not a drill... We need to spam the Network so that we can mount a counter attack all the brightest minds in the Ethereum world are in on this.

Green quickly led a collective known as "The Robin Hood Group" as a white hat hacker (a term denoting an ethical hacker) to pre-emptively drain the DAO before the malicious hackers completed their work. The counter-offensive was successful, limiting the amount of funds stolen. It did come at a considerable risk to Green – who recognized the dubious legal situation he found himself in at the time, given he was essentially stealing assets from the DAO. Green also faced a barrage of criticism from the community, which was unable to distinguish the good and bad guys. Green's team eventually returned all the funds that were drained to investors through a program that his team created.[77] The exact identity of the DAO hackers has not been definitively proven. *Forbes* journalist Laura Shin claims it is Toby Hoenisch, an Austrian programmer. Shin, in conjunction with blockchain analytics firm Chainalysis, traced the movement of funds between wallets – ending with Hoenisch – who denies the allegations.[78]

Like on the internet, hacking is an ever-present threat in crypto. Hacking groups have formed all around the world to target cryptocurrencies, but none are as famous (and as effective) as North Korea. The hermit kingdom is heavily involved in crypto-related hacking, even though most of its population doesn't even have access to the internet. Lacking a source of foreign currency, the North Korean government has backed hackers to steal cryptocurrency to help fund programs including its nuclear and ballistic weapons program. The United Nations estimates that hackers have been able to steal billions of dollars of cryptocurrency in recent times.

As the dust settled on the DAO hack, investors were left to tally losses. In the end, around 3.6 million ether, or about $50 million, was stolen.[79] This was around a third of the entire value of the DAO. The attack rocked the entire crypto world, with the price of ether plummeting. The loss of funds, trust and confidence left the grand experiment that was the DAO, shattered. It was unable to recover and was essentially wound up only a few months later.

Investor anger quickly turned towards Jentzsch and Slock.it, blaming the team for its failure to pick up on the bug. This was despite Jentzsch encountering huge pressure from the community to launch the DAO early, when Jentzsch wanted more time to test the code. Jentzsch described this period as the "hardest time of his life"[80] with social media channels ablaze with criticism from investors who lost their funds. At this point in time, the Ethereum network had been live for a little over one year, and the attack presented an existential threat, and heated debate. Should the hack stand? Should the hack serve as an example of why well-written and bug-resistant code is essential? Or should the stolen funds be restored?

Some argued the hack should stand, wanting to preserve the immutability of the Ethereum blockchain at all costs. Others took the opposite view, fearing the integrity of the Ethereum ecosystem was on the line, and not wanting to leave investors with a massive loss. Eventually, the decision was made to "hard fork" the Ethereum blockchain. This drastic measure had the effect of essentially creating a "blockchain time machine". It reverted the blockchain to its pre-hack position, which meant the hack never happened, and investors had their tokens back. A group of users who did not support the change continued operating the original blockchain, now known as Ethereum Classic.

And what of the bug that created all this mess?

Illustrating that the margin for error is so small in smart contract code, Omid Maleken wrote in his book, *The Story of the Blockchain*:

> The bug that was exploited by the hacker was, appropriately enough, found on line 666 of the smart contract code of The DAO. It was later determined that if a capital T in a command on that line had been lowercase, the theft would not have been possible.

While the DAO hack was a significant body blow to decentralized organizations, people were quick to realize the failure was not in the concept itself. Following the hack, DAOs continued to spring up across the crypto ecosystem ranging from governing the development of games (for example, the game "Illuvium") to running decentralized crypto exchanges. Currently, the largest DAO is Uniswap, which is in charge of the exchange of the same name (a decentralized exchange allows for trading between crypto without a central authority or third party). The Uniswap DAO has over 300,000 members and controls a treasury worth over $2 billion.[81]

While interesting, it was the ConstitutionDAO that really put the concept of DAOs into the mainstream. The spark for ConstitutionDAO came following the announcement that Sotheby's in New York was running an auction on November 18, 2021 for an original copy of the US Constitution, one of just 13 copies known to exist. The starting bid for the constitution was set at $15 million. The effort for the Constitution would be spearheaded by Graham Novak, a successful entrepreneur based in Atlanta, Georgia who founded NomadX, a platform that aggregated co-living and co-working for digital nomads. Having sold the company in 2019, Novak moved to the investment management company 28th Street Venture, eventually running crypto investments. Novak had been introduced to crypto from a customer of NomadX, who became a multi-millionaire from some early Bitcoin investments and now travelled the world on his earnings. Initially a crypto skeptic, the customer recommended Novak read the book Digital Gold by Nathaniel Popper, which charted the rise of Bitcoin.

The idea of programmatic money and Bitcoin immediately hooked Novak. His first foray into crypto was trying to make arbitrage profits trading Bitcoin and Litecoins on small exchanges, including one based in Zimbabwe. Although it was a fruitless endeavor, Novak was now a crypto devotee. Devouring any and all content in the crypto space, Novak embraced the idea of on-chain organization. At the time, DAOs had started a quiet resurgence, with new variants used to purchase NFTs. Intrigued by these possibilities, Novak started to think more deeply about how else to use DAOs.

He lit the fuse for ConstitutionDAO in a group chat with his college friends. On November 11, Noval's friend Allison jokingly posted a link to a Reuters article on Sotheby's auction for the US Constitution with: "anyone looking to get me a Christmas gift."

This was the opportunity Novak was waiting for.

Novak's inspiration was the almost poetic symmetry between the Constitution and the DAO. A keen American history student, he recognized that a decentralized and distributed organization could acquire one the of most important documents in the history of democracy and decentralized government. In little under an hour after Allison's message, Novak text messaged his friend Austin Cain with an admittedly "crazy idea." He stated: "[Let's] start an acquisition DAO (maybe through Party DAO) to literally buy the Constitution of the United States and turn it into an NFT. Easily meme-ified with references to Nic Cage and national treasure."

Cain didn't need any more convincing, he was in.

The task ahead of them was huge. Not only would they need to raise an estimated $15-20 million (the price guide from Sotheby's for the Constitution) using a new organizational structure that nobody had ever heard of – they would only have one week to do so. Novak and Cain messaged as many people as possible to get a team together, scheduling a kickoff call that night. If they were going to pull this off, virality would be their key to success. The team created a Discord and X account. The team's objective was to spread this far and wide, using Nicholas Cage's meme to do so. Novak explained that the use of memes was key, as:

> memes are a legitimate form of communication, it takes a complex idea and boils it down to something that is hyper-simplified to get to a core point. For ConstitutionDAO, this was a picture of Nicholas Cage holding the declaration of independence that says we are going to buy the Constitution. People do not need to understand all the nuances of smart contracts, funding mechanisms, DAOs – they just see "Buy constitution" and know exactly what we are doing.[82]

This approach worked – within 24 hours of the kick-off meeting, the Discord had 2,000 members and nearly $3 million in soft commitments. ConstitutionDAO quickly assembled a team of more than 20 core contributors, spread across the US and the world. Each played a specific role, from legal, partnerships, engineering, fundraising and media.

In the background, the team corresponded with Sotheby's on bid logistics. There was some apprehension from Sotheby's, evidently confused by the definition of a DAO and if it even had the legal capacity to bid. The auction house was not used to dealing with distributed decision making, appearing visibly shaken with the number of people who would jump on calls. Sotheby's told ConstitutionDAO it would only even consider allowing participation if it raised $10 million.

With this target in mind and the DAO assembled, the team was ready to start fundraising. Settling on Juicebox as the funding raising platform, contributors in ConstitutionDAO received a token called "$PEOPLE." This referenced the opening phrase of the Preamble of the United States Constitution, "We the People." For every 1 Ether contributed, contributors would receive 1 million $PEOPLE tokens in exchange. Holding $PEOPLE would confer a governance vote in ConstitutionDAO. On November 14, 2021, at 8:45pm the $PEOPLE token was created on the Ethereum blockchain.

The results were stunning.

Within just 10 minutes of ConstitutionDAO opening for contributions, it had raised over $250,000. Donations continued to flood in as media outlets started to pick up the campaign. NFT curation studio Metaversal donated $1 million, inspiring an anonymous donor to contribute an additional $4 million. In little under a week, ConstitutionDAO raised $47 million from more than 17,000 contributors. Contributions could be accompanied by some public text, leading to a flood of quotes that encapsulated the excitement around the project. One such contribution of 0.5 ether (around $1,000) by charliethompson.eth wrote the following quote from Ruth Bader Ginsburg: "We have the oldest written constitution still in force in the world, and it starts with three words: 'We, the people.'"

Another contributor of 0.2 ether (around $200) wrote, "first generation immigrant, proud owner of the US constitution." Novak and the team were stunned by the success of the fundraising effort. In what seemed to be an insurmountable task to raise $20 million in little under a week, ConstitutionDAO had more than doubled this target.

However, just a few days before the auction, a crisis threatened the entire project.

Raising funds in Ethereum had meant price risk for the bid. This could go two ways – if Ethereum increased in price, it would improve the bid position in US dollars. The converse position of a decline in the price of Ethereum could be fatal. In what could only be described as incredibly bad luck, ConstitutionDAO had raised funds around the all-time high of Ethereum's price. Ethereum's price started to decline – nearly 15% over the week (from $4,800 to around $4,000).

Sotheby's had initially told ConstitutionDAO it could participate in the auction and bid using the dollar value of Ethereum in US dollars with the requirement that if it won, it must convert the funds to US dollars. On auction day, Sotheby's started to get cold feet on this requirement fearing that if ConstitutionDAO won the bid and Ethereum continued to fall, it would not be able to pay the purchase price.

In what was a chaotic final day, crypto exchange FTX US stepped in and agreed to swap Ethereum at a guaranteed USD rate – purchasing Ethereum for $4,000 and guaranteeing buy back of the same amount if it lost the auction. Sotheby's finally gave ConstitutionDAO the greenlight to participate – a mere four hours before the auction started.

With the crisis averted, ConstitutionDAO's core team was optimistic about the chances of success. It had raised more than double Sotheby's original price guide. The internet too was abuzz in participation of the auction. The Constitution was last sold at auction in 1988, selling for $165,000. How much would the Constitution be sold for?

Sotheby's would live stream the auction.

Behind the scenes, Sotheby's told ConstitutionDAO it was not to reveal the identity of the bidder – with only a few members of the core team knowing the bidder's identity. As auction commenced, the live chat was ablaze with speculation about who ConstitutionDAO's bidder was.

The bidding started at $10 million and quickly descended into a frenzy. Within 30 seconds of bidding, bids went from $11 million, to $12 million to $14 million.

A bid then came in at $30 million, which visibly shocked the auctioneer. The bid came from Brooke Lampley, then Vice Chairman at Sotheby's, who the internet immediately assumed was representing ConstitutionDAO. Lampley had 15 minutes of internet fame, being the subject of numerous memes, but was representing another bidder. ConstitutionDAO's bidder was in fact David Schrader, Head of Private Sales at Sotheby's.

After a pause, Schrader put in a $31 million bid.

The bidding descended into a head-to-head battle between Schrader and Lampley, with bids moving in $1 million to $2 million increments.

The tension in the room was palpable.

Twice it looked like Schrader and ConstitutionDAO had won the auction, with the auctioneer nearly putting the hammer down before Lampley would come in with a higher offer. At a bid of $41 million, Schrader finally put his phone down, marking the limit of ConstitutionDAO's bidding. After auction house fees, the final amount was a record $43.2 million, making it the most expensive document ever sold.[83]

As the auctioneer put the hammer down to signal the end of the auction, both the livestream commentors and X was ablaze with euphoria that ConstitutionDAO had won. What added to the initial confusion was that the $41 million bid was below the $47 million ConstitutionDAO had raised. However, ConstitutionDAO could not have bid $47 million exactly, given a combination of the fall in the price of Ethereum, additional auction fees and costs on top of the bid amount, and an allocation to "insure, store and transport the document" if the group had been successful.[84]

The confusion ended with an official post by ConstitutionDAO, confirming it lost the auction. In a tweet announcing the outcome, ConstitutionDAO stated:

> Sotheby's has never worked with a DAO community before. We broke records for the most money crowdfunded in less than 72 hours. We have educated an entire cohort of people around the world – from museum curators and art directors to our grandmothers asking us what ether is when they read about us in the news – about the possibilities of web3. And, on the flip side, many of you have learned about what it means to steward an asset like the US constitution across museums and collections, or watched an art auction for the first time.

The question was then, who was the bidder being represented by Lampley?

In what would be considered a plot twist worthy of a Hollywood movie, the bidder came out to be none other than Kenneth Griffin, the hedge fund billionaire, seen as a major antagonist in the GameStop saga. The core ConstitutionDAO team immediately went into war room mode, planning to contact Griffin. The team's approach was straightforward. First the team would explain why a distributed democratic body should own the Constitution that talks about how to have large distributed democratic bodies. Next it would propose to raise additional funds to purchase the Constitution at the price Griffin paid.

ConstitutionDAO got in touch with a representative of Griffin, who offered, in the words of Novak, "The world's worst, most offensive deal you could possibly imagine."[85] Griffin's offer was for ConstitutionDAO to send its entire treasury to himself, who would then give it the right to mint an NFT of the Constitution. The

Griffin camp clearly misunderstood what ConstitutionDAO stood for – it wasn't a ragtag group of crypto degens, it was a collection of individuals who together wanted a stake in the most important document in American history.

Griffin told the *Wall Street Journal* that a key part of his motivation in purchasing the Constitution was that "there were important questions about whether a large decentralized group would be able to manage the responsibilities necessary to protect this rare document." Griffin had a history of cryptocurrency skepticism and criticism. While he has subsequently reversed some critiques, it appears likely he viewed ConstitutionDAO with the same contempt as cryptocurrencies more broadly, thus coloring his decision to buy the Constitution.

The result was disappointing on a few levels. A victory for ConstitutionDAO would have been a stunning illustration of the power and organizational ability of DAOs, forever etched in crypto folklore. In fact, one of the strengths of the DAO – its transparency – may have contributed to the loss. The publicity surrounding the exact amount raised by the DAO meant that Griffin (the founder of the hedge fund Citadel) knew precisely what the bidding limit was. Griffin was then able to swoop in to win the auction with a last-minute bid.

The fact the winner was a billionaire private investor speaks to some of the challenges American society faces. It is a disappointing result for a document with such symbolic value to be held privately and not "by the people". On a more positive note, the fact that a random collection of people united by a common purpose could directly compete and almost beat a billionaire demonstrates the power and potential of a DAO.

But what exactly was ConstitutionDAO's plan if it won the auction?

This, of course, would have been up to the holders of $PEOPLE as members of the DAO. There would first be a proposal period, where members of the DAO could put together a detailed proposal as to what to do with the Constitution. At the end of that period, DAO members could vote and implement the winning proposal.

The proposal was to display the Constitution at Federal Hall, the location of the 1st Congress when New York City was the United States capital in 1788. Federal Hall had hosted historical events, from the location of where the Bill of Rights was ratified to the inauguration of George Washington. The building, now run by the National Parks Service, planned an exhibition in 2026 (the 250th anniversary of the country) on the evolution of the Constitution over time. This included artifacts from American history but was missing one thing: an original copy of the US Constitution.

The proposal would have lent the US Constitution for the exhibition, including a description of the DAO and the circumstances of its purchase. While a great use of the Constitution, the positive thing about the DAO was that other equally worthy proposals were being discussed. These included having the Constitution go on tour around the US, to be featured in areas where people would usually not have the opportunity to see a copy. Others had floated the idea of a worldwide tour to display the Constitution, to showcase this piece of American history.

Regardless of what the final use would have been, in the end it was the people who would have decided – not based on the whims of a billionaire. As for ConstitutionDAO, the core team ultimately decided to wind up the DAO and return all funds raised – the ethical route forward. On November 24, the official ConstitutionDAO X account announced the decision:

> Ultimately, we've come to the decision that continuing on without the unifying mission of buying the constitution, setting up more official governance, and embarking on a new chapter is not something that we as a core team are able to support.

Of course, in typical crypto market fashion, just two days after this announcement, the price of $PEOPLE token exploded, rising more than 200%. Through no intention or action of the core team, the $PEOPLE token had become a meme coin trading at nearly 20 times the redemption value. $PEOPLE would reach a fully diluted valuation of nearly $1 billion before falling.

Where ConstitutionDAO failed, other DAOs' dreams of collective ownership have been realized. In 2021, PleasrDAO was created with a mission to (as stated on its website):

> collect digital art representing and funding important ideas, movements, and causes that have been memorialized on-chain as NFTs. PleasrDAO has set a precedent for bidding on unique pieces, many of which have powerful messages that transcend crypto.

PleasrDAO made headlines in 2021 for purchasing Wu-Tang Clan's one-of-a-kind unreleased album *Once Upon a Time in Shaolin*. The album was purchased from the United States Government for $4 million. The original album was owned by the infamous Martin Shkreli, who was dubbed in the media as "Pharma Bro" following his decision to increase the price of the lifesaving drug Daraprim by ~5500% (from $13.50 to $750 per pill) after acquiring the manufacturing license. The US Government seized the album after Shkreli was convicted on securities fraud charges.[86]

PleasrDAO used blockchain technology to distribute the ownership of the album by minting the ownership deed of the album as an NFT, allowing ownership of physical items to be evidenced in digital form. PleasrDAO has also made some additional high-profile purchases: they purchased an Edward Snowden "Stay Free NFT" for around $5.5 million, with the sale proceeds going to the Freedom of the Press Foundation. This was a deliberate choice by the DAO, given Edward Snowden leaked classified information on the activities of the US National Security Agency, showing widespread global and local surveillance of US citizens and foreigners by the US Government.[87]

In the middle of the Dogecoin bull run, PleasrDAO purchased an NFT tied to a Doge meme image. It secured a winning bid of over

$4 million, making it the most expensive meme NFT purchase of all time.[88]

We are gonna buy the Constitution (again)

The dream of a DAO owning a copy of the US Constitution is not dead. A year after the initial auction, Sotheby's announced the auction of another private copy of the original US Constitution. This copy had not been sold for over 125 years and was valued between $20-30 million. On this news, the core team of ConstitutionDAO got together again and put it to a vote as to whether to organize another bid – but ultimately decided against it.

In this vacuum, the crypto community came together to form ConstitutionDAO2. ConstitutionDAO2 was quickly set up from a combination of DAOs and organizations across the crypto space. The rallying cry time was slightly adjusted to: "We are gonna buy the Constitution! (again)"[89] While not taking a front-line position, Novak assisted ConstitutionDAO2 with advice and a playbook from the initial bid.

This influenced some key decisions from ConstitutionDAO2 – by allowing donations to be made both publicly and privately, it avoids the issue of other bidders knowing the DAO's maximum bid. As of the time of writing, the DAO had received ~$300,000 in public donations – with a reserve of private donations. Hours before the auction of the Constitution, Sotheby's indefinitely postponed the auction, stating it needed time "to provide interested institutional parties with additional time to pursue fundraising efforts for a possible acquisition."

It is unclear whether this copy will ever go to public auction. All hope, however, is not lost for ConstitutionDAO2, with another opportunity already in the works to buy a copy of the Constitution in a private sale.

The future of DAOs

Despite the failure of ConstitutionDAO to win the auction, the publicity was a watershed moment in the history of DAOs. This led to an almost exponential rise in the number of DAOs.[90] One particularly interesting DAO that has recently come to prominence is MoonDAO, which stated mission is "to create a self-sustaining, self-governing settlement on the Moon by 2030 to act as a launch point for humanity to explore the cosmos."

MoonDAO has sent two members to space on the Jeff Bezos-owned Blue Origin's New Shepard suborbital launch vehicle. The DAO raised over $8 million in funding and is guided by Pablo Moncada-Larrotiz, an original ConstitutionDAO member. The DAO plans to have a 2030 New Year's Eve Party on the Moon. Everyone is invited, but they are asking you to bring your own beers.

Another recent example is BlockbusterDAO which organized a crowdfunding effort to raise around $5 million from NFT sales. The funding would go towards buying the nostalgia-filled Blockbuster brand. Blockbuster, which famously refused to acquire Netflix only to go bankrupt a few years later, was purchased by the Dish Network. BlockbusterDAO aimed to resurrect the brand to create a "DeFilm" streaming studio and movie using decentralized decision-making by the DAO. After prolonged negotiations and pitch decks, Dish Network refused to sell the BlockbusterDAO rights. The IP rights were purchased in 2011 for $320 million – magnitudes lower than the BlockbusterDAO could muster.

ConstitutionDAO created a template for others to follow, showcasing the power of crypto and blockchain technology to harness grassroots movements. It cuts to the philosophical ethos underpinning crypto: decentralization can empower common-minded individuals to challenge the entrenched power dynamics in traditional corporate and financial structures. DAOs can help distribute power and decision-making into a more democratic forum.

Novak, reflecting on his experience, hoped ConstitutionDAO

would inspire others to push the periphery of what DAOs could be used for – from a digital, crypto-only governance tool to real world operations. Novak continued in this mission, founding Mezzanine Labs, focused on creating a protocol for creating on-chain companies, which he views as the next iteration of DAOs.

CHAPTER 7: HOW ONE WEB3 GAME WAS PLAYED BY 2% OF THE PHILIPPINES FOR A LIVING

"Well, as of now, I can quit my day job." – Gamer after earning $20,000 in one month playing *Axie Infinity*

As COVID-19 lockdowns swept across the world in 2020, many people escaped into the digital realm. From Zoom calls to day-long Netflix binges, seemingly anything digital experienced a massive increase in usage. Gaming was no exception. The large household names in gaming, like *Fortnite* and *Minecraft*, experienced a huge uptick in users. However, one of the largest surges in users came from the most unlikely source.

In 2017, a small team distributed across the world started developing a game. The gameplay itself wasn't anything ground-breaking, using a familiar "auto-battler" game mechanic where players can collect, breed, and battle cute little creatures called "Axies" (in the same mold as *Pokémon*). Taken in isolation, the game may have achieved moderate success. Instead, it became one of the most successfully indie-developed games of all time.

Why?

Blockchain, of course.

Axie Infinity became one of the first games to successfully integrate both cryptocurrencies and NFTs into gaming. Its breakout success became the catalyst for an entirely new type of game that integrated blockchain technology, referred to as "web3 gaming". At its peak, more than 2.8 million people were playing *Axie Infinity* every day.

How did they do it?

By paying people to play. But instead of paying players with actual cash, they paid them with magic internet money – cryptocurrencies. Playing and earning NFTs and cryptocurrencies in the game became so lucrative that players quit their jobs to start playing the game full-time. Players in the Philippines and Venezuela, particularly, would earn many multiples of the average wage just from playing the game. At its peak, around 2% of the adult population of the Philippines was playing the game – many as their full-time job.[91]

Axie Infinity became so popular that its cryptocurrencies and NFTs skyrocketed in value. Most famous is Axie NFT #2655 (better known as "Sir Gregory"), which fetched around $800,000 in a sale in July 2021. *Axie Infinity*'s success was not to last; it was brought down by a $600 million hack by North Koreans and a speculator crash in their game economy. Regardless, *Axie* helped spur the development of web3 gaming. *Axie Infinity*'s success propelled the concept of "web3 gaming" to the mainstream. Web3 gaming simply describes games that leverage blockchain technology, not traditional so-called "web2" games. Specifically, this takes the form of integrating cryptocurrency and NFTs into the gameplay experience.

While appearing to be novel use of blockchain technology, the idea of integrating digital tokens and NFTs into games is not a new concept. Take, for example, the massively multiplayer online role-playing game *World of Warcraft*, which has enjoyed enormous success since its 2004 release, with the game being played by over 2.3 million people (roughly equivalent to the entire population of Qatar). Such is their dedication, gamers have collectively played for nearly nine million hours since the game's release.[92] Set in the fantasy world of Azeroth, players can choose to play as one of two factions (the Alliance or the Horde) and create a character with a distinct race (e.g., elves, orcs, humans), class, and set of abilities. With their character, players can fight various monsters and creatures, complete quests and challenges, and fight against each other.

World of Warcraft housed a complex and dynamic in-game economy. The main in-game currency is gold, which can buy weapons, armor, and other goods. Gold can also be used to "craft" items in-game, creating or upgrading items to enhance gameplay. Gold can be obtained by completing quests, looting defeated enemies, and selling items. Players can also engage in the in-game economy to earn gold, buying items at a lower price and selling at higher prices in the in-game marketplace. In-game items like armor and weapons have varying degrees of rarity and utility in the game, with the rarest items (epic and legendary) highly coveted. These powerful items function both as a competitive advantage in the game as well as a status symbol to other players.

Players are renowned for spending thousands of hours "grinding" (i.e., spending time on repeating set of actions to gain experience or in-game currency) through the game to obtain these rare items. This inevitably leads to a huge real money demand for these items, with players shelling out cash to secure items that can go for many tens of thousands of dollars online. Players will even buy entire accounts from others, with sales clocking in at numbers north of $30,000. The developer of *World of Warcraft*, Blizzard Entertainment, has taken multiple steps to stamp out these transactions, including the ability for players to report suspicious activity and automated systems to ban accounts. Nevertheless, trading of this nature occurs all the time across the internet.

This is where NFTs and cryptocurrencies come in. "Gold" in *World of Warcraft* can be replicated simply as a cryptocurrency on the blockchain, with in-game items (e.g., swords and armor) being NFTs.

Okay, cool, but why does this matter?

The key advantage is that having in-game items such as NFTs allows players to have true digital ownership over items. Instead of storing items on the game developer's internal server (and vulnerable to deletion by the developer), the blockchain permanently stores

NFTs. Players are now free to trade, sell, borrow, or lend items outside of the game. Having a shared record on the blockchain can enable NFTs to be transferred across games, meaning a player could use a sword in *World of Warcraft* – and then use it in a completely different game. This opens the door to the potential of exciting (and potentially hilarious) cross-game experiences, like using your gun NFT from *Call of Duty* in *World of Warcraft*.

NFTs also create a direct mechanism for players to be rewarded for the time and effort they put into the game. In *World of Warcraft*, a player may spend thousands of hours leveling up their character and items. If the player moves on to another game, all that time, effort, and value is now locked in *World of Warcraft*. With NFTs, that player could sell these items on the marketplace to recoup some of their investment. This was what inspired Ed Bunting, the Chief Legal Officer at the crypto gaming platform Immutable, to become interested in web3 gaming. As a parent, his children would constantly be begging him to buy digital items in a game, only to move onto a new game a few weeks later. If games had NFTs instead, he could sell these NFTs for cash every fortnight, and then recycle them back into the latest games his children were interested in.

NFTs have also been used as a funding mechanic for game developers. Funding for game developers is an ever-present challenge with many small developers running out of cash well before their game is live. NFTs have opened a new funding channel for these developers, with game NFTs often sold well before the game is live. The Australian-based gaming company Illuvium raised a whopping $72 million from an NFT sale to help fund the development of its game.

Replacing in-game currency with cryptocurrency opens the door to interesting use cases. The key change is that cryptocurrencies can be freely traded on the market, giving them real-world value. This enables developers to give rewards to players and the ecosystem from these cryptocurrencies, promoting behavior like making user-generated content, identifying bugs, or suggesting game improvements. From this angle, cryptocurrencies can better distribute the value generated from the game to key contributors in a way that was not previously possible. Finally, games are increasingly turning to DAOs as a way to help govern their game. Some games have fully embraced the concept, such as Illuvium, which intends to create a fully decentralized and transparent game that is owned and governed by its players.

While the current crop of web3 games is experimenting with this new medium, the idea of web3 gaming can be traced back to one of the earliest NFT projects. In 2017, a project was launched on the Ethereum network called *CryptoKitties* which quickly became a craze in the crypto community. The game was relatively simple. Players could purchase, breed, and trade virtual cats. Each CryptoKittie has its own set of distinct traits, from fur color to eye shape and tail. Think cartoon kittens meet *Pokémon* cards. Players clamored to collect and breed as many rare CryptoKitties as they could, entranced by the novel world of NFTs.

Such was the popularity of the game that the Ethereum network started to slow with the sheer volume of transactions. This caused the fees to perform transactions on the network (called "gas fees") to surge as the game accounted for nearly 10% of all Ethereum transactions.[93] While *CryptoKitties* was a fun experiment in NFTs, it could hardly be considered a game. Australian based brothers, Robbie and James Ferguson, and Alex Connolly, built upon the premise of *CryptoKitties* with the launch of the game *Etherbots* (launched under the company "Fuel Games").

The Ferguson brothers had been inspired by the CryptoPunks NFT collection, and sought to combine NFTs with their lifelong love of gaming with a crypto video game. The founding trio, all law students, forwent a steady career as lawyers to dive into web3 gaming. After a grueling length of months, the team was able to create the first multiplayer competitive blockchain game. *Etherbots* built on the breeding mechanic in *CryptoKitties*, allowing players to combine parts obtained through purchasing crates to create a robot (known as "forging"). *Etherbots* also introduced both a gameplay and reward element, which would be an early foreshadowing of the development of rewards in the space.

The robots you create could battle against each other, with the winner receiving a large number of shards (which could be used to eventually forge more parts or to be sold). The game was a hit, surpassing the number of transactions of *CryptoKitties* in February 2018 and bringing in $1 million of revenue in its first week alone.

While *Etherbots* was innovative, the game didn't have deep gameplay mechanics like traditional games. The founding team set to sights on a larger ambition of creating a trading card game. Called *Gods Unchained*, the game was not unlike other popular trading card games like *Hearthstone* or *Magic: The Gathering Arena*. Players would create a deck of cards, which they could use to battle or trade with other players. The major innovation was replacing the cards with NFTs and launching a token (the "GODS" token) as the in-game currency. Launched in 2018, *Gods Unchained* has stood the test of time as one of the most successful and sustainable web3 games in market.

Not content at simply being a web3 gaming studio, the team rebranded the company to "Immutable" and built out a web3 gaming chain and platform, including a gaming specific wallet called "Passport". Immutable now aims to bring digital ownership to players, making it safe and easy to build web3 games. Immutable now has more than 400 games building on the platform and more than three million Passport signups.

I had tremendous luck in escaping professional services to join the world of web3 at Immutable. It has been a privilege to work with a group of remarkably talented people trying to navigate the ever-changing crypto landscape.

While the Ferguson brothers and Connolly were launching their web3 games, another founder by the name of Trung Nguyen would be embarking on a similar path. Based in Vietnam, Nguyen was the co-founder and CTO of Lozi, a social network for food bloggers to share dining experiences. Nguyen was intrigued by the complicated breeding mechanics of *CryptoKitties*. Each time a CryptoKittie was bred, a new, unique CryptoKittie was made, defined by its own set of so-called "cattributes."

Nguyen set out to create a game of his own, reaching out to his co-founder of Lozi, Tu Doan, and pitched the idea. Nguyen handled the blockchain and game economy aspects, while Doan focused on the creative aspects. Together, they slowly built a team to develop *Axie Infinity*, focused on adding a gaming layer to the core mechanics of *CryptoKitties*. Collecting and breeding would remain, but now you could use your NFTs to battle against other players. This resulted in a simple auto-battler gameplay loop.

To start, players must acquire three Axie NFTs, purchased in the Axie marketplace or through breeding two parent Axies (in a similar mold to *CryptoKitties*). Once assembled, players have turn-based battles similar to *Pokémon* games. They select an ability from their Axie to use in battle, with each player taking turns with the ultimate goal of defeating the other player. Nothing in this gameplay loop is particularly innovative – it was on the commercial and technological side where *Axie* shined.

Using two distinct cryptocurrencies – "Axie Infinity Shards" (AXS) and "Smooth Love Potion" (SLP) – Axie conducted a public and private sale of AXS, raising in excess of $3 million for game development. AXS is used in *Axie* as a "governance token," essentially analogous to cryptocurrencies that are used in DAOs for voting. This model is common in web3 gaming, as it can give players a powerful voice to influence the game's direction.

Axie used SLP to drive explosive growth in the game, turning the traditional commercial model of the video game industry on its head. Historically, the default distribution for games was selling a physical disk in a store like GameStop for $60-$100. Game publishers were content gatekeepers – they had relationships with brick-and-mortar retailers to distribute games and had the capital to fund the marketing and release. This model proved to be very profitable for publishers, but profits became increasingly eroded by game piracy. Why pay $60 for a game when you can download a free version online?

Over the course of the early 2000s, with the increase in usage of the internet, online methods of distribution became more popular. This provided the catalyst for a new distribution model: free-to-play. Under this model, games were distributed entirely free to players. Mobile games like *Farmville* and *Angry Birds* enjoyed tremendous success under this model. This had significant impacts on the industry. Firstly, it substantially increased the potential pool of players, as they no longer needed to invest upfront to play the game. Secondly, it essentially eliminated game piracy – with no incentive to pirate a game you can get for free. Finally, it changed gaming's commercial model. Instead of generating fixed income per sale, developers tried making money from in-game purchases. These purchases varied from additional payments to unlock content (e.g., Halo's multiplayer is now free to play, but single-player campaign requires a payment) to buying cosmetic items to be used in the game (e.g., skins to dress up your character in a costume).

This new model shifted gaming from "pay-to-play" to "free-to-play." *Axie Infinity* took this one step further, popularizing what has been known as "play-to-earn". In a complete 180, the game now pays players to play, using SLP. Given SLP was a publicly traded asset, gamers could be gifted SLP and immediately sell it for real money.

Axie Infinity deployed these tokens for free to players. Players could earn tokens by winning game battles or doing certain in-game actions (e.g., completing quests). For every game players won, they could directly ascribe a monetary value to their victory. Clearly, even for a non-gamer, getting paid to play a game is quite attractive. Inevitably, as there was money on the line, players quickly realized the earning potential of playing *Axie Infinity*. Players started to invest more money into *Axie* NFTs to join the party. With an upfront investment required, players quickly pivoted to finding the optimal strategies to earn the most amount of SLP.

The earning potential of *Axie Infinity* became an attractive proposition for players in developing countries. Amidst COVID-19 lockdowns that left many unable to work, people started to pivot to more "irregular" jobs. The Philippines and Venezuela together accounted for ~50% of *Axie Infinity* players.[94] *Axie Infinity* became a craze in the Philippines, with Filipinos clamoring to get a share of the money being made through the game. Many quit their jobs to play *Axie Infinity* full time, often earning two to three times their usual income all from the safety and comfort of home.

CoinDesk columnist Leah Callon-Butler traveled to the Philippines to record a short documentary on the *Axie Infinity* phenomenon titled "NFT Gaming in the Philippines." Focused on a rural province of Cabanatuan City, Nueva Ecija (located north of Manila), Callon-Butler profiled Filipinos and their experiences playing *Axie Infinity*. At the time of the documentary, the Philippine economy was still reeling from the impact of COVID-19 lockdowns, exacerbated by the fact that nearly 50% of the entire workforce earns a living working day-to-day. This put a large portion of the workforce financially vulnerable during the COVID pandemic, with around 7.3 million Filipinos out of work.[95]

With few other options, digitally-savvy Filipinos turned to *Axie Infinity*. One such example was Art Art, who invested $4 into three *Axie* NFTs.[96] After 15 days of playing, he made 1,000 pesos ($20), roughly equivalent to two days of the minimum wage there. News of his experience quickly spread, leading to hundreds of people on Art Art's street playing. Two elderly store owners, Lolo Silverio and Lola Vergie, also turned to *Axie Infinity*. Due to the lockdowns, they saw their daily earnings from their store plummet by more than 90%.[97] While minding the storefront, Lolo Silverio would play *Axie Infinity* to supplement their meager income (and as a chance to escape reality). The owners used the extra income to pay for necessities like medicine.

Stories like this are common across the Philippines with games like *Axie Infinity* seen as a pathway out of poverty. Undoubtedly, this illustrates a positive aspect of *Axie*'s game economy – providing a social good that other games could not claim. However, it obscured a fundamental flaw in their business model and game economy. The playing base was slowly turning to a majority of "extractive players" whose sole objective was to take more out of the game (by converting their AXS and SLP to cash) than they were putting in. Such a model is fundamentally unsustainable, as it relies on an ever-increasing number of new players in the game to support the model.

This model would plague the initial class of web3 games. Another game at the time of *Axie Infinity* would face similar issues. A new incarnation of the play-to-earn model came in the form of move-to-earn. Australian-based company STEPN pioneered this. The idea was simple – users would download an app and then buy an NFT of a runner. Users could then walk, jog or run while on the app and earn cryptocurrency tokens for doing so. While a great use case of using cryptocurrencies to incentivize people to exercise, it too would struggle to maintain prices of its NFTs and tokens without more new players entering the game.

Axie would also face criticism for the "scholar" program that evolved alongside the game. As the number of *Axie* players rose, the barriers to entry for new players became higher as the value of the cheapest *Axie* NFT started to increase. This meant the cost of assembling a "team" of *Axies* (a term referring to three *Axie* NFTs required to play) increased substantially. The net impact was that the playing base in developing countries could no longer afford the initial upfront cost to play the game.

The solution: player guilds.

The business model was a simple revenue share. Guilds would front up the capital to purchase the *Axie* NFTs and rent them to the player. The player would play *Axie Infinity*, often for 10 plus hours per day, keeping 70% of the income earned. The Guild would be paid the remaining 30%, essentially the equivalent of rental income. Over time, the owner of the NFTs became known to be a "manager," while the player was known as a "scholar." While the *Axie Infinity* developers did not officially sanction the program, it continued to exist in a grey market.

The scholar program was controversial from the onset. On one hand, managers argue they were simply filling a gap in the market.

In 2021, *Forkast News* interviewed an *Axie* manager going by their discord name, "Porky," who stated:

> The [scholarship program] is doing good, and those scholars
> — it's changed a lot of their lives…. They have enough money
> to improve their house, they are not in debt anymore, they can
> pay for their tuition fee for school, they can pay for medicines
> for their relatives, they can even support their relatives.

Critics argued the scholarship program was a predatory employment arrangement. Scholars grind out earnings on the game while the managers reap the rewards. This critique, however, could equally be applied to any capitalist system. Fortunately, the ask for scholars was to invest their time (not money), insulating their risk from the price of *Axie* NFTs crashing.

Objections to the scholarship program were muted during the bull run of SLP. SLP rose from less than one cent in July 2020 to a peak of 36 cents in May 2021. Managers and scholars alike were making hundreds, if not thousands, of dollars per day. It was looking quite rosy for *Axie Infinity*, with more users, higher prices for NFTs, SLP and AXS. Underneath the surface, there were problems brewing.

The core problem lies in the "tokenomics" design of SLP – referring to the economics of a cryptocurrency. SLP had an unlimited supply, which stood in contrast to other cryptocurrencies like Bitcoin (with a fixed cap of 21 million). SLP could be created at the discretion of the game developer, Sky Mavis, which was in a similar position to the US Federal Reserve – able to increase and decrease the supply of a currency at will. The temptation, therefore, is always to create more, particularly when the price is high. Without sufficient "sinks" – referring to how gamers spend currency – the game economy can collapse.

SLP reached a peak of 36 cents in mid-2021, only to capitulate just six months later to less than one cent – a stunning 99% loss. This had a crushing impact on many players, particularly pronounced in the Philippines. The opportunity to escape poverty had attracted many players who now saw the earning opportunity evaporate. Those who had invested substantial sums in the game were nursing heavy losses with many having to return to their regular jobs. Things then went from bad to worse for *Axie Infinity*. With their game economy in a tailspin, the last thing *Axie Infinity* needed was another crisis.

They got it in the form of North Korean hackers.

Sky Mavis had chosen to create their own blockchain for *Axie Infinity* to run on. Called "Ronin", this decision was due to the high costs for transactions on the Ethereum blockchain. These costs could mean that the fees to buy an *Axie* NFT could be higher than its actual price. Like buying a $4 coffee using a debit card, only to be charged an additional $5 fee from Mastercard or Visa.

Sky Mavis dialed up the scalability of this new blockchain allowing for cheaper and faster transactions. This came at the cost of both security and decentralization. Often referred to as the "Blockchain Trilemma", developers can pick two of the three major aspects of blockchain technology: decentralization, security, and scalability. Ethereum, while scoring strongly on decentralization and security, is not highly scalable, leading to higher costs for transactions.

The decision by Sky Mavis was eventually ruthlessly exploited by hackers. In March 2022, hackers struck the Ronin sidechain having spent time carefully studying its inner workings that included nine separate "validator nodes". Validator nodes are like referees in sports. They enforce the "rules of the game" of the blockchain, ensuring transactions follow network requirements. They ensure things such as the legitimacy of transactions (e.g., that the buyer has enough funds to buy an NFT). As in sports, if you can control the referee, you can control the game. The hackers gained control of the majority of the network (five of nine nodes) – known as a "51% attack" – enabling the ability to perform transactions at will. The hackers immediately set to work. Their target – the Sky Mavis treasury.

The hackers drained an incredible $625 million from the treasury, constituting 173,600 ether and $25.5 million USDC (a stablecoin that trades one to one with the US dollar). This was such a catastrophic loss for the company that Sky Mavis had to raise $150 million from investors in a so-called "rescue round."

There was a stunning amount of sophistication in the attack.

The Verge reported in 2022 that *Axie Infinity* was compromised by a phishing scheme targeting a Sky Mavis engineer. The hack, perpetrated by North Korean hackers known as "Lazarus", used a mix of social engineering and technical know-how. The hackers created a sham company on LinkedIn, adding bells and whistles to make it appear legitimate before reaching out to a Sky Mavis engineer under the guise of getting them to apply for a fake job. The hackers then proceeded to have multiple rounds of fake interviews. In the final round of interviews, the hackers then promised the engineer an extremely generous compensation package – the details of which were contained in a PDF containing the offer.

Eager to find out exactly how much this job would pay; the engineer opened the PDF which contained malicious code, enabling them to hack the Ronin sidechain. Law enforcement agencies recovered more than $30 million of these funds, but it appears like the hackers will retain the lion's share of their proceeds.[98] Sky Mavis subsequently implemented changes to the Ronin sidechain to increase its security, but the reputational impact remains.

Despite these setbacks, *Axie Infinity* and Sky Mavis have proven to be resistant. Although it has not reached the heights of the 2021 boom, the game still recorded ~500k monthly active players as of the end of 2022 (which would be considered the user numbers of a successful game). There remains a core committed playing group, still predominately based in the Philippines and Venezuela. In the web3 gaming industry, a common refrain is "Don't be like *Axie*," but this obscures some important points. *Axie Infinity* along with STEPN tried a radically innovative and new business model. With any innovation in this space, there were bound to be mistakes and missteps.

Axie Infinity has explicitly sought to distance itself from the "play-to-earn" brand it established, trying to focus the game around actually being fun for players. This may not be a great solace to players who lost money when the price of AXS/SLP and NFTs collapsed. It does, however, underline the importance of understanding risks when treating gaming NFTs and tokens as investment assets, particularly when they are intended to be mechanisms to play with the game. The industry is trying to learn its lesson from *Axie Infinity* and focus on making games people want to play. The web3 elements (cryptocurrencies and NFTs) are now being seen as a way to *enhance* the player experience.

In my view, web3 gaming is one of the major use cases for blockchain technology. Cryptocurrencies and NFTs already align with existing gaming features making adoption easier. There's tremendous potential for gamers to digitally own their assets, opening the world of NFTs across games, allowing for innovative teams to explore and experiment the new opportunities the technology unlocks. I have had the great fortune of working directly with a number of visionary gaming teams, from the Space Opera Massively Multiplayer Online Role-Playing Game (MMORPG) *Space Nation*, the mobile MMORPG *Treeverse* and Boomland studios, creator of a number of successful titles such as the action RPG *Hunters On-Chain*. I also had a unique opportunity to become immortalized on the blockchain as an NFT with *Space Nation*. As part of its "Space Nation Crew: The Immutables" NFT collection, there are now 9 NFTs with my likeness that can be played in-game (with my NFT titled "Nard"). When the collection launched, I had the fortune of being the first NFT traded, with the sale coming in for over $1,000.

These are among the more than 500 blockchain games being played worldwide, with billions of funding pouring into the space.[99] Despite *Axie Infinity*'s missteps, the future looks bright for the future of web3 gaming.

CHAPTER 8: HOW A $40 BILLION CRYPTOCURRENCY WENT TO ZERO IN 72 HOURS: THE COLLAPSE OF LUNA

"95% [of crypto companies] are going to die, but there's also entertainment in watching companies die too." – Do Kwon, eight days prior to the collapse of his crypto company

In 2022, Do Kwon was a crypto titan. The South Korean had a stellar resume: a Stanford University Computer Science graduate, working briefly as a software engineer at tech giants Apple and Microsoft. Feeling the entrepreneurial itch like so many Stanford peers, Do Kwon returned to South Korea to try to build his own company. What emerged was Terraform Labs and the Terra blockchain – a crowning jewel in the South Korean crypto landscape.

The Terra blockchain was powered by the cryptocurrency Luna and the stablecoin TerraUSD (UST). This blockchain enjoyed a meteoric rise in usage following its launch in 2018, quickly establishing itself as a major competitor to large blockchains like Ethereum, Binance Smart Chain and Solana. Simultaneously, the value of Luna had skyrocketed, giving Do Kwon a war chest many looked at with envy. This, of course, included a sizable personal sum that he had made from Luna.

This success made Do Kwon a messianic-like figure in crypto. His frequent tweets, youth and enviable lifestyle sprawled across social media inspired a loyal following who proudly titled themselves

"LUNAtics." This was, of course, also due to the tremendous returns early community members made from investing in Luna, with the cryptocurrency becoming the eighth largest in the industry.[100] Many LUNAtic had been made millionaires in a short space of time thanks to Do Kwon, who himself had become a billionaire (at least on paper).

In a tale of Shakespearean ilk, Do Kwon's empire collapsed. Waking up on May 9, 2022, not even in his wildest nightmares would Do Kwon have envisaged that 72 hours later, everything he built would crumble. This seismic event would not be confined to Luna only – its ripples would have a devastating impact on the industry, causing the entire crypto market to drop. It would devastate the LUNAtic community, with catastrophic losses. There appeared to be suicides linked to the event, including a Taiwanese man who jumped from his apartment after reportedly losing almost the entirety of his $2 million investment in Luna. The events that followed devasted a community, destroyed Do Kwon's fortune, made him a fugitive, and led him to face charges of up to 40 years in prison.

Do Kwon and algorithmic stablecoins

Do Kwon's foray into crypto started after he returned to South Korea to settle in Seoul following his stint in the US. It was around this time that he became interested in blockchain and crypto, becoming obsessed with Bitcoin and Ethereum. Despite this interest, he entered entrepreneurship through a different angle. He founded a telecommunications start-up, AnyFi, focused on creating a decentralized peer-to-peer Wi-Fi network, using smartphone-to-smartphone connections to expand the range of these urban networks. Do Kwon remained AnyFi CEO for just short of two years before he moved on to a grander ambition.

Not satisfied with expanding the Wi-Fi range, Do Kwon changed his target to revolutionizing the entire global economy. He was going to use blockchain technology to do it. Bitcoin was founded with the aspiration to be the world's decentralized currency. Yet, at the time, the

Bitcoin network had been live for under ten years, and global finance was still the domain of centralized banks. Cross-border payments were still almost exclusively governed by large multinational banks. There was clearly still a market opportunity for new types of digital currencies to emerge.

The failure of Bitcoin to seriously challenge traditional payment methods is mainly a function of Bitcoin's price volatility. This is readily apparent by looking at Bitcoin's price chart. Bitcoin's price can change extremely rapidly, often without any clear catalyst. Price volatility is the enemy of both consumers and merchants. On the merchant's side, there is apprehension to accept Bitcoin as a payment as its value could fluctuate such that after payment is received, the price could fall, resulting in the merchant receiving less than the original selling price. This adds both risk and complexity to operations for merchants, who now need to actively manage their Bitcoin holdings (e.g., selling them immediately on the market). This renders it not particularly appealing for businesses at present (notwithstanding the possibility for innovation in the space to help address these problems).

From the consumer perspective, a premium is placed on stability of currency. There is less appetite to hold a currency that may fall 10% in the next 24 hours when trying to manage your spending. This is also true if you want to send money overseas – you and the other party want certainty on the amount. While it is possible that eventually the price volatility of Bitcoin will ultimately settle to be more in line with fiat currency (making it more conducive as a medium of exchange), other players in the industry were ready to seize on Bitcoin's weakness.

Do Kwon turned to stablecoins to achieve the original vision of Bitcoin. Stablecoins would be able to address Bitcoin's volatility issue – trading one to one with a fiat currency. This would enable the benefits of blockchain technology for payments (being faster and cheaper than existing payment methods), without the downsides. Today, stablecoins are integral to crypto trading and operations. They are designed to trade at parity to a fiat currency like the USD or

EURO (or can also be traded against a commodity like gold). The largest stablecoin in the market is Tether (trading as USDT), which has almost always traded as one Tether equal to one USD.

In a world of crypto token volatility, stablecoins are a safe harbor. Having a constant stable value against fiat currency makes them both a medium of exchange and a store value. Stablecoins often function like the USD in financial markets – being the counterparty trading pair. So, for example, when a person wants to sell Bitcoin to buy another cryptocurrency, they would typically trade Bitcoin to USDT to then buy the cryptocurrency. They also function as tools for financial inclusion. Individuals can buy stablecoins to house their savings when banking services are unavailable or unreliable. Many view these cryptocurrencies as more reliable than their local banks given blockchain's transparency and security.

Stablecoins are also often used to send money both domestically and overseas. Organizing a transfer of funds from one currency to another through the banking system can be annoying at best and a nightmare at worst. Banks often charge exorbitant fees; the transfer can take days and sometimes weeks to land. Using a stablecoin, people can transfer money for a meager cost, receiving the funds in minutes. Given their use cases, stablecoins will remain a permanent fixture in crypto (and may eventually replace fiat currencies entirely one day). All positive so far.

But a central problem for issuers of stablecoins is ensuring they stay pegged one to one to the underlying fiat currency. Avoiding a "de-peg" (i.e., when the stablecoin trades at less than one to one for the fiat currency) is critical. Once de-pegged, the currency can quickly spiral downwards as holders lose confidence. Currently, major stablecoins in the market have cash-backed reserves: for every $1 of stablecoin issued, there is $1 of fiat currency held by the issuer for conversion.

This gives the stablecoin holder confidence it will not de-peg (provided they can immediately convert it back to USD, for example). But it's not ideal for the issuer, who is in it to make money. They prefer not to have this money sitting in a bank somewhere; instead, they would rather be able to invest it into other assets (or even not having to have one dollar of assets to cover one dollar of the stablecoin exactly).

The other issue with stablecoins is a philosophical one. Much of the foundations of crypto markets, particularly in the financial space, is to create a more robust, inclusive, and fair economic system (harking back to Satoshi Nakamoto and Bitcoin). Central to this vision is the ability of crypto to divorce itself from centralized backing norms and institutions. One of the primary centralized financial instruments is fiat currency, like the US dollar. The US dollar's supply is controlled by the Federal Reserve and is often used as a tool by the US Government for political ends (e.g., for sanctions against other countries). Having stablecoins directly backed by the USD goes against the ethos of a large part of the crypto market.

Searching for an alternative, a new type of stablecoin was created. What if instead of backing a stablecoin with actual currency, you could use an algorithm to manage it?

Enter algorithmic stablecoins.

The search for a working algorithmic stablecoin has been best described in a *CoinDesk* article as "crypto's equivalent of the philosopher's stone." The idea behind algorithmic stablecoins is to adjust the supply in response to demand, using a combination of smart contracts and complex algorithms. For example, if the stablecoin trades above its one-dollar US peg, the algorithm creates more stablecoins. The increase in supply should, in theory, result in the price returning to one dollar. Conversely, if the stablecoin falls below the one-dollar US peg, supply drops and the price would return to peg.

Algorithmic stablecoins offered the tantalizing possibility of having all the benefits of a stablecoin without holding all the reserve currency. This algorithmic stablecoin would be the founding idea behind Terraform Labs. Do Kwon turned to Daniel Shin, a fellow South Korean with a similar background, as a co-founder. Shin moved to Washington D.C. when he was nine. He attended the prestigious University of Pennsylvania's Wharton School, majoring in Finance and Marketing. Like Do Kwon, he had an entrepreneurial streak, founding two organizations while completing his degree.

Together, their ambition was to make Terraform Labs the leading payment provider in the world, with algorithmic stablecoins at its core. Not only did they want to have stablecoins as a feature, they also aimed to create an entire decentralized economy.[101] This objective is reflected in their 2019 whitepaper, stating:

> While many see the benefits of a price-stable cryptocurrency that combines the best of both fiat and Bitcoin, not many have a clear plan for the adoption of such a currency…. There is demand for a decentralized, price-stable money protocol in both fiat and blockchain economies. If such a protocol succeeds, then it will have a significant impact as the best use case for cryptocurrencies.

But creating a new digital currency for the world to use would not be easy. To achieve this ambition, Do Kwon needed capital and a thriving ecosystem to build it.

The capital part was easy.

Investors were entranced by the two founders, enabling Terraform Labs to raise more than $200 million from investors. These included heavyweights in crypto venture capital, such as Arrington Capital and Coinbase Ventures.[102] Terra was pitched in investment rounds as "a protocol of money that ensures price-stability by algorithmically expanding and contracting supply. Terra's Stability Reserve makes a decentralized guarantee of solvency, protecting it from the speculative and regulatory risks that other currencies are exposed to."[103]

With a war chest now secured, they would need to build an ecosystem around it. Having a price-stable cryptocurrency is well and good – but it will only promote real change if people use it. This formed the genesis of Terra's strategy, which coalesced around their two cryptocurrencies: Luna and UST.

Luna launched in January 2019 with an initial coin offering to investors. The seed sale was priced at 16 cents per token, with the private sale at 80 cents. Luna was pitched as the cryptocurrency of the entire platform, used to issue stablecoins. It was intended to be a price stability mechanism for the stablecoin while also being used for staking and network governance purposes. Luna was instrumental in Terra's strategy to create a widely-adopted stablecoin.

Luna would be used to support the stablecoins in the ecosystem through an algorithm that used arbitrage to keep it. The design was as follows, using the example of UST pegged to one USD (noting Terra had other stablecoins pegged to other currencies):

- **One UST falls below its one USD peg:** Let's say one UST falls to .90 USD. People holding one UST can go to Terra and directly convert it to one dollar worth of Luna (in theory making a 10-cent profit). The UST is then "burnt" (i.e., digitally destroyed), meaning the supply of UST decreases. Economics 101 suggests the price goes up when supply goes down. The idea, then, is that enough individuals would perform this action, causing UST supply to go down enough that the price would rise back to the peg.

- **One UST rises above its one USD peg:** Conversely, let's say UST rises to 1.10. People holding one dollar of Luna can exchange it for one UST (in theory, making a 10-cent profit). This UST would be created, meaning the supply of UST would rise. As the supply of UST rises, so too should the price fall. This action would continue until UST falls back to its one USD peg.

Essentially, Terra was designed to leverage economic incentives to maintain its peg. Holders could profit by transferring between UST and Luna whenever UST de-pegged. This incentive would ensure that UST would never de-peg and be a stablecoin forever.

Flawless, right?

From the onset, this model was predicated on the assumption that Luna itself had value. In 2018, a prescient Linda Xie described exactly the flaw in the model that would come to pass four years later.

In a message on a group chat, Xie, a former product manager of the US-based crypto exchange Coinbase, wrote:

> I'm not a monetary expert, but it seems to me that Terra suffers from the death spiral. So in this example Terra is the stablecoin and Luna is the collateral. If Terra were to fall and break the peg, then it would depend on Luna to save Terra. But Luna would fall as investors would panic, and then Terra would continue to fall, and then they would just each keep contributing to each other's demise. This is exactly what happened to Nubits, like 3 years ago. I'm kind of surprised this idea is being tried again when it's so trivially broken.[104]

The central argument from Xie is that Luna must have fundamental value for the entire system to hold. If Luna had no fundamental value, the death spiral would eventuate, and the complicated algorithmic stablecoin mechanism would be powerless to stop it.

Do Kwon, whether due to hubris or willful blindness, would aggressively and publicly attack critics of this model. In November 2021, a X user with the handle "FreddieRaynolds" described a trading strategy that could result in a collapse of the protocol. The strategy would require an estimated $1 billion of capital to execute. It involved a series of trades involving the borrowing and lending of Luna and UST. Executing these trades was estimated to net the trader a healthy $50 million profit.

Do Kwon replied to FreddieRaynolds' X thread, stating: "Probably the most retarded thread ive read this decade. Silence is a perfectly acceptable option if stupid. Billionaires in my following, go ahead, see what happens." This was characteristic of Do Kwon's X personality. He was often hostile to anyone who questioned himself or the protocol. The enormous wealth Do Kwon had accumulated had clearly got to his head, with a common refrain calling people "poor" on X. A prime example of this was a response to the user Frances_Coppola, who again raised the issue of a death spiral for

Luna. Do Kwon replied to Frances_Coppola as follows: "I don't debate the poor on X, and sorry I don't have any change on me for her at the moment."

Whether or not Do Kwon took the flaw in Terra's model seriously, he may have tried to mitigate it by creating an ecosystem around the cryptocurrency. In this way, it may have been possible to bootstrap some inherent value in Luna which would prevent users from selling immediately if the price went down. There were two main mechanisms for this: 1) get stablecoins used in everyday commerce (so they could function like actual currencies); and 2) incentivize users to hold the currencies.

To execute this, Terra partnered with mobile payments app CHAI. The South Korean company was to be a test case for using decentralized stablecoin payments in day-to-day commerce. In the press release accompanying the announcement, CU (South Korea's largest convenience store chain) was adding support for CHAI across its more than 10,000 locations. This partnership was critical to the aspirations of Terra. Having a real-world use case for the platform would support both the demand and price of the token.

Terra and Do Kwon anchored heavily on this partnership in their communications to investors and the public. However, following the collapse of Terra, the SEC, in its filing against Terraform Labs and Do Kwon, stated:

> Investors bought in, purchasing LUNA and other Terraform crypto assets, based in part on Terraform's and Kwon's claims that Chai payment transactions were being processed and settled on the Terraform blockchain. But in reality, Chai payments did not use the Terraform blockchain to process and settle payments. Rather, Defendants deceptively replicated Chai payments onto the Terraform blockchain, in order to make it appear that they were occurring on the Terraform blockchain, when, in fact, Chai payments were made through traditional means.

The second initiative that Terra marketed was the decentralized "Anchor" protocol. Anchor functioned as a money market for lenders and borrowers for stablecoins on Terra. Holders of UST could deposit into Anchor and earn interest, with that pool available for loans to borrowers (who provide other crypto as collateral) and pay an interest rate. This arrangement wasn't innovative; it functioned similarly to a typical bank engaged in borrowing and lending (aside from the platform being decentralized).

The interest rate Anchor offered on UST grabbed attention. It was 19-20%. Before interest rate rises in 2022, this represented around 400 times the interest rate on a typical US bank savings account. This rate resulted in substantial cash inflows into UST and the Terra ecosystem with users wanting to get a piece of the seemingly risk-free return. Anchor eventually attracted around 72% of all UST onto the platform. [105] [106]

In crypto – as in life – there is no such thing as a free lunch. The 20% return had to be generated from somewhere. It was partially generated from the interest paid by borrowers of UST on the platform but it was not enough to cover the ever-growing deposits. In February 2022, with UST reserves dwindling, Terraform Labs injected $450 million of UST into the platform to sustain the 20% yield.[107] Anchor's 20% return proved to be extremely controversial. Many labeled it unsustainable and functioning like a Ponzi scheme requiring constant inflows of new capital to sustain it. Defenders argued it was a form of "loss leader" deliberately designed to attract users to the Terra ecosystem.

I nearly deposited money into Anchor, highly attracted to the returns given the near 0% deposit rate in Australian banks at the time. Fortunately, upon reading about concerns around the UST model, I decided against it.

Despite Do Kwon's attacks on anyone questioning the robustness of Terra and UST, in January 2022, the Luna Foundation Guard (FG) was created to explicitly protect the UST peg. Terra's X post announcing the creation stated: "FG is a non-profit organization mandated to build reserves supporting the $UST peg amid volatile market conditions and allocate resources supporting the growth and development of the Terra ecosystem."

The Foundation initially raised $1 billion to support its operations by selling Luna. Over the following months, it would make a series of Bitcoin purchases – the largest of which was 27,000 in a week.[108] By early May 2022, the Foundation had accumulated around $3.5 billion in Bitcoin which placed it in the top 10 Bitcoin holders in the world.[109] It aimed to hold $10 billion worth.[110] In typical lambaste fashion, Do Kwon stated that his goal was to build a war chest of Bitcoin that would rival even Satoshi Nakamoto.

Following the creation of the Luna FG, Luna continued to go from strength to strength. Luna had risen from ~$5 in mid-2021, reaching a high of $116 in April 2021 (a 23x return).[111] To put this into perspective, a pre-seed investor in Luna who invested $10,000 would have seen their investment rise to over $7 million. X was ablaze with LUNAtics posting about their gains and wondering how high Luna would go. Do Kwon, too, was at the peak of his powers. In April 2022, his wife gave birth to a baby girl, whom Do Kwon named Luna. In a tweet, Do Kwon announced the birth, stating: "My dearest creation named after my greatest invention."

To outsiders, it appeared that Do Kwon was untouchable. The astronomic rise in the price of Luna had given him unparalleled crypto credibility. When he tweeted, people listened. Many laughed and defended his trash-talking tweets. His influence sat on par with Ethereum co-founder Buterin, Binance founder Changpeng Zhao (better known as CZ), and now-disgraced FTX founder Sam Bankman-Fried. Luna's success also made him an incredibly wealthy man. His net worth was estimated at over $1 billion. The UST peg resilience boosted his confidence: in April 2021, amongst a broad crypto crash, UST de-pegged; by May it UST dropped to $0.9457 but quickly returned to its one-dollar peg.

Do Kwon and Terraform Labs hailed this as proof of the algorithm working as intended, evidence of its "automatic self-heal[ing]."[112] In the subsequent SEC filing against Do Kwon, it is alleged that this return to peg was not at all a function of the algorithm. Instead, it is alleged that Do Kwon secretly engaged a third party to purchase a large amount of UST to restore the peg.[113] UST would later de-peg again, but this time, no back-door dealing would be able to save Terra.

The collapse of Luna and UST

In March 2022, Anchor protocol's DAO passed a governance vote. Reflecting concerns over the sustainability of Anchor's high savings rate, the DAO voted in a mechanism to adjust the rate in response to market supply and demand. Known as "Proposal 20", the governance vote meant the interest rate was now variable changing by a maximum of 1.5% up or down each month.[114] At the time, Anchor had roughly four depositors for each borrower. It was clear to everyone the savings rate of 20% was going in one direction – down.

At this point, Anchor had become Terra's equivalent of a "too big to fail" bank. With around $12.6 billion of UST locked into Terra (around 72% of the total amount), any rotation out could have dire consequences for the peg. In an April 2022 article on *Decrypt*, Liam J. Kelly stated (in response to Anchor's decision): "If this rotation [of investors out of UST to other stablecoin] were to happen en masse, it could be catastrophic for the health of UST as well as LUNA. Still, a lot needs to happen before we call it quits for Terra." Despite Terra and Do Kwon's efforts, there was little reason for most UST investors to hold onto UST aside from the returns on Anchor. Many investors realized the interest rate on Anchor would continue to fall. This lit the fuse that would burn Terra to the ground.

At the start of May 2022, Luna was sitting at approximately $80, with a market capitalization of around $30 billion. On May 7, 2022, around $2 billion worth of UST was taken out of Anchor (around 16% of the total deposits).[115] To put this in perspective, if the same percentage amount was taken from the bank deposits of JP Morgan, it would total nearly $380 billion. Even a well-capitalized bank like JP

Morgan would struggle to deal with such outflow. Murky circumstances surround this withdrawal. It may have been directly attributed to widespread concern of the lowering of interest rates on UST. Others speculate this was a coordinated George Soros-style attack on the peg, like those described on X which Do Kwon had viciously attacked.

Whatever the reason – investors wanted out – quickly.

There were two main ways to dispose of UST: convert it to one dollar's worth of Luna or sell it on a stablecoin exchange like Balancer (involving swapping UST for another stablecoin like Tether). On May 9, around $285 million of UST was sold on Balancer for other stablecoins. This mammoth amount caused UST to lose its peg, falling to $0.985.[116] While stablecoins will often fall below their peg only to regain it subsequently, this was not the case for Terra. Investors in UST and Luna immediately started to panic. Unable to adequately sell UST in exchanges like Balancer, they turned to redeeming UST for Luna. The supposed arbitrage mechanism meant redeemers would burn their UST and mint Luna, which is what investors flocked to do. With Luna supply increasing, the price plummeted. Luna holders raced to sell out in whatever way they could.

The death spiral warned about a few years earlier – and one that Do Kwon criticized as baseless – was now a reality.

In what can only be described as a brutal crash played out live on X, Luna and UST investors had their entire investment destroyed. On May 10, just a day after the de-peg, Luna crashed 52%, and UST was sitting 38 cents below its peg at 62 cents. Two days later, Luna was down to $0.02 – more than 99% down from May 9. The Luna FG started a desperate attempt to stave off destruction. Firstly, it deployed a large amount of its non-UST stablecoin holding to try to rebalance trading pools on Curve. From May 8 to May 12, the Foundation sold around $50 million of stablecoins to buy UST.

This was insufficient to stop the bleeding so the Foundation turned to its $2.8 billion of Bitcoin. It deployed its Bitcoin balance in defense of the peg. Through Jump Crypto, the Foundation sold its entire Bitcoin holding to buy UST and Luna. The Foundation even dipped into its own proprietary capital reserves spending $613 million in a vain attempt to defend the peg.[117] These actions managed to temporarily move UST from $0.64 to $0.93.

Do Kwon took to X to calm the masses, tweeting first: "Deploying more capital – steady lads." Then later: "getting close…stay strong Lunatics." Nothing Do Kwon could tweet, or any amount of capital the Foundation deployed, could save Terra or Luna.

On Friday, May 13, 2022 (an ominous date perceived as unlucky in popular culture), Terra halted its blockchain on block 7607789. This block was labeled "the crypto coroner."[118] Luna was sitting at just $0.008, while UST was at $0.19. According to blockchain analytics firm Elliptic, investors in UST and Luna lost an estimated $42bn.

The sheer speed and demise of Terra shocked even its harshest critics. Worse still, in the social media age, it was played out in real time. For anyone involved in the crypto space (regardless of whether they held Luna/UST or not), it was a horrendous time. X, Reddit, and Discord were full of stories of investors who had lost their entire savings. The Terra Luna subreddit had a pinned post directing users to the International Suicide Hotline after a slew of users posted their suicidal thoughts.[119] [120] It is estimated that nearly 280,000 South Koreans lost money in the collapse, with a further 230,000 Indians.[121] Numerous suicides and attempted suicides were linked to Terra Luna's collapse, reflecting the devastation of the event.[122]

The collapse of Terra caused a domino effect in the crypto industry, reminiscent of the events during the GFC. In a classic case of financial contagion, in the following months crypto lender Celsius filed for bankruptcy. At its peak, Celsius managed nearly $12 billion of assets. The next domino to fall was Three Arrows Capital. The hedge fund managed $10 billion of crypto assets before facing a liquidity crunch due to Terra's collapse. This failure resulted in crypto broker Voyager Digital collapsing, as Three Arrows Capital could no longer service a $665 million loan. Broadly, crypto markets also crashed in the aftermath, with Bitcoin falling 65% throughout 2022.[123]

Do Kwon was humbled. His tweets took a contrite tone – in sharp contrast to his usual belligerent style. His fortune was erased. His status as a titan of crypto was but a fleeting memory. Post-collapse, Do Kwon launched a new version of Terra, with the original being referred to as "Terra Classic."[124] The new chain acknowledged the issues with the algorithmic stablecoin design, forgoing this element in the latest incarnation. The new Terra aimed to retain the core builders and community members of Terra Classic but, well over a year after the event, the new Terra is a shadow of its former status.

Amid one of the fastest and largest destructions of value in corporate history, one question was on everyone's minds: What would happen to Do Kwon?

In a bizarre spectacle, Do Kwon continued to tweet and conduct interviews with the proverbial sword of Damocles sitting over his head. In September 2022, he had his first interview after the collapse of Terra. While taking responsibility for the failure, he defended against allegations that Terra was a Ponzi scheme, noting the earliest investors had lost the most money from the crash (not typical of a Ponzi scheme where the early investors tend to make outsized returns). The interviewer pressed him on how much he personally lost but Do Kwon simply acknowledged he was "down infinite."[125]

It was clear to most that Do Kwon would be charged for his involvement in the Terra collapse. It was not a matter of if, but when, he would face charges. Before Terra's collapse, Do Kwon had moved to Singapore. South Korean prosecutors prepared their case after the collapse, raiding the house of Terra co-founder Shin. Prosecutors issued an arrest warrant for Do Kwon in September, with Interpol issuing a red notice on Do Kwon in the same month.[126]

Do Kwon denied he was evading authorities. On September 17, he tweeted: "I am not 'on the run' or anything similar – for any government agency that has shown interest to communicate, we are in full cooperation and we don't have anything to hide." In interviews, Do Kwon dodged questions about where he was located. He argued that it was due to personal security reasons rather than attempting to evade the South Korean authorities.

In a bizarre scene on the *UpOnlyTV* podcast, we return to the "Pharma Bro" and convicted fraudster Martin Shkreli. Appearing with Do Kwon, in an awkward interaction, Shkreli told Do Kwon, "Hey Do, I just want to let you know, jail is not that bad." The pressure was mounting on Do Kwon. In October, South Korea announced it would cancel his passport making it impossible for him to leave Singapore. A day after this announcement, South Korean authorities confirmed he had already left the country for Dubai.

In February 2023, the US SEC officially charged Terraform Labs and Do Kwon. Regulators accused him of "orchestrating a multi-billion dollar crypto asset securities fraud"[127] and a "fail[ure] to provide the public with full, fair, and truthful disclosure as required for a host of crypto asset securities, most notably for Luna and TerraUSD."[128] After months on the run, Do Kwon was finally arrested on March 23, 2023 in Montenegro. He allegedly carried a fake Costa Rican passport under a different name and was apprehended as he tried to board a flight to Dubai along with Han Chang-joon, the chief financial officer of Terraform Labs.

As of the time of writing, Do Kwon is in jail in Montenegro – with both the South Korean and US Governments vying to extradite him to face trial.

What next for Algorithmic stablecoins?

With the high-profile failure of Terra, appetite understandably waned for algorithmic stablecoins. The central purpose of stablecoins (as the name implies) is that they are stable. Investors and market participants became much more alert to potential risks in holdings, leading to greater scrutiny over other stablecoins. While a successful algorithmic stablecoin is still possible, crypto markets have trended towards fiat backed stablecoins like USDC and USDT. Addition stablecoins may come in the form of Central Bank Digital Currency (CBDC), issued by central banks, which could eventually completely replace digital currency altogether.

CHAPTER 9: HOW TO GO FROM $26 BILLION TO $0: THE DOWNFALL OF SAM BANKMAN-FRIED AND FTX

"Being comfortable with risk is very important. We tend not to have things like stop-losses, I think those aren't necessarily a great risk-management tool." — Caroline Ellison, CEO of Alameda Research, whose risk positioning contributed to the collapse of FTX

Sam Bankman-Fried (SBF) was an enigmatic figure in crypto. He represented aspects of the counterculture of crypto, absconding from the usual social norms to which we are accustomed. His eccentricities included sleeping on a bean bag in the middle of an open-plan office, dressing in a worn baggy t-shirt, and driving around in an old Toyota Corolla.

At 30 years old, SBF founded the crypto exchange FTX in 2019. In a few short years, the exchange became one of the world's largest and most successful, making over $1 billion in revenue in 2021 with a $32 billion valuation. This meteoric rise catapulted him to the very center of the crypto industry and earned him the title "JP Morgan of crypto."[129] With the larger-than-life Do Kwon out of the picture, SBF would now only compete with CZ, the founder of Binance, for global prominence as the "face" of crypto. The relationship between SBF and CZ started on friendly terms with Binance investing in FTX. Like two great powers competing for hegemony, their relationship soured as FTX began to compete for market share and influence against

Binance. Their feud escalated to the point that the actions of CZ led to the downfall of SBF's empire, leading to one of the largest and swiftest corporate collapses in history.

In a story mirroring Do Kwon's, SBF would be reduced from a multi-billionaire (with a wealth estimated at $26 billion) to broke. He would be arrested and extradited to the US for trial on charges of criminal fraud and money laundering. He was found guilty on seven charges, and now faces up to 120 years in prison. The rise and collapse of SBF seems more like a work of fiction than reality. It involves stories of a possible "orgy house" in the Bahamas, allegations of rampant drug use, large political donations, and financial speculation that would shock even the greatest degen shitcoin trader.

The beginning

SBF was born on March 6, 1992 in Stanford, California. His family reads almost like a dean's honors list: his parents are Stanford Law School professors; his aunt the dean of Columbia University's Mailman School of Public Health. Undoubtedly, with such gifted minds raising him, SBF would be destined for a noteworthy career. He attended the prestigious Massachusetts Institute of Technology, graduating in 2014 with a bachelor's degree in physics.

After graduation, SBF joined Jane Street Capital, a renowned proprietary trading firm, focusing on creating complicated mathematical models to develop trading strategies for asset markets (e.g., equities and bonds). Such strategies are typically extremely lucrative, using high frequency trading to obtain a market edge. These firms typically compensate exceptionally well and, therefore, have a high talent bar for hiring. Interviews are usually done over multiple grueling stages, involving a series of games and mental math, with a small fraction of applicants receiving an offer. Those who do make it through the interview process obtain the cultural capital that is having the name of Jane Street Capital on their resume – typically read as "this person is a genius".

SBF left Jane Street after a little over three years, a rare occurrence for an institution known for high employee retention. For a short time, he joined the Centre of Effective Altruism as a director of development. "Effective Altruism", a philosophical movement that involves using evidence and reason to precisely determine how to do the most good for society, would form a crucial part of his public persona. It is not simply a philosophy taught within the four walls of a university class; it has practical intention with adherents taking action to implement their worldview.

Initially formalized by professors at Oxford University, its practitioners include Dustin Moskovitz (co-founder of Facebook) and Peter Singer (a philosopher at Princeton University). The movement aims to bring an alternative worldview to the modern world, encouraging people to think differently about the things they care about. Singer described effective altruism as a counter to consumerism culture, stating, "It's clearly an alternative to the consumer lifestyle that says what you do is earn money to buy a nice house and a nice car, and after a few years you renovate the house and turn over the car and go to expensive resorts and so on."

Throughout his time in crypto, SBF became evangelical for effective altruism. He stated in a YouTube video titled "The Most Generous Billionaire": "I wanted to get rich, not because I like money but because I wanted to give that money to charity." He signed up for the "Giving Pledge", a campaign founded by Warren Buffet and Bill Gates. The pledge encouraged wealthy individuals to promise to dedicate the majority of their wealth to charitable causes. The current pledge list includes the likes of Elon Musk, Mark Zuckerberg, and George Lucas.

SBF pledged to donate the majority of his wealth (keeping only around 1% of his earnings). He stated in a *Bloomberg* article, "You pretty quickly run out of really effective ways to make yourself happier by spending money.... I don't want a yacht." His demeanor towards wealth was in sharp contrast to many in crypto. X is awash with conspicuous displays of wealth and a desire for material goods flowing from crypto investments. This is perhaps best illustrated by an almost universal desire to make enough money to buy a "Lambo" (shorthand for the luxury car Lamborghini). A common crypto meme is to post "wen lambo" – shorthand for asking when the price of an NFT or cryptocurrency will go to the moon. As with every crypto meme, it eventually became a reality with a cryptocurrency called "Wen Lambo" and a 10,000 NFT collection with the same name launched.

SBF's departure from this prevailing ethos in the crypto community was in part why he was able to create such a positive public persona. He did not drive around in a lambo; no, an old Toyota Corolla would do just fine. Reporters would often gush over this fact, as if proof of the positive intent of SBF, who at the time was worth more than $20 billion. They would, however, omit the fact that he was living in a lavish $35 million penthouse in the Bahamas, set up with a rooftop pool, view of the ocean and two spas.[130]

His public appearance added to, at least externally, the perception that he was disinterested in the trappings of wealth. SBF was notorious for his ill-fitting attire. He dressed in scruffy shorts and an oversized FTX t-shirt that looked like he had slept in it the night before. Positive media stories abounded. SBF even earned himself the "white knight" of crypto label. While in part due to SBF and FTX often bailing out other crypto projects, it led to a near-deification of SBF.

The origin of the myth around SBF can be traced back to his first foray in cryptocurrencies. In October 2017, coincidentally the same year CZ founded Binance, SBF and Tara MacAulay founded the cryptocurrency trading firm Alameda Research. MacAulay was a fellow devotee of effective altruism, which proved to be a lucrative source of both funds and talent for the fledging firm. Alameda secured a staggering $170 million in trading capital, sourced from wealthy effective altruists. In what would later be mythologized, Alameda Research would profit heavily from the "kimchi premium" (a term to denote the gap in the higher price of Bitcoin in non-US exchanges, mainly in South Korea and Japan). With crypto markets still relatively nascent (particularly compared to traditional equity markets), large arbitrage opportunities were still available. And SBF aimed to capitalize on these through Alameda Research.

In Alameda's most famous trade, SBF set his sights on the premium paid for Bitcoin in Japan – around 10% higher than in the US. If you bought Bitcoin in the US and sold it in Japan, you would make an instant risk-free 10% return. Free money, right? The actual process wasn't so simple; it involved dealing with a maze of different banks and regulations (with many banks simply refusing to work with crypto projects). Nevertheless, SBF and Alameda overcame these obstacles to make nearly $20 million.

This became a staple story in the narrative of SBF, positioning him as a genius trader exploiting pricing inefficiencies. This obscured the complete chaos that was the early stages of the firm. SBF created an incredibly demanding work environment and expected employees to work 18-hour days, sacrificing any semblance of a work-life balance in the process.[131] Alameda was so chaotic, an employee discovered that nearly $4 million of the XRP token had gone missing. The funds were recovered, but the event eroded employee confidence in SBF. MacAulay, the management team, and half the employees left Alameda in 2018.

SBF retained a Jane Street Capital alumni, Caroline Ellison, a talented mathematician he met while mentoring her equities trader's cohort. Over a coffee in 2018, SBF convinced Ellison to leave her stable position to take (in her own words) a "blind leap into the unknown."[132] She quickly rose up the ranks at Alameda Research and in 2021 became the co-CEO with Sam Trabucco. A year later, she was the sole CEO when Trabucco stepped down. Ellison had an on-again off-again romantic relationship with SBF, dating across two separate stretches. Their relationship eventually ended.

FTX is created

After two years running Alameda Research, SBF turned his attention to the lucrative crypto exchange market. In 2019, along with Garry

Wang (another Jane Street alumni), SBF created FTX (short for "Futures Exchange"). FTX was able to differentiate itself from the large incumbents at the time (mainly Coinbase and Binance) through its focus on crypto derivative products. Seizing on crypto's speculative elements, FTX offered options, leveraged products, and prediction markets. Most famously, FTX opened up a futures contract, "TRUMP-2020," which allowed users to bet on the outcome of the 2020 US Presidential election.

FTX is best described as being in the right place at the right time. With crypto markets entering a bull market in 2020, there was a strong desire for more higher-risk leveraged products. FTX's liquid markets became the perfect haven for hardcore degen crypto traders. Binance and its founder, CZ, quickly recognized the potential of FTX. A mere six months after creating FTX, Binance invested $100 million into the company in exchange for a 20% stake. Binance also took a position in FTX's token (FTT). At the time of the announcement in 2019, CZ stated:

> The FTX team has built an innovative crypto trading platform with stunning growth. With their backgrounds as professional traders, we see quite a bit of ourselves in the FTX team and believe in their potential to become a major player in the crypto derivatives markets... We are pleased to have an excellent partner joining the Binance ecosystem and aim to grow the crypto market together.

What started as a cozy relationship quickly soured. The position that Binance took in FTX's token FTT was the spark that blew up the entire business.

The boom period (2020-2022)

FTX saw explosive growth shortly after its inception. Revenue grew an astounding 1,000% from $89 million to just over $1.02 billion in a year.[133] Fueled by stunning revenue growth, FTX went on a marketing and sponsorship binge. It signed on as the official sponsor of Major League Baseball, with its logo emblazoned on every umpire. It signed a 19-year, $135 million agreement with the NBA club Miami Heat to rename the stadium "FTX arena." A Super Bowl ad followed costing a whopping $6.5 million for a 30-second spot featuring Larry David. In it, David comically rejected a series of inventions, from the wheel, the toilet, and coffee. The ad ended with a man recommending Larry try FTX, stating:

> It is a safe and easy way to get into crypto.
> [Larry replies] I don't think so, and I'm never wrong about this stuff.
> [The ad concludes with a graphic:] Don't be like Larry.

In retrospect, viewers of the ads would have been much better off being exactly like Larry.

With sponsorship deals in full swing, FTX continued to rake in more capital investments. In July 2021, FTX raised a further $900 million. This raise valued the company at around $18 billion making it one of the most meteoric rises in valuation in corporate history. The funding round reads like a *Who's Who* list of venture capital firms. One investor was Softbank, famous for its founder and CEO Masayoshi "Masa" Son, who would write aggressively large cheques including a $10 billion investment in Uber and a $18 billion + investment in WeWork (famously depicted in the TV series "WeCrashed").

Another investor was Sequoia Capital, one of the most successful and prestigious venture capital firms. Sequoia Capital made its name for a series of early-stage investments in tech giants like Apple, Instagram, LinkedIn and Google, amongst others. In its first meeting with SBF, partners at Sequoia Capital were reportedly enamored by SBF's vision for FTX. After nailing a series of questions, the partners typed to each other over Zoom, "I LOVE THIS FOUNDER", "I am a 10 out of 10", and "YES!!!"[134]

While the partners heaped praise on SBF, it turned out that throughout the entire meeting, SBF was, in fact, playing the popular multiplayer online battle arena game *League of Legends*. His *League of Legends* talent notwithstanding, he established himself during this period as one of the kings of the crypto industry. He amassed a fortune and built a positive brand around him. Despite this, cracks were beginning to show with his initial benefactors, CZ and Binance.

Relationship with CZ deteriorates

By mid-2021, with FTX's market share of crypto traders increasing, CZ and Binance started to view FTX as a major competitor. Binance reportedly stonewalled an attempt by FTX to apply for a license in Gibraltar of a subsidiary, with Binance refusing more than twenty times to provide the necessary details to apply for the license. This, in retrospect, formed a quasi-declaration of war between the two crypto giants – neither SBF nor CZ would be playing Mr. Nice Guy.

Frustrated, SBF decided to buy back Binance's initial stake in FTX. The deal was worth $2 billion, representing a nearly twenty-times return by Binance in only a couple of years. The payment was made in part with FTT. CZ reported a different version of events, stating, "Sam was so unhinged when we decided to pull out as an investor that he launched a series of offensive tirades at multiple Binance team members, including threatening to go to 'extraordinary lengths to make us pay.'" Regardless of who was right or wrong, the battlelines between the two were set.

SBF increasingly started to lobby for crypto regulation. Regulation is perennially a divisive topic in crypto and to cover it in detail is beyond the scope of this book. Nevertheless, harking back to the founding of Bitcoin, much of the rationale behind creating blockchain technology was precisely to avoid the need for government regulation or intervention. The philosophical basis for crypto – centered around financial sovereignty and privacy – could be undermined by far-reaching or overzealous regulation. Many who have been burned by dodgy operators, rug pulls, or scams would attest to the importance of investor protections and consumer safeguards in crypto.

Regardless of what camp you sit on, SBF's foray into active lobbying for crypto regulation was unpopular in the industry. It opened up speculation that SBF was trying to use the US political machine to undermine CZ and Binance.[135]

The first line of attack for SBF was to leverage tensions between China and the US. CZ was born in China but moved to Canada at age 12. His country of birth has often been viewed with suspicion, despite him only being only a Canadian citizen (China does not allow dual citizenship). Playing this angle, SBF, in a since-deleted tweet, stated: "excited to see him [CZ] repping the industry in DC going forward! uh, he is still allowed to go to DC, right?"

The second was to write a blog post on FTX titled "Possible Digital Asset Industry Standards" containing a set of standards the crypto industry could voluntarily enact before a regulatory framework was legislated. Many – particularly in the decentralized finance (DeFi) space – criticized this proposal and SBF's lobbying as a form of regulatory capture,[136] aiming to entrench the power of centralized exchanges like FTX at the expense of DeFi exchanges (such as Uniswap). DeFi is a catch-all term covering the replacement of traditional financial service providers (e.g., banks) and products (e.g., savings deposits, loans) in an open, permissionless, and decentralized way using blockchain. Ryan Sean Adams, founder of Bankless (a popular crypto mailing list and podcast), was succinct in his critique, tweeting: "Sam. With respect. This absolutely sucks." Others criticized SBF's suggestion DeFi protocols complied with US foreign asset laws. By enforcing US sanctions (along with the requirement for protocols to register as brokers or dealers), DeFi proponents argued this would destroy the innovative potential of DeFi and transform it back to centralized finance.

Before the collapse of FTX, SBF was legendary for the size and frequency of his political donations. He reportedly contributed $40 million to the Democrats during the 2022 elections and $5.2 million to

Joe Biden's 2020 presidential campaign. Republicans didn't miss out. In a phone call with YouTuber Tiffany Fong, he stated, "All my Republican donations were dark…. The reason was not for regulatory reasons, it's because reporters freak the f—k out if you donate to Republicans. They're all super liberal, and I didn't want to have that fight."

SBF once noted to Ellison on the effectiveness of political contributions, stating, "you could get very high returns in terms of influence by spending relatively small amounts of money."[137]

A sleepover party

Like many individuals in the FTX story, Ellison was, let's say, unusual. In an April 2021 tweet, she stated: "nothing like regular amphetamine use to make you appreciate how dumb a lot of normal, non-medicated human experience is." SBF, too, tweeted in September 2019 about drug use: "stimulants when you wake up, sleeping pills if you need them when you sleep."

Rumors abound about potential rampant drug use at Alameda and FTX. *New York Times* journalist Andrew Sorkin stated to SBF point blank in an interview, "it sounds like this is a bunch of smart kids on Adderall having a sleepover party." SBF confirmed he wore an Emsam patch and took Adderall.[138] Both drugs are stimulants, but SBF claims he used both for legitimate medical uses (as a treatment for depression and ADHD, respectively).[139]

Combined with drug use were rumors of polyamorous relationships.[140]

Terra collapses

Problems with FTX and Alameda came to a head around the collapse of Terra Luna. Despite FTX and Alameda being separate, distinct organizations on paper, they were anything but. Notably, FTX and Alameda together held the lion's share of FTT tokens – around 90%.[141] The FTT token had been worth nearly $10 billion at its peak, trading at around $3-6 billion throughout 2022.[142] Holding such a large percentage of FTT meant Alameda had limited options for getting liquidity for their holdings. If they were to sell FTT in large quantities, it would almost certainly tank the price.

With limited options to use FTT, Alameda used it as collateral for loans. This allowed Alameda to borrow more capital to generate additional trading income. But if FTT's price dropped, lenders could call on these loans as the value of the collateral fell below their loan amount. Additionally, Alameda held so-called "Sam Coins"; specifically cryptocurrencies that SBF heavily supported. These cryptocurrencies would have a large correlation with FTT, making Alameda's risk position worse in the event of a downturn.

Following the Terra Luna collapse, contagion spread across the crypto ecosystem. With investor confidence rattled as the value of Luna fell, so too did the prices of other cryptos. FTT was no exception, seeing its value more than halve from nearly $7 billion to ~$3.3 billion during the crisis.[143] Alameda was under threat of insolvency, with loans potentially being called in by lenders and an inability to cover these with liquid assets. FTX started to lend more money to Alameda. When asked how FTX approved the increase in liabilities, SBF simply stated, "I don't feel good about not knowing the answer."[144]

The source of Alameda's funds was egregious. It wasn't from its profits – instead, FTX was lending customer funds to Alameda. To the tune of $10 billion.

This arrangement left both FTX and Alameda in a highly vulnerable position. Everything could crash with a further decline in the value of FTT, a run on the FTX exchange, or investors calling in loans. Over a few weeks in November 2022, that is precisely what happened.

The collapse of FTX and Alameda

The crisis for FTX and Alameda began in earnest on November 2, 2022. It started first with an article published by the crypto news outlet

CoinDesk which reported a large proportion of Alameda's assets were in the illiquid FTT, based on a balance sheet that FTX sent to crypto lender Genesis Global Capital. This immediately stoked fears about Alameda's financial position. What happened next was either one of the most ingenious moves in corporate history, or a serendipitous decision by CZ. On November 6, 2022, CZ tweeted:

> As part of Binance's exit from FTX equity last year, Binance received roughly USD 2.1 billion equivalent in cash (BUSD and FTT). Due to recent revelations that have come to light, we have decided to liquidate any remaining FTT on our books.

A few hours later, CZ tweeted, giving more light on the decision:

> Liquidating our FTT is just post-exit risk management, learning from LUNA. We gave support before, but we won't pretend to make love after divorce. We are not against anyone. But we won't support people who lobby against other industry players behind their backs. Onwards.

The bad blood between SBF and CZ dramatically came to the fore in the most public of fashion.

The decision to liquidate an estimated $580 million of FTT rattled investor confidence. Fearful of the price impact of such a large block of FTT being sold on the market, FTT's price declined. The perilous financial position of Alameda and FTX was unbeknownst to the broader market. Now CEO of Alameda, Caroline Ellison tweeted to CZ, in an attempt to minimize the damage: "if you're looking to minimize the market impact on your FTT sales, Alameda will happily buy it all from you today at $22!"

Twenty-two dollars represented a slight discount to the market price of FTT at the time. Many subsequently pointed to this being the final nail in the coffin for FTX. By suggesting a twenty-two dollar price tag, Ellison revealed the floor price for FTT. The market knew that if the price fell below twenty-two dollars it would be a point of no return.

A death spiral for FTT began, with the price collapsing over the next few days. Simultaneously, there was concern over the safety of deposits on the FTX platform. In scenes reminiscent of a bank run, users rushed to withdraw cryptocurrency and cash from the FTX platform.[145] Withdrawals were reportedly around the $6 billion mark. This placed enormous pressure on FTX's reserves to cover the withdrawals (already depleted from the use of customer funds to loan to Alameda). FTX was forced to halt customer withdrawals altogether.

Desperately attempting to cover the shortfalls, SBF raced to raise nearly $8 billion in capital from investors to avoid bankruptcy. On November 8, another bombshell dropped, with the most unlikely savior potentially coming to the rescue. With the crisis initially started by CZ, in what appeared to be a "4D" chess move, CZ's Binance would acquire FTX. Across a series of tweets, SBF noted:

> Things have come full circle, and http://FTX.com's first, and last, investors are the same: we have come to an agreement on a strategic transaction with Binance for http://FTX.com (pending DD etc.)…. A *huge* thank you to CZ, Binance, and all of our supporters. This is a user-centric development that benefits the entire industry. CZ has done, and will continue to do, an incredible job of building out the global crypto ecosystem, and creating a freer economic world.

CZ replied: "This afternoon, FTX asked for our help…. There is a significant liquidity crunch. To protect users, we signed a non-binding [letter of intent], intending to fully acquire FTX.com."

The proposed deal saw Binance acquire one of its biggest competitors, coming into backstop the liquidity crunch being experienced by FTX.[146] It was a stunning humbling moment for SBF, who had been at CZ's throat just a few weeks earlier. The announcement created a temporary sense of calm across the crypto industry. Still recovering from the Terra Luna disaster, many viewed the collapse of FTX as a potential existential threat to the industry. The tentative sense of optimism that a crisis could be averted was shattered just a day later as Binance tweeted:

> As a result of corporate due diligence, as well as the latest news reports regarding mishandled customer funds and alleged US agency investigations, we have decided that we will not pursue the potential acquisition of http://FTX.com... In the beginning, our hope was to be able to support FTX's customers to provide liquidity, but the issues are beyond our control or ability to help.

Peering into FTX's books likely uncovered how bad the situation was, making an acquisition to save the embattled company impossible. The price of FTT continued to plummet, wiping out nearly 80% of its value in a few short days.

Sequoia – whose partners had gushed over SBF – disclosed it had written down its $210 million investment to zero dollars in a public letter. It conducted a "rigorous due diligence process" at the time of investing.[147] In a subsequent interview, billionaire venture capitalist and co-host of *The All-In* podcast Chamath Palihapitiya revealed SBF had approached his firm Social Capital for fundraising.[148] Palihapitiya quickly realized there were numerous red flags about SBF and FTX; first and foremost, the lack of a board of directors. According to Palihapitiya, the pitch from FTX "didn't make a lot of sense"[149] and his team at Social Capital prepared two pages of recommendations for FTX (for Social Capital to consider an investment).[150]

FTX's response to this request was to call back and tell Social Capital to "go fuck yourself."[151]

At the point of no return, SBF admitted defeat on November 11. SBF started a twenty-two-tweet thread with the following: "I'm sorry. That's the biggest thing. I fucked up, and should have done better." In the thread, SBF admitted FTX International had insufficient liquidity to meet customer deposits, attributed to "poor internal labeling." Later that day, SBF stepped down as FTX CEO and was replaced by a court-appointed CEO and liquidator, John Ray III, who had a career in high-profile corporate bankruptcies, including Enron.

FTX then filed for Chapter 11 bankruptcy protections, bringing an abrupt end to one of the most successful crypto exchanges.

SBF is arrested

In a scenario reminiscent of the lead-up to Do Kwon's arrest, there was a sense that charges would inevitably be filed against SBF following the collapse of FTX. In the month following FTX's bankruptcy filing, SBF engaged in several interviews and tweets – many of which would make a criminal defense lawyer shake their head in disbelief. SBF was arrested by the Royal Bahamas Police Force on December 13, 2022, and extradited to the US on twelve criminal charges, from conspiracy to commit wire fraud, to campaign finance violations.[152] The charges allege that SBF used around $8 billion in customer deposits to:

> support the operations and investments of FTX and Alameda; to fund speculative venture investments; to make charitable contributions; to enrich himself; and to try to purchase influence over cryptocurrency regulation in Washington, D.C. by steering tens of millions of dollars of illegal campaign contributions to both Democrats and Republicans.[153]

FTX co-founder Gavin Wang and Caroline Ellison both pleaded guilty to several charges (including fraud), agreeing to testify against SBF.[154]

SBF was released on bail after posting a $250 million bond. This was described by Assistant US Attorney Nicolas Roos as "the highest ever pre-trial bond" with SBF's parents (amongst others) putting their home up as collateral for the bond.

The aftermath

The collapse of FTX and Alameda was another body blow for the crypto market. Still reeling from the Terra Luna disaster, crypto's white knight was replaced with a villain. As crypto markets tried to process what happened, more details of malfeasance around FTX were revealed. Ray III stated in FTX's bankruptcy filing:

> I have over 40 years of legal and restructuring experience. I have been the Chief Restructuring Officer or Chief Executive Officer in several of the largest corporate failures in history. I have supervised situations involving allegations of criminal activity and malfeasance (Enron)… never in my career have I seen such a complete failure of corporate controls and such a complete absence of trustworthy financial information as occurred here. From compromised systems integrity and faulty regulatory oversight abroad, to the concentration of control in the hands of a very small group of inexperienced, unsophisticated and potentially compromised individuals, this situation is unprecedented.[155]

More details of the failed and risky Alameda investments emerged. Blockchain transaction research by a X user with the handle @ jconorgrogan found several dubious and downright crazy investments, including:

- A $135,000 investment in a token called "CUMMIES" used to power payments on a blockchain-based adult platform called "CumRocket" (covered in more detail in Chapter 1)[156]
- A $20,000 purchase of "TENDIES", a shitcoin launched in 2020[157]
- ~600 NFTs purchased in "CarolineDAO". CarolineDAO's X states that it is "a shadowy society dedicated to math and beauty… SimpDAO for Caroline Ellison"[158] This is an example of the trend of "SimpDAOs" in crypto, with the

term "simp" referring to a person (typically a young male) who is overly desperate for attention/affection from another (typically a female).[159] SimpDAOs are formed from groups of largely males focused on a particular female figure (e.g., DuaLipaDAO, MiaKhalfiaDAO)[160]

- An $18,000 investment in Pebble – an NFT of a picture of a rock

Alameda Research received special privileges in trading, which included the ability to have a negative account and to have unlimited withdrawals. Compliance firm Argus alleged Alameda used insider information to "front run" crypto listings on FTX. When cryptocurrencies are first listed on a major exchange, they typically experience a sharp price increase (due to the additional liquidity and exposure). Based on blockchain transaction research, Argus argues Alameda leveraged this inside information to purchase eighteen different cryptocurrencies before an official FTX listing. This totaled approximately $60 million of investments. Given the advantages Alameda enjoyed, it is a wonder it did not make more money from its trading activities.

SBF would stand trial in October 2023, pleading innocent to all seven charges of fraud and money laundering. The trial in part became a character assessment of SBF – was he the well-meaning effective altruist who had unintentionally gone astray? Or was he a conman who had carefully cultivated this image to disguise his fraud?

SBF's defense largely relied on the contention that it was Ellison's mismanagement that resulted in FTX's downfall. The main line of attack was to discredit prosecution witnesses (mainly Wang and Ellison), on the basis their testimonies against him were motivated by saving themselves through plea deals. Nevertheless, the long list of prosecution witnesses provided compelling testimony to SBF's guilt.

Most notable was Ellison's testimony, in which she stated SBF had "directed" her to "commit crimes" during her tenure at Alameda. This specifically related to using FTX customer funds for Alameda's own investments. Ellison also confirmed Alameda enjoyed special privileges, such as having a near-$65 billion credit line and no requirements to post collateral (with FTX having no other customers with more than a $1 billion line of credit). These privileges were not disclosed to any customers or investors. Ellison at one point broke down in tears during the testimony, stating she "felt a sense of relief that I didn't have to lie anymore."[161]

Testimony from Peter Easton, an accounting professor, shed some light on what happened to funds on FTX. Alameda had been spending customer funds not only on investments, but also on political and charitable contributions, and properties. Of the $11.3 billion of customer funds lent to Alameda, nearly $200 million went to FTX insiders. With limited options available to the defense, SBF took the stand to testify. This is a risky approach in criminal proceedings, as it opens the defendant up to cross-examination by the prosecution.

SBF's testimony cast himself as the innocent and unaware CEO, with illegal actions taken by others in the company without his knowledge. This gamble backfired, as the prosecution ruthlessly cross examined SBF providing numerous examples of hard evidence that SBF indeed had knowledge that he denied. One such example was the prosecution asking whether SBF was publicly promoting regulations on consumer protections because they were important to him or whether it was really for PR. SBF stated that it was not, only for the prosecution to get SBF to read a message he had written in relation to consumer protections which stated, "Yeah. Just PR. Fuck regulators."

In a short 3-hour deliberation by the jury, SBF was found guilty on all seven counts and subsequently sentenced to 25 years in prison. His sentence is being served in the notorious Metropolitan Detention Center in Brooklyn – notable for also housing singer R. Kelly and the aforementioned "Pharma Bro" Shkreli. SBF continues to leverage his crypto knowledge, reportedly giving crypto investment tips to prison guards. In an interview post-conviction, SBF maintains his innocence, stating he was "set up to be the fall guy" with his major error being negligence that made FTX "vulnerable to a bank run and devious actions of its competitors."[162] SBF has subsequently lodged an appeal to overturn his conviction.

It seems that CZ has emerged the clear winner in his feud with SBF. He denies his initial tweet to sell FTT was part of a "master plan" to destroy his rival.[163] In all likelihood, CZ intended to inflict some damage from this tweet on SBF but surely couldn't have anticipated the house of cards that FTX had been at the time. In a subsequent tweet, CZ was scathing in his assessment of SBF:

> SBF perpetuated a narrative painting me and other people as the "bad guys." It was critical in maintaining the fantasy that he was a "hero." SBF is one of the greatest fraudsters in history, he is also a master manipulator when it comes to media and key opinion leaders.

The U.S. Department of Justice commenced an investigation in Binance, suspecting a violation of the Bank Secrecy Act (BSA). Binance would eventually plead guilty and agreed to pay a $4.3 billion penalty for these violations. CZ pleaded guilty to one count of violating the BSA. The judge found that CZ "accepted responsibility" of the failures for Binance to comply with the BSA and found "no evidence that the defendant was ever informed" of any illegal activity at Binance.[164] CZ received a four-month prison sentence and agreed to pay a $50 million fine as part of the settlement.

The FTX collapse resulted in another downward leg in crypto markets to the tune of $170 billion, with yet another stream of negative news articles about the industry. FTX's collapse seemingly vindicated the view that crypto was nothing more than a Ponzi scheme. The truth, in retrospect, is more nuanced. Nakamoto's creation of Bitcoin was itself a direct response to the corporate failures of the banking industry in the lead up to the GFC. These very same failures of corporate controls and governance were repeated by FTX, although under the guise of a crypto trading platform. This was ultimately a failure of trust: customers and investors put their trust in FTX and

SBF (as they did in large banks prior to the GFC), and fell victim to a mix of greed, negligence and incompetence.

In this sense, the collapse of FTX is a vindication of the entire founding ethos of crypto. Nakamoto's vision was to create a decentralized world that would not depend on trusting a large organization to do the right thing, rather a trustless system based on code. There are countless people working in crypto to make this vision a reality – and failures like FTX simply crystallize why this vision is so important.

CHAPTER 10: $6.4 BILLION OF FREE MAGIC MONEY: UNISWAP AND THE AIRDROP REVOLUTION

"Thanks u [sic], I used the coins to buy myself a goat during this Easter[sic]." –
X user @OpanyRichard after receiving a $100 airdrop of Worldcoin

In the summer of 2020, amongst the mania of NFTs and meme coins, a new obsession emerged in the crypto community. With crypto in a bull market, simply buying and holding crypto yielded a great return. But surely you could do something else with all these coins sitting in your wallet?

Enter "Decentralized Finance", or DeFi (discussed in Chapter 9). A flood of new DeFi protocols emerged during this period, later termed "DeFi summer". This period was a mix of new entrepreneurial protocols, as well as a sense of risk and excitement as degens experimented with new ways to earn coin yields through a range of things like "liquidity pools". Against this backdrop, an enterprising crypto enthusiast would have no doubt come across Uniswap. The premier "Decentralized Exchange" (DEX), Uniswap allows users to swap between different cryptocurrencies. Making a simple trade on Uniswap prior to September 2020, say ten dollars of Ethereum to ten dollars of the stablecoin tether (USDT), would have proved lucrative. To the tune of $16,000.

Enter airdrops.

The culmination of the DeFi summer was Uniswap's airdrop of

its token UNI. This distribution to over 250,000 wallets of Uniswap users, at its peak, was worth a whopping $6.4 billion.

The best part? It was free.

Users got free money, straight to their wallets. Uniswap's airdrop was one of the highest profile airdrops in crypto history, leading to more than $30 billion in free money from airdrops being distributed to crypto users, to date.

Uniswap and DeFi

Created in 2018, Uniswap was a pioneer in the world of DeFi. DeFi is a logical extension of the philosophy underlying Bitcoin's creation. Bitcoin's main objective was to replace traditional currencies with a decentralized and open digital currency that could be used by anyone around the world with an internet connection. However, currencies are just one of the many financial services we interact with daily. DeFi simply extends this philosophy to all financial services.

DeFi created a parallel financial system that is both open and permissionless. Want to send some USD overseas? You could go through your bank that will charge fees and take multiple days to process. Or you could just send USDC (a stablecoin) for less than a cent that will arrive in the recipient's wallet in less than five minutes. Have some cash you want to park in a savings account? You can do this with crypto, through protocols like Compound, in which users can deposit their crypto and earn an interest rate (similar to a savings account) or borrow crypto and pay an interest rate (with interest rates determined by the relative supply and demand for lending).

DeFi offers promise in developing countries for individuals without access to traditional financial infrastructure (e.g., living in a remote village). Through their smartphone, people could send money overseas, obtain a loan, or put their money into a savings account – all by clicking a few buttons. The potential to boost financial inclusion is an understated DeFi benefit. It has no banks or centralized parties to gate-keep access to financial services. Discrimination against individuals based on ethnicity or gender (as happens on an international scale)[165] is simply not possible in DeFi, given the anonymity of interactions. If you meet the criteria of a smart contract to borrow or lend, nobody can stop you.

DEXs are core to the DeFi ecosystem. Uniswap put them on the map.

DEXs represent a remarkable innovation only truly possible through blockchain technology. In centralized exchanges for asset trading, a buyer and seller must always be matched. For example, if I use a centralized exchange (e.g., Binance) to purchase Bitcoin, I would put in a bid for, say, $40,000 to purchase one Bitcoin. A seller with one Bitcoin would have to then go onto Binance and put in a sell order for $40,000. At this point, Bitcoin would change hands (through the operations of the central party). This system works well in liquid and highly traded markets (e.g., large equity markets like the NASDAQ or for very liquid cryptos like Bitcoin). It does not work very well for illiquid assets or tokens. Without enough buyers and sellers in a market, you will have to pay significantly above the true market price if you want to buy a large amount. The converse is true for sellers, being required to sell at a steep discount.

The major innovation for DEXs to solve this problem was using an "Automated Market Maker" (AMM). AMMs are smart contracts that form the counterparty to the buying and selling tokens. This means you no longer need to match a buyer to a seller to execute a trade. Instead, AMMs use a pre-funded pool of assets to execute trades. Depending on the order size, the AMM will use the algorithm in the smart contract to determine the price (with larger orders having a more significant price impact).

Crypto asset holders can earn a return from these operations via a process called "liquidity mining" which is, essentially, lending crypto assets. Hence, the AMM has enough crypto assets to execute the transaction. If you deposit these assets into the AMM's smart contract, you are "locking" your assets in (similar to a loan). In return, every time the AMM processes a transaction, you receive a fee from the transactions. Often, these fees can return >20% over the course of the year (with some well in excess of 100%).

But scammers can exploit this mechanic. Returning to our chapter on shitcoins, this is one of the major methods for a rug pull. Scammers will provide some liquidity to the AMM, but when the price rises, they will quickly sell all of the scam tokens (receiving a valuable token in return). This means that genuine sellers will be unable to execute any trades (as the AMM has run out of the other tokens to sell into).

Uniswap experienced rapid growth during the DeFi Summer, with more than $20 billion of cryptocurrency traded on its platform and more than $1 billion of liquidity since launch. On the back of this, Uniswap decided to launch its governance token "UNI" which allowed holders to vote on governance decisions, mainly around the deployment of the protocol's treasury. The most common launch strategy to the public at this time was an Initial Coin Offering (ICO), essentially the same as an IPO in equity markets (i.e., the public could purchase cryptocurrency for a fixed price for the first time).

Uniswap took a different path. Instead of getting the public to pay for the token, it was given out for free. The criteria for this were straightforward: if you interacted with Uniswap before September 1, 2020 (e.g., did a swap on the platform or provided liquidity) you were eligible for at least 400 UNI tokens. At launch, 400 UNI tokens were worth between $1-2,000, before skyrocketing to nearly $16,000 nine months later. To put this in perspective, it would take an individual in India on an average salary nearly four years to make this amount of money – compared to literally two minutes to make a swap on Uniswap.

Things got even more crazy for a small subset of power users on Uniswap. Roughly 250 of these users received 250,000 UNI tokens, worth over $11 million at their peak. At face value it seems absurd that anyone would give out this amount of money for free. While airdrops have a distinct character in crypto, they can be thought of in many ways as conceptually analogous to frequent flyer/airline miles programs that exist today. With frequent flyer programs, you are rewarded with points for going on flights or purchasing something on the airline's platform. These points can subsequently be used to redeem flights or other benefits and perks. They have an economic value attached – if 1,000 points can purchase a flight that is worth $1,000, then the points are worth one dollar each.

In a similar vein, in crypto you interact with a protocol or perform an action, and you get rewarded with a token with economic value. Often these tokens can be used directly to use services on the protocol or give the holders other benefits. The major difference between the two is that in crypto there is an open market for these tokens. One can buy and sell them very easily (including converting them to cash). This is extremely difficult for frequent flyer points; indeed, some airlines will block users if they find them trying to buy and sell points.

The economic rationale of airdrops can be thought of as: 1) a mechanism to attract users; 2) a means to retain these users; and 3) a reward to incentivise users for positive engagement. In crypto markets, it is also a mechanism to decentralise the protocol. This was a major reason Uniswap decided to airdrop; it was able to circulate its token to over 250,000 wallets. If it had preceded down an ICO route, it is likely the token would be held by only a small number of users, making governance decisions highly centralised.

Airdrops evolve

While Uniswap's airdrop was not the first, it would be the largest and most influential in crypto history, establishing airdrops as a common GTM strategy for protocols. The honor for the first airdrop would instead go to "Auroracoin". Labelled the "cryptocurrency of Iceland" and intended to be an alternative to both Bitcoin and Iceland's currency (the Icelandic krona), Auroracoin was given for free to everyone on in Iceland's nation ID database in 2014. Other high value airdrops include "ApeCoin" from the aforementioned Yuga Labs (the parent company of the NFT collection BAYC). Each owner of a BAYC NFT was eligible to receive 10,000 ApeCoins. This airdrop became the second largest in history, with nearly $3.6 billion worth of tokens given out at ApeCoin's all-time high.

This amounted to more than $200,000 per Bored Ape Yacht Club NFT.

Coming into 2024, airdrops would become the primary means for protocols to launch tokens to the public. As more protocols followed Uniswap's lead, a new class of users emerged. Seeing the vast amount of free money on offer, "airdrop farmers" would interact with a protocol purely for the chance to receive an airdrop. The most sophisticated of these users are called "Sybils." The term Sybil is taken from the title of a 1973 book of the same name by Flora Schreiber. The book describes the real-life treatment of Sybil Dorsett (a pseudonym to protect the patient's identity) for dissociative identify disorder (previously known as multiple personality disorder). Sybil had a range of mental health issues (attributed to abuse by her mother), which manifested in sixteen different personalities.

Sybil would be used initially in computer security (for a Sybil attack) but was adopted in crypto as referring to a single user of multiple wallets. Creating a wallet is incredibly easy in crypto, so easy that you can easily download a program to create thousands of wallets in a few minutes. The allure of using multiple wallets for farming airdrops was clear – if one wallet would get $16,000 from Uniswap, why not just create ten and get $160,000?

This same logic could apply to a hundred, a thousand, or even tens of thousands of wallets. These Sybils, often referred to as "industrial Sybils", would create automated bots to interact across all wallets in order to qualify for a separate airdrop on each. Some industrial Sybils, fearing detection, created "Sybil farms" where people were employed on a salary of one to three dollars per day, typically from India and the Philippines, to farm airdrops across multiple wallets. The creator of the Sybil farm would pay their wages and front up the capital for each wallet and would keep the proceeds.

These industrial Sybils have seen enormous success, capable of receiving millions from an airdrop. The rise of Sybils created a form of arms race between protocols and Sybils. Airdrops can be seen as a zero-sum game. If a protocol gives out 10% of its tokens at a $1 billion valuation, there is $100 million of value to go around. If Sybil wallets end up accounting for 70% of wallets, assuming an equal distribution amount per wallet, this means that $70 million of value is flowing to Sybils instead of real users.

This presents a huge problem for protocols, as Sybil wallets will churn immediately once they receive their airdrop. Additionally, they are likely to sell their token immediately – negatively impacting the token's price. However, there is a delicate balance here as protocols may in many instances not mind Sybils initially farming their airdrop as they increase their user metrics, helping to raise money from investors (notwithstanding these are artificially inflated numbers).

A common approach from protocols is to explicitly screen out Sybils from receiving any tokens. This typically takes the form of detailed data analysis to identify "clusters" of wallets traced back to one user. As this style of analysis becomes more sophisticated, so are the Sybils, who are resorting to more complicated mechanisms to disguise their activities.

LayerZero founder and CEO Bryan Pellegrino took to X to fight a self-proclaimed war against Sybils. LayerZero, a bridging protocol which allows users to move funds across different blockchains, was one of the most hyped and eagerly anticipated airdrops of 2024. Pellegrino was intent on ensuring only real users received LayerZero's "ZRO" token airdrop. To combat Sybils, Pellegrino first opened a page for Sybils to self-report, promising they would receive 15% of their allocation of ZRO. If they were later identified as a Sybil, they would receive zero. Just over 800,000 wallets self-reported as a Sybil, illustrating the scale of industrial Sybils.

The second phase involved a "Sybil bounty hunt" in which users could submit their own analysis of Sybil clusters. If LayerZero agreed with their analysis, the submitter would receive 15% of the Sybil's allocation. What was in effect a crowd-sourced Sybil hunt was initially received negatively, but Pellegrino's transparency and constant tweets won over the community.

LayerZero's airdrop, along with other airdrops in 2024, were extremely lucrative for those participating. I became obsessed with farming airdrops in December 2023, often spending more than five hours per day interacting with different protocols. Amongst the many airdrops I received, the most lucrative was the ZKsync airdrop. The $ZK token was airdropped in June 2023, and I was fortunate to receive the maximum allocation of tokens worth nearly $30,000 at the time of launch.

Airdrops can be a lifechanging windfall for recipients, particularly those in developing countries. A wholesome example is Richard Opany, a man based in Kenya who received $100 in airdrop from Worldcoin and tweeted that he had used the proceeds to purchase a goat. The tweet went viral, with crypto users sending Opany money to purchase more goats.

There is, however, a dark side to airdrops.

Many users who farm airdrops have high expectations as to the amount of money they will receive. With airdrops becoming more saturated over time, the amount per wallet has reduced. This can often result in a project receiving death threats at the time of distribution by disgruntled users, often referred to as "e-beggars" in crypto. There are also examples of exploitation of the criteria for an airdrop. Often, protocols will keep the criteria for an airdrop hidden from the public; however, if someone leaks the criteria, an individual can ruthlessly exploit this.

A suspected case of this is the Jupiter airdrop. Jupiter, a DEX on the Solana blockchain, had a hyped airdrop. Shortly before the cut-off date for receiving an allocation, a Sybil managed to qualify for more than $1 million of tokens across 9,246 wallets. X users suspected this was an insider or someone who leaked the criteria, although the founder of Jupiter denied it was an insider stating, "someone guessed the airdrop a few days before and farmed it super hard."

The future of airdrops

Despite the difficulties in combating Sybils and e-beggars, airdrops remain a popular distribution method for protocols. Airdrops have evolved, generally moving away from a retrospective design used by Uniswap (i.e., retrospectively awarding tokens for past activities) to more points-based programs (where users earn points for doing a range of specified activities) that eventually convert to tokens in an airdrop. This style of design is a natural response to the increase in the number of Sybils with points often weighted to the amount of capital provided to the protocol (meaning there is less of an incentive to use multiple wallets).

Airdrops are also used in crypto as a market share acquisition strategy against competitors. Known as a "vampire attack", there are numerous examples in crypto, such as the NFT marketplace Tensor, which was able to gain market share on competitor Magic Eden by having an airdrop program. Other crypto wallets, such as Rainbow wallet and Rabby, use an airdrop program to attract users from the largest wallet provider MetaMask. This is possible in crypto as user transactions are publicly available, allowing protocols to specifically target users on competitor platforms.

CONCLUSION

Crypto certainly has some absurd and crazy aspects.

Excess is often the focus of crypto talk – the rampant speculation and the bad actors who have profited from it. I've also looked at the crazy valuation of particular crypto assets, and some of the losses that people have experienced from this strange Magic Internet Money. But let's consider the tremendous positive potential and impact of the industry. From the tremendous goodwill and generosity of the Dogecoin community, the egalitarianism and empowerment available through DAOs, the potential for gamers to own their assets, to the ability of digital artists to now earn a respectable living through their craft. There are other amazing, impactful crypto stories that haven't been told.

My first exposure to crypto dates back to early 2015. At the time I was a teacher's assistant for a personal finance subject as part of a commerce degree at the University of Melbourne. In a class I prepared for my students, I drew up a chart of the price of Bitcoin, which in November 2013 peaked at around $1,100 only to decline to under $200. In that class I told my students, "This is a classic case of a bubble – rampant speculation on something with no value."

I sincerely hope that my students were not listening to me.

At the time I had such little understanding of the technology, and therefore it was so easy to dismiss it simply as a Ponzi scheme or a bubble. I have now had the fortune of being able to spend my time learning about blockchain – from writing an academic article to working with a bunch of highly intelligent and driven people at Immutable as we apply the technology in the video game industry.

I also (rather proudly) see myself as a crypto degen, holding more NFTs, tokens and meme coins than I would like to admit.

Whenever I tell someone I work in crypto I almost inevitably get a response along the lines of "Isn't crypto just a massive scam?" or an expression of confusion when I try to explain what crypto is. I can't blame them. It can be complicated and intimidating at first, particularly when many people's notions of crypto are based on sensationalized media headlines. My hope is that by reading this book you gain a deeper understanding of the crypto industry now, and do not immediately think "scam". At its core, crypto is just a technology, with capacity to do tremendous good.

Bad actors are what gives it the potential to exploit others. Like any nascent industry or technology, bad actors lurk and seek to take advantage of the information asymmetry or exploit innocent individuals. As someone in the crypto world, I firmly believe we should hold these people to account. Too often, these actors can tar the reputation of the space more generally. I also believe that holding up a mirror at the absurdities can help crypto move forward. It is possible to think that buying a picture of a rock for $5 million is insane while still believing NFTs have potential to transform different markets (like gaming) and give users power.

Looking forward, crypto continues to gain mainstream adoption. Bitcoin and Ethereum now trade freely on global stock exchanges as exchange-traded funds. Central banks around the world are exploring issuing their own cryptocurrency for payments. There are emerging fields of academic research on cryptocurrency, covering topics like the economic theory behind airdrops Most importantly, regulators around the world are increasingly viewing the technology not with suspicion, but rather as a positive force, crafting a regulatory framework that preserves its innovative potential while curbing some of the excesses around it.

GLOSSARY

Algorithmic stablecoin – Stablecoins that attempt to maintain their target value by implementing various market incentives and mint/burn techniques. These are distinct from asset-backed stablecoins, which ostensibly maintain reserves of US dollars or other assets to back their price

Altcoin – "alternative" cryptocurrencies; that is, cryptocurrencies that aren't Bitcoin

Annual percentage yield (APY) – the rate of return on an investment, which includes the effect of compounding interest

Bag – crypto slang for a large quantity of a specific cryptocurrency. Alternatively (but less frequently) used to refer to the contents of an individual's crypto portfolio

Bagholder – an investor who continues to hold large amounts of a specific coin or token, regardless of its performance

Bear market – when prices of assets in a market fall by 20% or more from recent highs, it is called a bear market. As a result, investor confidence is low, and the economy and market turn pessimistic

Bull market – a bull market in crypto and stock markets refers to a time during which the prices of assets grow dramatically. These markets act as a source of motivation for both investors and purchasers

Burning – the process in which users remove tokens from circulation. This can apply to various assets including cryptocurrencies, where it is done to reduce the number of coins in circulation, or to NFTs, where it makes the NFT impossible to ever trade again. The process of burning involves sending the token to a wallet address that is unable to send tokens, permanently locking it there

Coin – alternative word for cryptocurrency or token

Cryptocurrency – a digital asset recorded on a blockchain

Decentralized autonomous organization (DAO) – an organization represented by rules encoded as a computer program that is transparent, controlled by the organization members and not influenced by a central government

Decentralized exchange (DEX) – cryptocurrency exchange that facilitates trading of cryptocurrencies without a centralized party

Degen – short for "degenerate". Slang in crypto as an individual taking extremely speculative investments, often with limited information

Digital collectible – alternative word used for NFTs

ERC-20 – a token created using the standard for new tokens on the Ethereum blockchain. Named as it was the twentieth issue posted on the discussion board Ethereum Request for Comments

Fiat – legal tender issued by a government (e.g., the US dollar)

Fear Uncertainty Doubt (FUD) – any negative commentary or false information. Typically used by crypto projects to describe information that has any negative impact on the price of their token or NFT

Peg – specified price for the rate of exchange between two assets. In the case of stablecoins, coins are often pegged to fiat currencies – for example, one Tether is pegged to one US dollar

Ponzi scheme – a form of fraud that lures investors and pays profits to earlier investors with funds from more recent investors. The scheme leads victims to believe that profits are coming from legitimate business activity. A Ponzi scheme can maintain the illusion of a sustainable business as long as new investors contribute new funds, and as long as most of the investors do not demand full repayment and still believe in the non-existent assets they are purported to own

Private key – the cryptographic string of numbers and letters that grants access to tokens and NFTs

Protocol – set of rules for computers running a network

Poocoin – a website providing charts and portfolio management for tokens on the Binance Smart Chain

Pump and dump – artificially inflating the price of a token or NFT. This may involve dissemination of false or misleading information, organized price manipulation or leveraging of crypto influencers with the information to increase the price (pump) to subsequently sell (dump)

Rug pull – the crypto project's team suddenly abandons the project, exploits code in the smart contract or pulls liquidity from a DEX

Non-fungible token (NFT) – a non-interchangeable unit of data stored on a blockchain that can be sold and traded

Shitcoin – A coin with no obvious potential value or usage

Smart contract audit – a process in which an individual or company checks a blockchain-based project for flaws in its code, as well as tries to determine the legitimacy of the project based on other factors (identity of its creators, etc.)

Stablecoins – cryptocurrencies that are pegged to another cryptocurrency (or basket of cryptocurrencies), fiat money (e.g. the US dollar), or to exchange-traded commodities

Web3 – an idea for a new iteration of the World Wide Web based on the blockchain, which incorporates concepts including decentralization and token-based economics

Web3 gaming – the use of blockchain technology (i.e., tokens and NFTs) for games. Examples include replacing digital "skins" with NFTs

Whitehat – a security researcher who operates ethically to identify vulnerabilities and report them to the project. In crypto, whitehats are known to execute known exploits on projects that are actively being exploited in order to safeguard the funds until they can be returned to a secure address belonging to the project operators

ACKNOWLEDGEMENTS

Writing this book has been a labor of love for well over a year. It has been a source of both great satisfaction and frustration all at once – particularly since the world of crypto moves so quickly that I often had to go back and rewrite chapters with new information.

It has also been a humbling experience. Trying to piece together this strange world of crypto exposed how much I still did not know. It involved hundreds of hours of research and interviews. It would not have been possible without the voluminous amount of research and content produced across the crypto world, from crypto news outlets, podcasts and across X. A special thanks to Graham Novak for his patience and time in answering my questions help me bring out one of the most fascinating events in crypto.

Thank you to my agent Tom Gilliat who took a chance on a first-time author. Your guidance, feedback and encouragement has been invaluable along the way.

To the Good Prose Studios team, Erin O'Dwyer, Linda McSweeny and Teresa Goudie, for your editing, proofreading and guidance. In particular, I thank Linda McSweeny for her exceptional copyediting, which helped tremendously in bringing the text to life.

A huge thanks to my friends who read early drafts of the manuscript. Your feedback and advice were deeply appreciated. In particular, I thank Aman Gadgil, Andrew Dick, Luke Bilotta, Julian Mangione, Michael Cardamone, and Thomas Atlassian.

Special thanks to Sarah Kasner for her love and support throughout the entire journey. Putting up with a crypto obsessed partner is not the easiest task.

To the Immutable Founders, Alex Connolly, Robbie and James Ferguson who took a chance on hiring a random management consultant. The growth and opportunities afforded by working in a web3 company made this book possible.

To my parents, John and Diana, and sisters Natalie and Sarah for the love and support across this journey.

Finally, to Satoshi Nakamoto for making this all possible.

NOTES

I conducted a number of interviews for this book.

For cryptocurrency prices I used https://coingecko.com/ or
CoinMarketCap.com for prices, market capitalization, fully diluted
valuation, and trading volume. NFT prices were sourced from the
relevant marketplace in which they were listed (generally Opensea or
Magic Eden).

Further reading

Introduction

Perper, Rosie. "What is a Rug Pull? How to Protect Yourself From
    Getting 'Rugged'." *CoinDesk*, August 30, 2022. www.coin-
    desk.com/learn/what-is-a-rug-pull-how-to-protect-yourself-
    from-getting-rugged/.

Chapter 1: The Rise of Shitcoins

Frankenfield, Jake. "What Is Shitcoin?" *Investopedia*, June 24, 2021.
    https://www.investopedia.com/terms/s/shitcoin.asp.
Know Your Meme. "Shitcoin." January 12, 2021. https://knowyour-
    meme.com/memes/shitcoin.
Pollock, Darren. "The Cream of the Crypto Crop: 10 Best Perform-
    ing Assets in 2017." *Cointelegraph*, January 3, 2018. https://
    cointelegraph.com/news/the-cream-of-the-crypto-crop-10-

best-performing-assets-in-2017.

Hayes, Adam. "Tulipmania: About the Dutch Tulip Bulb Market Bubble." *Investopedia*, updated June 25, 2024. https://www.investopedia.com/terms/d/dutch_tulip_bulb_market_bubble.asp.

CNET. "Pets.com Raises $82.5 Million in IPO." February 10, 2003. https://www.cnet.com/tech/tech-industry/pets-com-raises-82-5-million-in-ipo/.

Goldman, David. "10 Big Dot.com Flops." *CNNMoney*, March 2, 2015. https://money.cnn.com/gallery/technology/2015/03/02/dot-com-flops/index.html.

International Banker. "The Dotcom Bubble Burst (2000)." September 29, 2021. https://internationalbanker.com/history-of-financial-crises/the-dotcom-bubble-burst-2000/.

DeepFuckingValue. "User Profile of DeepFuckingValue." *Reddit*. https://www.reddit.com/user/DeepFuckingValue/.

Roaring Kitty. "100%+ Short Interest in GameStop stock (GME) – Fundamental & Technical Deep Value Analysis." July 28, 2020. YouTube, 56:31. https://www.youtube.com/watch?v=GZTr1-Gp74U

Herrig, Andrew. "How This Redditor Made $46M with GameStop – and Sparked a Revolution Along the Way." *Wealthy Nickel*, April 19, 2021. https://wealthynickel.com/keith-gill-wall-street-bets-gamestop/.

The Washington Post. "Testimony of Keith Patrick Gill, Aka 'Roaring Kitty.'" *The Washington Post*, updated February 19, 2021. https://www.washingtonpost.com/context/testimony-of-keith-patrick-gill-aka-roaring-kitty/dbb18b2e-400c-4a10-8fc5-156e8856cfd1/.

Hesp, Mike. "SafeMoon Coin - Why Is It a Scam?" AnycoinDirect. April 20, 2022. https://anycoindirect.eu/en/blog/safemoon-coin-why-is-it-a-scam.

Harper, Christopher. "What Is SafeMoon - the New Cryptocurrency and How It Compares to DogeCoin." *BirminghamLive*, April

23, 2021. https://www.birminghammail.co.uk/news/uk-news/what-safemoon-new-cryptocurrency-how-20453449.

Daly, Lyle. "If You'd Bought $1,000 Worth of SafeMoon When It Launched, Here's How Much You'd Have Now." *The Ascent*, July 10, 2021. https://www.fool.com/the-ascent/cryptocurrency/articles/if-youd-bought-1000-worth-of-safemoon-when-it-launched-heres-how-much-youd-have-now.

Classaction. "Class Action Complaint: Bill Merewhuader et al. v SafeMoon LLC et al." Filed February 17, 2022. www.classaction.org/media/merewhuader-et-al-v-safemoon-llc-et-al.pdf.

Knight, Robert D. "Jake Paul Exposed as $2.2M Serial Crypto Scammer." BeInCrypto, March 8, 2022. https://beincrypto.com/jake-paul-exposed-as-2-2m-serial-crypto-scammer/.

"SafeMoon to Implement Operation Phoenix in Gambia." Investing. May 17, 2021, https://www.investing.com/news/cryptocurrency-news/safemoon-to-implement-operation-phoenix-in-gambia-2508301.

u/CamperCrimson. "The #SafeMoonSqueeze Has Begun." r/SatoshiStreetBets. *Reddit*, June 24, 2021. https://www.reddit.com/r/SatoshiStreetBets/comments/o4fimb/the_safemoonsqueeze_has_begun/.

Germain, Atahabih. "Soulja Boy and Lil Yachty Named in Suit Accused of Misleading Crypto Buyers in 'Pump and Dump' Scheme." *Atlanta Black Star*, February 24, 2022. https://atlantablackstar.com/2022/02/24/soulja-boy-and-lil-yachty-named-in-suit-accused-of-misleading-crypto-buyers-in-pump-and-dump-scheme/.

Francheschi-Bicchierai, Lorenzo. "What Happened to SafeMoon, the Hyped-up Crypto That Promised Riches?" *Vice*, May 9, 2022. https://www.vice.com/en/article/wxdmj9/what-happened-to-safemoon-the-hyped-up-crypto-that-promised-riches.

@juicetothemoon. "$MOJO Enthusiast. The first ever crypto powered energy drink!" X, accessed September 2, 2023.

https://X.com/juicetothemoon.

Khalili, Joel. "The Not-So-Subtle Art of the Meme Coin." *Wired*, May 23, 2023. https://www.wired.com/story/meme-coin-cryptocurrencies/.

CumRocket. "CumRocket." Accessed September 2, 2023. https://www.cumrocket.io/.

@DogshitCrypto. "Lost all your gains due to the market SHITTING the bed?" X, May 19, 2021. https://X.com/DogshitCrypto/status/1394982981446639621.

Kumar, Harsh. "Omicron Coin: All You Need To Know About the Covid Variant Namesake". *Outlook India*, updated December 2, 2021. https://www.outlookindia.com/website/story/business-news-omicron-coin-all-you-need-to-know-about-the-covid-variant-namesake/403549

Nomayo, Osato. "AnubisDAO Funds Move for the First Time, Eight Months After Rug Pull." *The Block*, June 24, 2022. www.theblock.co/post/154004/anubisdao-funds-move-for-the-first-time-eight-months-after-rug-pull.

Gorman, Kelly. "Influencers Are Being Paid to Promote Scammy Altcoins." *Mashable*, May 10, 2022. www.mashable.com/article/influencers-altcoin-scams.

Mitchelhill, Tom. "Kim Kardashian Shills Shitcoin, Gets Fined $1.26m." *The Chainsaw*, October 4, 2022. https://thechainsaw.com/defi/crypto/kim-kardashian-shilling-crypto-sec/.

Coffeezilla. "ADIN ROSS LIED About MILF – Token Scam."Posted August 3, 2021. YouTube, 12:56. https://www.youtube.com/watch?v=ZPlYxwmTkeg

Binder, Matt. "Inside the Shady World of Influencers Promoting Cryptocurrency." *Mashable*, June 25, 2021. https://mashable.com/article/influencers-altcoin-scams.

iancey, Cas. "Soulja Boy Tweets $24K Pay-To-Play Deal with SafeMoon Clone — Then Deletes It." *Protos*, May 31, 2021. https://protos.com/soulja-boy-safermars-deleted-tweet-oopsie-celeb-touting-violations/.

Banergee, Avinandan. "The ASIC Reveals Data about Crypto 'Pump and Dump' Schemes on Telegram." *Blockchain Council*, December 29, 2021. https://www.blockchain-council.org/news/the-asic-reveals-data-about-crypto-pump-and-dump-schemes-on-telegram/.

BBC. "Squid Game Crypto Token Collapses in Apparent Scam." *BBC News*, November 2, 2021, sec. Business. https://www.bbc.com/news/business-59129466.

Murray, Alan, and Zillman, Claire. "One of Warren Buffett's Most Famous Sayings Is about to Come True." *Fortune*, October 3, 2022. https://fortune.com/2022/10/03/warren-buffett-famous-quotes-swimming-naked-interest-rates-debt-zombies/#:~:text=One%20of%20Warren%20Buffett.

Chapter 2: The Million Dollar photo of a Rock: NFTs

Etherrock. "Ether Rock – Pet Rocks on the Blockchain." Accessed June 5, 2024. https://etherrock.com/.

Sigalos, MacKenzie. "Somebody Just Paid $1.3 Million for a Picture of a Rock." *CNBC*, August 23, 2021. https://www.cnbc.com/2021/08/23/people-are-paying-millions-of-dollars-for-digital-pictures-of-rocks.html.

Ongweso Jr., Edward. "Someone Sold a $1 Million Clipart Rock NFT for Under a Penny by Mistake." *Vice*, March 11, 2022. https://www.vice.com/en/article/someone-sold-a-dollar1m-clipart-rock-nft-for-under-a-penny-by-mistake/

Rosenfeld, Meni. "Overview of Colored Coins." December 4, 2012, https://allquantor.at/blockchainbib/pdf/rosenfeld-2012overview.pdf

McCoy, Jennifer and McCoy, Kevin. "Mccoyspace: Quantum." May 2, 2014. https://www.mccoyspace.com/project/125/.

Exmundo, Jex. "Quantum: The Story behind the World's First NFT." *NFT Now*, March 21, 2023. https://nftnow.com/art/quantum-the-first-piece-of-nft-art-ever-created/

Christie's. "10 Things to Know about CryptoPunks, the Original

NFTs" April 8, 2021. https://www.christies.com/features/10-things-to-know-about-CryptoPunks-11569-1.aspx.

Yuga Labs. "The Fucking Metaverse Ep. 2 Highlights: Larva Labs Founders Matt Hall and John Watkinson." Video of a Podcast creation. Posted December 14, 2022. YouTube, 22:57. https://www.youtube.com/watch?v=5l2lss4FExE.

Medved, Matt. "Inside CryptoPunks' Early Days: From 'Deafening Silence' to Digital Revolution." *NFT Now*, October 10, 2023. https://nftnow.com/features/cryptopunks-documentary-larva-labs-interview/.

Abbruzzese, Jason. "This Ethereum-Based Project Could Change How We Think about Digital Art." *Mashable*, June 16, 2017. https://mashable.com/article/cryptopunks-ethereum-art-collectibles.

Ginsburg, Randy. "Celebrities Who Own CryptoPunks: 15 Famous NFT Owners." *NFT Now*, April 11, 2022. https://nftnow.com/collectibles/from-celebrities-to-ceos-meet-15-of-the-most-famous-cryptopunk-holders/.

Forbes. "Profile: Shalom Meckenzie." *Forbes*, September 3, 2023. https://www.forbes.com/profile/shalom-meckenzie/?sh=1fc8c9e343e9.

Escalante-De Mattei, Shanti. "Company Behind Bored Ape Yacht Club Buys CryptoPunks." *ARTnews*, March 14, 2022. https://www.artnews.com/art-news/news/bored-ape-yacht-club-buys-crypto-punks-1234621792/.

Thomas, Eve. 2023. "The Rise and Fall of NFTs." *Verdict*, July 12, 2023. https://www.verdict.co.uk/the-rise-and-fall-of-nfts/?cf-view.

Covalent. "How Nike Won with NFTs." February 3, 2023. https://www.covalenthq.com/blog/how-nike-won-with-nfts/.

NBA TopShot. "LeBron James Drops Triple-Double in Title-Clinching Game of 2020 Finals - Owned by Easyaces." Accessed January 20, 2024. https://nbatopshot.com/moment/c1c29a9a-327f-47fe-a570-f4bd806b1ae3.

@coinmarketcope. "Imagine Mistakingly Listing Your 1m Rock NFT for 444 WEI ($0.001) and It Selling in a Sniper Bot's 1 Block Tx. That's What Just Happened." X, March 10, 2022. https://X.com/coinmarketcope/status/1501802006364635139.

@etherpebble_32. "When Your 1M Rock NFT Sells for 444 WEI by Mistake, That's a Huge L." X, March 10, 2022. https://X.com/etherpebble_32/status/1501873934479859719.

OpenSea. "a ToN oF coke." June, 2021. https://opensea.io/collection/a-ton-of-coke

Gómez-Upegui, Salomé. "Meet the Colombian Artist Trying to Move a Ton of Cocaine... NFTs." *Input*, September 17, 2021. https://www.inverse.com/input/culture/camilo-restrepo-a-ton-of-coke-cocaine-drugs-nft-art.

Tran, Ken. "Trump's 'Major Announcement' of NFT Collection Draws Ridicule but Sells Out." *USA TODAY*, December 16, 2022. https://www.usatoday.com/story/news/politics/2022/12/16/donald-trump-nft-trading-card-collection/10908893002/.

Taylor, Josh. "Donald Trump's Digital Trading Card Collection Sells Out in Less than a Day." *The Guardian*, December 17, 2022. https://www.theguardian.com/us-news/2022/dec/17/donald-trumps-digital-trading-card-collection-sells-out-in-less-than-a-day

CollectTrumpCards. "Trump Digital Trading Card NFTs." Accessed December 6, 2023. https://collecttrumpcards.com/.

Liang, Annabelle. "NFT of Jack Dorsey's First Tweet Struggles to Sell." *BBC News*, April 14, 2022. https://www.bbc.com/news/business-61102759.

Handagama, Sandali. "Buyer of Jack Dorsey's First Tweet Reportedly Arrested in Iran." *CoinDesk*, May 18, 2021. https://www.coindesk.com/markets/2021/05/17/buyer-of-jack-dorseys-first-tweet-reportedly-arrested-in-iran/.

Cuthbertson, Anthony. "NFT Millionaire Beeple Says Crypto Art

Is Bubble and Will 'Absolutely Go to Zero.'" *The Independent*, March 24, 2021. https://www.independent.co.uk/tech/nft-beeple-cryptocurrency-art-b1821314.html.

Sundaresan, Vignesh. "Vignesh Sundaresan." Accessed July 20, 2023. https://vigneshsundaresan.com/about/.

Hoogendoorn, Robert. "Beeple, B20 and the Rise of Digital Art." February 25, 2021. https://dappradar.com/blog/beeple-b20-and-the-rise-of-digital-art.

NFTevening. "B20 Token: An Introduction to Fractional NFT Art with Beeple's Cryptoart." Updated April 10, 2024. https://nftevening.com/b20-token-an-introduction-to-fractional-nft-art-with-beeples-cryptoart/.

Castor, Amy. "Metakovan, the Mystery Beeple Art Buyer, and His NFT/DeFi Scheme." March 14, 2021. https://amycastor.com/2021/03/14/metakovan-the-mystery-beeple-art-buyer-and-his-nft-defi-scheme/.

Schneider, Tim. "'This Was a $69 Million Marketing Stunt': Why Crypto Purists Say Beeple's Mega-Millions NFT Isn't Actually an NFT at All." *Artnet News*, March 18, 2021. https://news.artnet.com/market/beeple-everydays-controversy-nft-or-not-1952124.

Knight, Oliver. "Hack of Vitalik Buterin's X Account Leads to $691K Stolen." *Coindesk*. September 11, 2023. https://www.coindesk.com/business/2023/09/11/691k-stolen-as-hackers-take-over-vitalik-buterins-x-account/.

Hategan, Vlad. "Dead NFTs: The Evolving Landscape of the NFT Market." dappGambl. 2024. https://dappgambl.com/nfts/dead-nfts/

Chapter 3: The $450 Million dollar lost Password

Wieczner, Jen. "Mt. Gox and the Surprising Redemption of Bitcoin's Biggest Villain." *Fortune*, April 19, 2018. https://fortune.com/longform/bitcoin-mt-gox-hack-karpeles/.

Baydakova, Anna. "Where the Mt. Gox Money Went: New Details in the BTC-e Exchange Case." *CoinDesk*, June 9, 2023. https://www.coindesk.com/consensus-maga-zine/2023/06/09/where-the-mt-gox-money-went-new-de-tails-in-the-btc-e-exchange-case/.

Tuwiner, Jordan. "Mt Gox Hack Explained: Date, History & More (2014)." Buy Bitcoin World Wide. October 23, 2023. https://buybitcoinworldwide.com/mt-gox-hack/.

Popper, Nathaniel. "Lost Passwords Lock Millionaires out of Their Bitcoin Fortunes." *The New York Times*, January 12, 2021. https://www.nytimes.com/2021/01/12/technology/bit-coin-passwords-wallets-fortunes.html.

What Next? "$250 MILLION of Bitcoin lost, an ETF could have prevented this!" Posted July 25, 2022. YouTube, 12:32. https://www.youtube.com/watch?v=cZr97E5PgzQ.

BBC News. "This man threw away $6 million worth of Bitcoins - BBC NEWS." Posted November 29, 2013. YouTube, 3:12. https://www.youtube.com/watch?v=0tMXLDVpPs8.Top of Form

BBC. "Bitcoin: Newport Man's Plea to Find £210m Hard Drive in Tip." *BBC News*, January 15, 2021. https://www.bbc.com/news/uk-wales-55658942.

Howells, James. "Profile: Howelzy." LinkedIn. Accessed July 10, 2023. https://www.linkedin.com/in/howelzy/?originalSub-domain=uk.

Interledger Foundation. "Vision." Accessed July 7, 2023. https://interledger.org/vision.

CoinDesk. "Stefan Thomas: 'I Didn't Sleep For a Year' Re-Imple-menting Bitcoin." Posted April 20, 2019. YouTube, 3:07. https://www.youtube.com/watch?v=Owi9xLU5Z9c.

DW Deutsch. "Bitcoin: Stefan Thomas vergisst Passwort zu Mil-lionen-Schatz | DW Interview." Interview in German, post-ed January 17, 2021. YouTube, 11:04. https://www.youtube.com/watch?v=YACDMLsClW4.

Vanguard X. "Learn the Story of the Programmer Who Lost Mil-

lions in Bitcoin." March 1, 2022. https://vanguard-x.com/
blockchain/lost-millions-in-bitcoin/.

u/nathanielpopper. "Here's What Satoshi Wrote to the Man Responsible for the First Bitcoin Transaction." r/Bitcoin.
Reddit, May 23, 2015. https://www.reddit.com/r/Bitcoin/
comments/36vnmr/heres_what_satoshi_wrote_to_the_
man_responsible/.

Laszlo. "Bitcoin Forum: 'Pizza for bitcoins?'" Bitcoinpizzaindex.
net. May 10, 2010. https://bitcoinpizzaindex.net/images/
pizza-for-bitcoins.png.

"Bitcoin Pizza Index." Bitcoinpizzaindex.net. November 15, 2024.
https://bitcoinpizzaindex.net/.

Arslanian, Henri, Donovan, Robert, Blumenfeld, Matthew, and
Zamore, Anthony. "El Salvador's Law: A Meaningful Test
for Bitcoin." 2021. https://www.pwc.com/gx/en/finan-
cial-services/pdf/el-salvadors-law-a-meaningful-test-for-bit-
coin.pdf

Mancini, Jeannine. "El Salvador's Bitcoin Boom: How the World's
First Crypto Nation's Big Bet Is Stabilizing Its Economy,
Proving Critics Wrong, and Paying Back Its Debt." *Yahoo
Finance*, March 28, 2023. https://finance.yahoo.com/news/
el-salvadors-bitcoin-boom-worlds-151436258.html.

Lockett, Jon. "Man Who Got Bitcoin Worth £250million for Pizza in 2010 Admits He BLEW IT." *The Sun*, May 24, 2021.
https://www.thesun.co.uk/news/15049566/other-bit-
coin-pizza-jeremy-sturdivant-fortune-hanyecz/.

Bilton, Nick. "Disruptions: Betting on a Coin with No Realm." *Bits
Blog*, December 22, 2013. https://archive.nytimes.com/bits.
blogs.nytimes.com/2013/12/22/disruptions-betting-on-bit-
coin/.

Lockett, Jon. "Man Who Spent Bitcoin Now Worth £306MILLION
on 2 Pizzas Says He Has No Regrets." *The Sun* (US), May
22, 2021. https://www.the-sun.com/news/2935660/bit-
coin-pizza-laszlo-hanyecz-crypto-currency/.

Chapter 4: How a dog meme became worth more than the GDP of Sri Lanka

99bitcoins. "Bitcoin Obituaries - Bitcoin Declared Dead 350+ Times." Accessed August 5, 2023. https://99bitcoins.com/bitcoin-obituaries/.

Curry, David. "Binance Revenue and Usage Statistics (2024)." *Business of Apps*, updated October 7, 2024. http://www.businessofapps.com/data/binance-statistics/.

Cointree. "What is Dogecoin?" October 17, 2024. https://www.cointree.com/learn/what-is-dogecoin/.

World Crypto Index. "Jackson Palmer Bio." 2018. https://www.worldcryptoindex.com/creators/jackson-palmer/#:~:text=Early%20Life.

Noyes, Jenny. "An Interview with the Creator of Dogecoin: The Internet's Favourite New Currency." *Junkee*, January 22, 2014. https://junkee.com/an-interview-with-the-inventor-of-dogecoin-the-internets-favourite-new-currency/27411.

Gilbert, Daniel. "What Is Dogecoin? The Meme That Became the Hot New Virtual Currency." *International Business Times* (UK), December 20, 2013. https://www.ibtimes.co.uk/what-dogecoin-meme-that-became-hot-new-virtual-currency-1429847.

Epicenter Podcast. "#280 Jackson Palmer: Dogecoin – wow! so meme. such community. very charity. much story." Video of a podcast, posted March 27, 2019. YouTube, 1:21:23. https://www.youtube.com/watch?v=mtutzjz9g34&ab_channel=EpicenterPodcast.

Kay, Grace. "The History of Dogecoin, the Cryptocurrency That Surged after Elon Musk Tweeted about It but Started as a Joke on Reddit Years Ago." *Business Insider*, February 9, 2021. https://www.businessinsider.com/what-is-dogecoin-2013-12.

Cawrey, Daniel. "How Dogetipbot Turned a Spoof Altcoin into a Tipping Phenomenon." *CoinDesk*, April 10, 2014. https://www.coindesk.com/markets/2014/04/10/how-dogetipbot-turned-a-spoof-altcoin-into-a-tipping-phenomenon/.

Dogecoin Foundation. "Dogecoin Foundation: Do Only Good Ev-
      eryday." 2024. https://foundation.dogecoin.com/.

Rizzo, Pete. "Dogecoin Foundation to Raise $50k for Kenya's Water
      Crisis." *CoinDesk*, March 12, 2014. https://www.coindesk.
      com/markets/2014/03/11/dogecoin-foundation-to-raise-
      50k-for-kenyas-water-crisis/.

Zucker, Joseph. "Jamaican Bobsled Team Qualifies for 2014 Sochi
      Winter Olympics." *Bleacher Report*, January 19, 2014. https://
      bleacherreport.com/articles/1927933-jamaican-bob-
      sled-team-qualifies-for-2014-sochi-winter-olympics

Hern, Alex. "It's Bobsleigh Time: Jamaican Team Raises $25,000 in
      Dogecoin." *The Guardian*, January 20, 2014. https://www.
      theguardian.com/technology/2014/jan/20/jamaican-bob-
      sled-team-raises-dogecoin-winter-olympics

u/unicornbuttsex. "Guys, Let's Do It Doge NASCAR Style." r/
      dogecoin. *Reddit*, 2013. https://www.reddit.com/r/doge-
      coin/comments/20mwde/guys_lets_do_it_doge_nascar_
      style/.

Hern, Alex. "Dogecoin Raises $55,000 to Sponsor Nascar Driver."
      The Guardian, March 27, 2014. https://www.theguardian.
      com/technology/2014/mar/27/nascar-dogecoin-spon-
      sor-josh-wise-talladega-superspeedway.

Griswold, Alison. "Thousands of Dollars in Dogecoin Are Miss-
      ing." *Slate Magazine*, May 13, 2014. https://slate.com/busi-
      ness/2014/05/doge-vault-hack-millions-of-dogecoins-have-
      disappeared-from-the-online-wallet.html.

Shu, Catherine. "Such Hack. Many Dogecoin. Very Disappear. So
      Gone. Wow." *TechCrunch*, December 26, 2013. https://tech-
      crunch.com/2013/12/25/dogecoin-hack/.

u/ NeutralityMentality. "Friday 3PM EST: Save DogeMas Meeting
      Reimbursement." r/dogecoin. *Reddit*, 2013. https://www.
      reddit.com/r/dogecoin/comments/1ts263/friday_3pm_
      est_save_dogemas_meeting_reimbursement/.

u/ NeutralityMentality. "Remember Save Dogemas, the community fundraiser for victims of the Christmas Day hacking of Dogewallet.com?" r/dogecoin. *Reddit*, 2014. https://www.reddit.com/r/dogecoin/comments/236kfm/remember_save_dogemas_the_community_fundraiser/

Katje, Chris. "EXCLUSIVE: Billy Markus on Creating Dogecoin, the Negatives of Cryptocurrency, NFTs and Elon Musk." *Benzinga*, April 29, 2022. https://www.benzinga.com/markets/cryptocurrency/22/01/22155866/exclusive-dogecoin-co-creator-billy-markus-on-the-negatives-of-cryptocurrency-nfts-and-elo.

u/billymarkus2k. "True Value: An Open Letter from Billy Markus." r/dogecoin. *Reddit*, 2020. https://www.reddit.com/r/dogecoin/comments/lfl5iz/true_value_an_open_letter_from_billy_markus/.

Nagarajan, Shalini. "Dogecoin Creator Sold All His Coins 6 Years Ago after Getting Laid Off." *Markets Insider*, February 12, 2021. https://markets.businessinsider.com/currencies/news/dogecoin-creator-sold-coins-years-ago-laid-off-cryptocurrency-mania-2021-2-1030077260.

Rizzo, Pete. "Dogecoin Founder Exits Crypto Community Citing 'Toxic' Culture." *CoinDesk*, April 24, 2015. https://www.coindesk.com/markets/2015/04/24/dogecoin-founder-exits-crypto-community-citing-toxic-culture/.

Hakki, Tim. "Dogecoin Creator Jackson Palmer: 'I Wish It Was the End of Crypto, but It's Not.'" *Decrypt*, May 30, 2022. https://decrypt.co/101641/dogecoin-creator-jackson-palmer-i-wish-it-was-the-end-of-crypto-but-its-not.

Palmer, Jackson. "What in the Web3?! (w/Molly White of "Web3 is going just great")," May 2022, in *Griftonomics*, podcast, 51:12, https://open.spotify.com/show/6cQRqiNM5tvt1xrAVcQABK.

Benson, Jeff. "Elon Musk's Dogecoin and Bitcoin Tweets: A CryptoX Timeline." *Decrypt*, April 5, 2022. https://decrypt.

co/97015/elon-musk-dogecoin-bitcoin-tweets-crypto-X-timeline.

@elonmusk. "Dogecoin might be my fav cryptocurrency. It's pretty cool." X, April 2, 2019. https://x.com/elonmusk/status/1113009339743100929?lang=en%3A.

Mccrank, John. "Elon Musk on Crypto: To the Mooooonnn! And Back Again." *Reuters*, May 13, 2021. https://www.reuters.com/article/crypto-currency-bitcoin-musk-idCNL1N-2N027X.

Abrego, Javier. "Elon Musk Twitter Impact: 35MM Followers in 8 Month." Tweet Binder. October 20, 2022. https://www.tweetbinder.com/blog/elon-musk-twitter/.

TripleA. "Global Cryptocurrency Ownership Data 2021." January 4, 2023. https://triple-a.io/crypto-ownership-data/.

Shepherd, Jack. "22 Essential X Statistics You Need to Know in 2022." *The Social Shepherd*, January 3, 2023. https://thesocialshepherd.com/blog/X-statistics.

Peters, Jeremy W. "The Elusive Politics of Elon Musk." *The New York Times*, April 16, 2022. https://www.nytimes.com/2022/04/16/business/elon-musk-politics-X.html.

@elonmusk. "Dogecoin is the People's Crypto." X, February 4, 2021. https://X.com/elonmusk/status/1357241340313141249?lang=en.

Locke, Taylor. "'I Just Became a Dogecoin Millionaire': This 33-Year-Old Invested His Savings in the Meme Cryptocurrency with Inspiration from Elon Musk." *CNBC*, April 22, 2021. https://www.cnbc.com/2021/04/22/reddit-trader-im-a-dogecoin-millionaire-inspired-by-elon-musk.html.

u/ iUsedToCallDogeDodge. "Hey Guys, I Just Became a Dogecoin Millionaire!" r/dogecoin. *Reddit*, 2021. https://www.reddit.com/r/dogecoin/comments/mrsx8e/hey_guys_i_just_became_a_dogecoin_millionaire/.

Major, Jordan. "There Are Now over 1,000 DOGE-Made Millionaires after Dogecoin Price Skyrockets." *Finbold*, November 1,

2022. https://finbold.com/there-are-now-over-1000-doge-made-millionaires-after-dogecoin-price-skyrockets/.

Graffeo, Emily. "A Mysterious Dogecoin Whale Who Owns $15 Billion of the Cryptocurrency Added Another 420.69 Coins." *Business Insider India*, May 20, 2021. https://www.businessinsider.in/stock-market/news/a-mysterious-dogecoin-whale-who-owns-15-billion-of-the-cryptocurrency-just-bought-another-420-69-coins/articleshow/82809588.cms?

Sharma, Sunil. "Can Meme Numbers like '420' and '69' Make a Difference? Musk Believes So." *CoinGape*, November 15, 2021. https://coingape.com/can-meme-numbers-like-420-69-make-a-difference-musk-believes-so/.

Sigalos, MacKenzie. "Dogecoin Plunges Nearly 30% during Elon Musk's SNL Appearance." *CNBC*, May 9, 2021. https://www.cnbc.com/2021/05/08/dogecoin-price-plummets-as-elon-musk-hosts-saturday-night-live-.html.

Vasquez, Zach. "Saturday Night Live: Elon Musk Stumbles, Cast Bumbles in Brutally Awkward Episode." *The Guardian*, May 9, 2021. https://www.theguardian.com/tv-and-radio/2021/may/09/saturday-night-live-elon-musk.

King, Hope. "Elon Musk Reveals He Has Asperger's Syndrome." *Axios*, April 15, 2022. https://www.axios.com/2022/04/15/elon-musk-aspergers-syndrome.

Zhao, Christina. "Read Full Transcript of Elon Musk's Opening Monologue on 'SNL.'" *Newsweek*, May 9, 2021. https://www.newsweek.com/snl-read-full-transcript-elon-musks-opening-monologue-saturday-night-live-1589849.

@elonmusk. "Do you want Tesla to accept Doge?" X, May 11, 2021. https://x.com/elonmusk/status/1392030108274159619.

Kharpal, Arjun. "Dogecoin Jumps 9% after Elon Musk Says It Can Be Used to Buy Tesla Merchandise." *CNBC*, January 14, 2022. https://www.cnbc.com/2022/01/14/dogecoin-jumps-after-elon-musk-says-its-can-be-used-buy-tesla-merch.html.

Contessoto, Glauber. "'I've Lost Nearly $3m on Dogecoin.'" *Newsweek*, June 24, 2022. https://www.newsweek.com/dogecoin-millionaire-cryptocurrency-price-crash-bitcoin-1717417.

Stempel, Jonathan. "Elon Musk $258 Billion Dogecoin Lawsuit Expands." *Reuters*, September 8, 2022. https://www.reuters.com/markets/us/elon-musk-258-billion-dogecoin-lawsuit-expands-2022-09-07/.

Coinspeaker. "Elon Musk Linked to Mysterious Whale Dogecoin Wallet amid Recent Crypto Hype." Binance Square, April 5, 2023. https://www.binance.com/en/feed/post/385461.

u/AndreiFromAlberta. "Mystery Solved: The Billionaire Dogecoin Whale AKA 'The Most Important Man in Dogecoin.'" r/dogecoin. *Reddit*, 2020. https://www.reddit.com/r/dogecoin/comments/lkwnny/mystery_solved_the_billionaire_dogecoin_whale_aka/.

Barsby, Oliver. "Shiba Inu Founder?" Gfinityesports.com. December 23, 2022. https://www.gfinityesports.com/article/shiba-inu-founder-who-created-shiba-inu-coin-who-is-ryoshi-name-SHIB.

Kendall, Will. "Shiba Inu Timeline and Price History: What Could You Buy If You Had Bought SHIB." CoinMarketCap, November 23, 2021. https://coinmarketcap.com/academy/article/shiba-inu-timeline-and-price-history.

Crawley, Jamie. "Vitalik Buterin Burns $6B in SHIB Tokens, Says He Doesn't Want the 'Power.'" *CoinDesk*, May 17, 2021. https://www.coindesk.com/markets/2021/05/17/vitalik-buterin-burns-6b-in-shib-tokens-says-he-doesnt-want-the-power/.

McGimpsay, Patrick. "Floki Inu Explained: A Movement and a Meme-Coin in One." *Forbes Advisor*, January 10, 2024. https://www.forbes.com/advisor/in/investing/cryptocurrency/what-is-floki-inu/#

Shiba Inu Docs. "Swap Functionality." Accessed August 18, 2024. https://docs.shibatoken.com/shibaswap/shibaswap-functionality/swap.

ET Spotlight Special. "Elon Musk's Dog Sends Canine Cryptos Doge, Floki Soaring." *The Economic Times*, February 16, 2023. https://economictimes.indiatimes.com/news/new-updates/ elon-musks-tweet-about-his-dog-sends-canine-cryptos-doge-floki-soaring/articleshow/97940732.cms?from=mdr.

@TeslaOwnersSV. "Dogecoin was invented as a joke and yet fate loves irony." X, April 2, 2023. https://X.com/teslaownersSV/status/1643339912866045952.

Chapter 5: The $65-billion-dollar question: Who is Satoshi Nakamoto?

Nakamoto, Satoshi. "Bitcoin: A Peer-to-Peer Electronic Cash System." Accessed August 18, 2024. https://bitcoin.org/bitcoin.pdf.

u/Dunamisx. "First forum's post 13 years ago by Satoshi introducing Bitcoin." Bitcointalk (forum post), February 12, 2022. https://bitcointalk.org/index.php?topic=5385493.0.

@Narodism. "Here's an interview with @jgarzik who was an early core Bitcoin dev." X, October 12, 2024, https://x.com/Narodism/status/1844774934326772026

Goodman, Leah. "The Face behind Bitcoin." *Newsweek*, March 6, 2014. https://www.newsweek.com/2014/03/14/face-behind-bitcoin-247957.html.

Carter, Rebekah. "How Many Bitcoins Does Satoshi Nakamoto Have?" *BanklessTimes*, July 30, 2024. https://www.banklesstimes.com/how-many-bitcoins-does-satoshi-nakamoto-have/.

Nakamoto, Satoshi. "Bitcoin P2P e-cash paper." The Nakamoto Institute. Accessed August 18, 2024. https://satoshi.nakamotoinstitute.org/emails/cryptography/15/#selection-32.23-32.24..

Sweet, Ken. "Bank to Pay $31M for Avoiding Mortgages to Minorities, Largest Such Settlement in U.S. History." *PBS NewsHour*, January 12, 2023. https://www.pbs.org/newshour/economy/bank-to-pay-31m-for-avoiding-mortgages-to-minorities-largest-such-settlement-in-u-s-history.

World Bank. "Global Findex Database 2021 Reports Increases in Financial Inclusion around the World during the COVID-19 Pandemic." July 21, 2022. https://www.worldbank.org/en/news/feature/2022/07/21/covid-19-boosted-the-adoption-of-digital-financial-services.

Lee, Timothy. "Five Years of Bitcoin in One Post." *The Washington Post*, January 3, 2014. https://www.washingtonpost.com/news/the-switch/wp/2014/01/03/five-years-of-bitcoin-in-one-post/.

Elliot, Francis, and Duncan, Gary. "Chancellor Alistair Darling on Brink of Second Bailout for Banks." *The Times*, January 3, 2009. https://www.thetimes.com/article/chancellor-alistair-darling-on-brink-of-second-bailout-for-banks-n9l382mn62h?msockid=3634337da4db69f-1258327faa54a681a

Nakamoto, Satoshi. "Re: Bitcoin v0.1 released." *Mail Archive*, January 25, 2009. https://www.mail-archive.com/cryptography@metzdowd.com/msg10152.html.

Bitcoin Forum. "Satoshi." Bitcointalk, accessed August 18, 2024. https://bitcointalk.org/index.php?action=profile;u=3;s=-showPosts.

Andresen, Gavin. "Eleven Years Ago Today." Gavin Andresen's Blog, April 6, 2022. http://gavinandresen.ninja/eleven-years-ago-today.

Hearn, Mike. "Holding Coins in an Unspendable State for a Rolling Time Window." Mike's Homepage, accessed August 18, 2024. https://plan99.net/~mike/satoshi-emails/thread5.html.

u/Sergio_Demian_Lerner. "Satoshi's Fortune lower bound is 100M USD (DEBATE GOING ON, DO NOT TWEET!)." Bitcointalk (forum post), April 13, 2013. https://bitcointalk.org/index.php?topic=175996.msg1832533#msg1832533.

BitMEX Research. "Does Satoshi Have a Million Bitcoin?" BitMEX

Blog, August 20, 2018. https://blog.bitmex.com/satosh-is-1-million-bitcoin/.

George, Benedict. "How Can Satoshi Nakamoto Have a Birth-day? The Significance of April 5." *CoinDesk*, April 4, 2022. https://www.coindesk.com/learn/how-can-satoshi-nakimo-to-have-a-birthday-the-significance-of-april-5/.

Davis, Joshua. "The Crypto-Currency." *The New Yorker*, October 3, 2011. https://www.newyorker.com/magazine/2011/10/10/the-crypto-currency.

Wallace, Benjamin. "The Rise and Fall of Bitcoin." *Wired*, November 23, 2011. https://web.archive.org/web/20140326095105/http://www.wired.com/maga-zine/2011/11/mf_bitcoin/all/.

Redman, Jamie. "The Many Facts Pointing to Dorian Nakamoto Being Satoshi Nakamoto – Featured Bitcoin News." *Bitcoin News*, February 17, 2020. https://news.bitcoin.com/ma-ny-facts-dorian-nakamoto-satoshi/.

AP Archive. "A California man named Dorian Prentice Satoshi Nakamoto denies having anything to do with Bitcoin. H." Posted August 3, 2015. YouTube, 3:39. https://www.you-tube.com/watch?v=3dje9JyIjSc&ab_channel=APArchive.

Musil, Steven. "Dorian Nakamoto solicits donations to sue News-week." *CNET*, October 13, 2014. https://www.cnet.com/culture/dorian-nakamoto-solicits-donations-to-sue-news-week/.

Herper, Matthew. "Linguistic Analysis Says Newsweek Named the Wrong Man as Bitcoin's Creator." *Forbes*, March 10, 2014. https://web.archive.org/web/20140319123716/http://www.forbes.com/sites/matthewherper/2014/03/10/data-analysis-says-newsweek-named-the-wrong-man-as-bitcoins-creator/.

Juola, Patrick. "How a Computer Program Helped Show J.K. Rowl-ing Write a Cuckoo's Calling." *Scientific American*, August 20, 2013. https://www.scientificamerican.com/article/how-a-computer-program-helped-show-jk-rowling-write-a-cuckoos-calling/.

Musil, Steven. "Dorian Nakamoto Solicits Donations to Sue News-week." *CNET*, October 13, 2014. https://www.cnet.com/culture/dorian-nakamoto-solicits-donations-to-sue-news-week/.

Keoun, Bradley. "'Rare Pepe' Steeped in Bitcoin History Fetches $500K on NFT Market OpenSea." *CoinDesk*, August 31, 2021. https://www.coindesk.com/markets/2021/08/31/rare-pepe-steeped-in-bitcoin-history-fetches-500k-on-nft-market-opensea/.

Buckbee, Michael. "What Is PGP Encryption and How Does It Work?" Varonis, April 6, 2020. https://www.varonis.com/blog/pgp-encryption.

Chaum, David. "Blind Signatures for Untraceable Payments". In *Advances in Cryptology*, edited by D. Chaum, R. L. Rivest, and A. T. Sherman. Springer, 1983. https://doi.org/10.1007/978-1-4757-0602-4_18

Alloway, Tracy, and Weisenthal, Joe. "Meet the Godfather of Crypto, Who's Been Working on Digital Currency since the Early 80s." *Bloomberg*, May 27, 2019. https://www.bloomberg.com/news/articles/2019-05-27/meet-the-godfather-of-crypto-who-s-been-working-on-digital-currency-since-the-early-80s.

Greenberg, Andy. "Bitcoin's Earliest Adopter Is Cryonically Freezing His Body to See the Future." *Wired*, August 29, 2014. https://www.wired.com/2014/08/hal-finney/.

Wuckert Jr, Kurt. "Faketoshi Series (Hal Finney): The Men Who Are Not Satoshi—Part 3." *CoinGeek*, January 10, 2023. https://coingeek.com/faketoshi-series-hal-finney-the-men-who-are-not-satoshi-part-3/.

Kapilkov, Michael. "Previously Unpublished Emails of Satoshi Nakamoto Present a New Puzzle." *CoinDesk*, January 10, 2023. https://www.coindesk.com/markets/2020/11/26/previously-unpublished-emails-of-satoshi-nakamoto-present-a-new-puzzle/.

@DocumentingBTC. "The #bitcoin whitepaper appears to be hidden in every Apple Mac computer running macOS Catalina or newer.." X, April 5, 2023. https://X.com/DocumentingBTC/status/1643760765814358018.

Rowden, Seth. "What Is Satoshi Last Message To The World?" Bitkan. December 7, 2022. https://bitkan.com/learn/what-is-satoshi-last-message-to-the-world.

Migliaresi, Giorgia. "4 Famous Programmers Who Coded Their Way to The Top." Primo. June 6, 2017. https://www.primo-toys.com/4-famous-programmers-coded-way-top/.

Szabo, Nick. "Smart Contracts." 1994. https://www.fon.hum.uva.nl/rob/Courses/InformationInSpeech/CDROM/Literature/LOTwinterschool2006/szabo.best.vwh.net/smart.contracts.html.

Sharma, Rakesh. "Bit Gold: Meaning, Overview, and Differences from Bitcoin." Investopedia. Updated April 9, 2024. https://www.investopedia.com/terms/b/bit-gold.asp.

Szabo, Nick. "Shelling Out: The Origins of Money." Satoshi Nakamoto Institute. 2002. https://nakamotoinstitute.org/shelling-out/.

Hajdarbegovic, Nermin. "Linguistic Researchers Name Nick Szabo as Author of Bitcoin Whitepaper." *CoinDesk*, April 16, 2014. https://www.coindesk.com/markets/2014/04/16/linguistic-researchers-name-nick-szabo-as-author-of-bitcoin-whitepaper/.

Wuckert Jr, Kurt. "Faketoshi Series (Nick Szabo): The Men Who Are Not Satoshi—Part 1." *CoinGeek*, April 6, 2022. https://coingeek.com/faketoshi-series-nick-szabo-the-men-who-are-not-satoshi-part-1/.

@NickSzabo4. "Not Satoshi, but thank you." X, July 7, 2014. https://X.com/NickSzabo4/status/485970285254815745.

Voorhes, Adam. "Is Bitcoin's Creator This Unknown Australian Genius? Probably Not." *Wired*, updated March 30, 2019.

https://www.wired.com/2015/12/bitcoins-creator-sa-toshi-nakamoto-is-probably-this-unknown-australian-ge-nius/.

Au, Sean. "Craig Wright explains why a Japanese name was used as the inventor of bitcoins." Presentation from the 2017 Future of Bitcoin Conference. Posted July 14, 2017. YouTube, 3:28. https://www.youtube.com/watch?v=NERqjAOzdh0&ab_channel=SeanAu.

Pearson, Jordan. "Craig Wright's New Evidence That He Is Satoshi Nakamoto Is Worthless." *Wired*, May 2, 2016. https://www.vice.com/en/article/vv77z9/craig-wright-satoshi-nakamo-to-evidence-signature-is-worthless.

@dakami. "Satoshi signed a transaction in 2009…." X, May 3, 2016. https://X.com/dakami/status/727135599702876160.

@Narodism. "Satoshi wrote code that was not usual…" X, October 10, 2024. https://x.com/Narodism/sta-tus/1844017533336142025.

@marouane53. "Fact check: Todd's reply…" X, October 10, 2024. https://x.com/marouane53/status/1844041487492812893.

@PixOnChain. "This is Peter Todd…." X, Octo-ber 9, 2024. https://x.com/PixOnChain/sta-tus/1843820900678086889?s=03.

Tidy, Joe. "Peter Todd: I Am Not Bitcoin Inventor, Says Man Named in HBO Film." BBC News. October 9, 2024. https://www.bbc.com/news/articles/c62m73my0dno.

Lutz, Sander. "Is Craig Wright's Campaign to Convince the World That He Invented Bitcoin Over?" *Decrypt*, December 23, 2022. https://decrypt.co/117830/is-craig-wrights-campaign-to-convince-the-world-that-he-invented-bitcoin-over.

Hunt, Elle, and Farrell, Paul. "Reported Bitcoin 'Founder' Craig Wright's Home Raided by Australian Police." *The Guardian*, December 9, 2015. https://www.theguardian.com/technolo-gy/2015/dec/09/bitcoin-founder-craig-wrights-home-raid-ed-by-australian-police.

Redman, Jamie. "The Many Facts Pointing to Cypherpunk Len Sassaman Being Satoshi Nakamoto." Bitcoin News. March 5, 2021. https://news.bitcoin.com/the-many-facts-pointing-to-cypherpunk-len-sassaman-being-satoshi-nakamoto/.

Shumba, Camomile. "Craig Wright Is Not Satoshi, Didn't Author Bitcoin Whitepaper, Judge Rules." *CoinDesk*, March 15, 2024. https://www.coindesk.com/policy/2024/03/14/craig-wright-not-satoshi-didnt-author-bitcoin-whitepaper-judge-rules/.

White, Keira. "Was the First Reply to the Bitcoin White Paper Satoshi Themself? In-Depth Theory." *Cointelegraph*, November 18, 2021. https://cointelegraph.com/news/was-the-first-reply-to-the-bitcoin-white-paper-satoshi-himself-in-depth-theory.

Chapter 6: How a Group of internet strangers nearly bought the US Constitution – the story of DAOs

Ethereum. "DEVCON1: Slock.it - Christoph Jentzsch." Devcon one presentation. Posted January 7, 2016. YouTube, 23:34. https://www.youtube.com/watch?v=uy6P5_WQoUI&ab_channel=Ethereum.

Software Engineering Daily. "DAO Reflections and Slock.it with Christoph Jentzsch - Software Engineering Daily." March 23, 2018. Podcast, 53:26. https://softwareengineeringdaily.com/2018/03/23/dao-reflections-and-slock-it-with-christoph-jentzsch/.

Malekan, Omid. The Story of the Blockchain: A Beginner's Guide to the Technology Nobody Understands. Triple Smoke Stack, 2018. Kindle.

Waters, Richard. "Automated Company Raises Equivalent of $120M in Digital Currency." *CNBC*, May 17, 2016. https://www.cnbc.com/2016/05/17/automated-company-raises-equivalent-of-120-million-in-digital-currency.html.

Valenzuela, Virginia. "The History of the DAO." *SuperRare Mag-*

azine, November 17, 2021. https://superrare.com/maga-zine/2021/11/17/the-history-of-the-dao/.

Popper, Nathaniel. "A Venture Fund with Plenty of Virtual Capi-tal, but No Capitalist." *The New York Times*, May 22, 2016. https://www.nytimes.com/2016/05/22/business/deal-book/crypto-ether-bitcoin-currency.html?_r=1.

The Economist. "The DAO of Accrue." *The Economist*, May 19, 2016. https://www.economist.com/finance-and-econom-ics/2016/05/19/the-dao-of-accrue.

Newforum. "Griff Green Explains the Backstory of DAOs and How the DAO Hack Unfolded." Medium. August 16, 2022. https://medium.com/coinmonks/griff-green-explains-the-backstory-of-daos-and-how-the-dao-hack-unfolded-d7039a73a071.

Green, Griff. "LinkedIn Profile." LinkedIn. Accessed August 11, 2024. https://www.linkedin.com/in/griffgreen/?original-Subdomain=ch.

Ahonen, Elias. "Griff Green: Doge-Loving Hippy Hacker Steals Crypto Before Bad Guys Can." *Cointelegraph*, May 12, 2021. https://cointelegraph.com/magazine/griff-green-doge-lov-ing-hippy-hacker-steals-crypto-before-bad-guys-can/.

Stankovic, Stefan. "Has the DAO Hacker That Almost Killed Ethe-reum Been Identified?" Crypto Briefing. February 22, 2022. https://cryptobriefing.com/has-the-dao-hacker-that-almost-killed-ethereum-been-identified/.

Di Salvo, Mat. "Former Crypto CEO Denies Responsibility for $11 Billion Ethereum DAO Hack." *Decrypt*, February 22, 2022. https://decrypt.co/93547/crypto-ceo-denies-11-billion-ethereum-dao-hack.

Lyngaas, Sean. "Here's How North Korean Operatives Are Trying to Infiltrate US Crypto Firms." *CNN*, July 10, 2022. https://edition.cnn.com/2022/07/10/politics/north-korean-hack-ers-crypto-currency-firms-infiltrate/index.html.

Popper, Nathaniel. "A Hacking of More than $50 Million

Dashes Hopes in the World of Virtual Currency." *The New York Times*, June 17, 2016. https://www.nytimes.com/2016/06/18/business/dealbook/hacker-may-have-removed-more-than-50-million-from-experimental-cybercurrency-project.html.

Sotheby's. "Sotheby's to Auction One of Only Two First Printings of the U.S. Constitution Remaining in Private Hands." Sotheby's. November 1, 2022. https://www.sothebys.com/en/articles/sothebys-to-auction-one-of-only-two-first-printings-of-the-u-s-constitution-remaining-in-private-hands.

Irwin, Kate. "ConstitutionDAO Hits $30M in Ethereum Raised, One Day before Sotheby's Auction." *Decrypt*, November 18, 2021. https://decrypt.co/86359/constitutiondao-hits-30m-ethereum-raised-one-day-before-sothebys-auction.

McCormick, Packy. "Let's Buy the US Constitution." Not Boring by Packy McCormick. November 15, 2021. https://www.notboring.co/p/lets-buy-the-us-constitution.

Sotheby's. "Sotheby's $43.2M Sale of Constitution Shatters Record for Any Historical Document." Fine Books & Collections. November 19, 2021. https://www.finebooksmagazine.com/fine-books-news/sothebys-432m-sale-constitution-shatters-record-any-historical-document.

Sotheby's. "LIVE from Sotheby's New York | The Now & Contemporary Evening Auctions With U.S. Constitution Sale." Livestreamed auction, posted November 19, 2021. YouTube, 4:18:04. https://www.youtube.com/watch?v=1TBa-9Lx-3vc&ab_channel=Sotheby%27s.

Hills, Megan C. "First-Edition Copy of US Constitution Sells for Record $43.2 Million." *CNN Style*, November 19, 2021. https://edition.cnn.com/style/article/us-constitution-sothebys-sale/index.html.

Patel, Nilay. "From a Meme to $47 Million: ConstitutionDAO, Crypto, and the Future of Crowdfunding." *The Verge*, December 7, 2021. https://www.theverge.com/22820563/constitution-meme-47-million-crypto-crowdfunding-blockchain-ethereum-constitution.

@ConstitutionDAO. "Community: We did not win…." X, November 18, 2021. https://X.com/ConstitutionDAO/status/1461498841820192771.

Crow, Kelly. "Ken Griffin on Why He Spent $43 Million to Buy the U.S. Constitution." *Wall Street Journal*, August 9, 2022. https://www.wsj.com/articles/ken-griffin-constitution-museum-11660068328.

Feldman, Ella. "A Group of Crypto Investors Is Trying to Buy the Constitution—Again." *Smithsonian Magazine*, December 9, 2022. https://www.smithsonianmag.com/smart-news/crypto-investors-buy-the-constitution-dao-180981264/.

Wright, Keira. "PleasrDAO Adds $4M OG NFT Wu-Tang Clan Album to Its Collection." *Cointelegraph*, October 21, 2021. https://cointelegraph.com/news/pleasrdao-adds-4m-og-nft-wu-tang-clan-album-to-its-collection.

Escalante-De Mattei, Shanti. "Sotheby's Sale of U.S. Constitution Is Suddenly Postponed, Causing Uncertainty for Crypto Enthusiasts." *ARTnews*, December 14, 2022. https://www.artnews.com/art-news/news/constitution-sothebys-postponed-constitutiondao-2-1234650138/.

Irwin, Kate. "A DAO Is Trying to Buy the US Constitution—Again." *Yahoo Finance*, December 7, 2022. https://finance.yahoo.com/news/dao-trying-buy-us-constitution-201444374.html.

@WAGBTC. "We are gonna buy the Constitution! (again)" X, December 7, 2022. https://X.com/WAGBTC/status/1600327951148457989

Tan, Eli. "A DAO That Literally Wants to Party on the Moon Just Sent a Viral YouTuber to Space." *CoinDesk*, August 6, 2022. https://www.coindesk.com/business/2022/08/06/a-dao-that-literally-wants-to-party-on-the-moon-just-sent-a-viral-youtuber-to-space/.

Newar, Brian. "DAO Aims to Raise $5M to Resurrect Blockbuster Video." *Cointelegraph*, December 30, 2021. https://cointelegraph.com/news/dao-aims-to-raise-5m-to-resurrect-blockbuster-video.

Hayward, Andrew. "BlockbusterDAO Hits R3WIND: What's next after Failing to Buy Nostalgia Brand." *Decrypt*, July 2, 2022. https://decrypt.co/104322/blockbusterdao-hits-r3wind-whats-next-after-failing-to-buy-nostalgia-brand.

Chapter 7: How one web3 game was played by 2% of the Philippines for a living

Russel. "To Axie Infinity and Beyond – A Record Sale of 369 ETH." *NFT Plazas*, July 23, 2021. https://nftplazas.com/axie-infinity-and-beyond/.

Bergin, Lauren. "How Many People Play World of Warcraft? WoW Player Count & Population Tracker (2024)." Dexerto. August 9, 2024. https://www.dexerto.com/world-of-warcraft/how-many-people-play-world-of-warcraft-wow-player-count-population-tracker-1842964/.

Epic Drop. "7 Most Expensive WoW Items EVER SOLD!" Posted August 3, 2020. YouTube, 8:17. https://www.youtube.com/watch?v=mS2bVS5LKl8&ab_channel=EpicGamer.

Jade, Charles. "Blizzard Bans a Gold Rush." *Ars Technica*, March 15, 2005. https://arstechnica.com/uncategorized/2005/03/4700-2/.

BBC. "CryptoKitties Cripple Ethereum Blockchain." *BBC News*, December 6, 2017. https://www.bbc.com/news/technology-42237162.

Callon-Butler, Leah. "Most Influential 2021: Trung Nguyen." *CoinDesk*, December 8, 2021. https://www.coindesk.com/business/2021/12/08/most-influential-trung-nguyen/.

PLAY-TO-EARN. "PLAY-TO-EARN | NFT Gaming in the Philippines | English." Posted May 13, 2021. YouTube, 18:09. https://www.youtube.com/watch?v=Yo-BrASMHU4&ab_

channel=PLAY-TO-EARN.

Keller, Lachlan. "Axie Infinity Fans Play Their Way to Payday as Game Token Prices Soar." *Forkast*, July 16, 2021. https://forkast.news/axie-infinity-fans-play-their-way-payday-game-token-prices-soar/.

Gottsegen, Will. "The Bigger Problem with Axie Infinity." *Coin-Desk*, April 4, 2022. https://www.coindesk.com/opin-ion/2022/04/04/the-bigger-problem-with-axie-infinity/.

"A Trust and Liability Analysis: Ronin Hack." Vircon Legal. April 13, 2022. https://virconlegal.com/a-trust-and-liability-analy-sis-ronin-hack/.

Robertson, Adi. "Axie Infinity's Blockchain Was Reportedly Hacked via a Fake LinkedIn Job Offer." *The Verge*, July 6, 2022. https://www.theverge.com/2022/7/6/23196713/axie-infin-ity-ronin-blockchain-hack-phishing-linkedin-job-offer.

Grieg, Jonathan. "More than $30 Million Seized from North Korean Hackers Involved in Axie Crypto-Theft." *The Record*, September 8, 2022. https://therecord.media/more-than-30-million-seized-from-north-korean-hackers-involved-in-axie-crypto-theft.

Callon-Butler, Leah. "How the Play-to-Earn Industry Can Rebuild Better After the Ronin Attack." *Nasdaq*, April 7, 2022. https://www.nasdaq.com/articles/how-the-play-to-earn-in-dustry-can-rebuild-better-after-the-ronin-attack.

Chapter 8: How a $40 Billion Cryptocurrency Went to Zero in 72 Hours: The Collapse of Luna

Shen, Muyao, and Regan, Michael P. "Inside Bitcoin Whale Do Kwon's $10 Billion Plan to Prop up Terra, Luna Coin." *Bloomberg*, April 19, 2022. https://www.bloomberg.com/news/features/2022-04-19/terraform-s-do-kwon-s-huge-bit-coin-buys-catch-crypto-billionaires-attention?leadSource=u-verify%20wall.

Jin, Min-ji. "The LUNAtics aren't so crazy about Do Kwon anymore." *Korea JoongAng Daily*, May 20, 2022. https://korea-joongangdaily.joins.com/2022/05/20/business/finance/korea-terraform-labs-Luna/20220520144215830.html.

Coinage. "Inside Crypto's Largest Collapse with Terra Founder Do Kwon | Coinage Episode 0 Part I." Video interview, posted August 16, 2022. YouTube, 29:46. https://www.youtube.com/watch?v=5g9ycHS0xtU&ab_channel=Coinage.

Everington, Keoni. "Taiwanese Man Commits Suicide after Losing Nearly NT$60 Million from Luna Crypto Crash" *Taiwan News*, May 26, 2022. https://www.taiwannews.com.tw/en/news/4551502.

PitchBook. "Company Profile: Anyfi." Accessed August 19, 2024. https://pitchbook.com/profiles/company/500828-05#overview.

Thurman, Andrew. "Olympus DAO Might Be the Future of Money (or It Might Be a Ponzi)." *CoinDesk*, December 5, 2021. https://www.coindesk.com/policy/2021/12/05/olympus-dao-might-be-the-future-of-money-or-it-might-be-a-ponzi/.

Yaffe-Bellany, David, and Griffith, Erin. "How a Trash-Talking Crypto Founder Caused a $40 Billion Crash." *The New York Times*, May 18, 2022. https://www.nytimes.com/2022/05/18/technology/terra-luna-cryptocurrency-do-kwon.html.

Sandor, Krisztian, and Genç, Ekin. "The Fall of Terra: A Timeline of the Meteoric Rise and Crash of UST and LUNA." *CoinDesk*, May 20, 2022. https://www.coindesk.com/learn/the-fall-of-terra-a-timeline-of-the-meteoric-rise-and-crash-of-ust-and-luna/.

Sopov, Vladislav. "Terra (LUNA) Collapse Predicted 4 Years Ago; Check out This Visionary Statement." U Today. July 23, 2022. https://u.today/terra-Luna-collapse-predicted-4-years-ago-check-out-this-visionary-statement.

@FreddieRaynolds. "A few weeks ago I responded to….." X, November 26, 2021. https://X.com/FreddieRaynolds/status/1463960623402913797.

@stablekwon. "I don't debate the poor on X, and sorry I don't have any change on me for her at the moment." X, July 1, 2021. https://x.com/stablekwon/status/1410491186196795398.

Sulemanji, Nawaz. "CHAI Mobile Payments App Sees $54 Million in Blockchain Transactions." *Yahoo Finance*, October 29, 2019. https://finance.yahoo.com/news/chai-mobile-payments-app-sees-154534077.html.

United States District Court, Southern District of New York. *Securities and Exchange Commission v. Terraform Labs PTE LTD. and Do Hyeong Kwon*, No. 1:23-cv-1346 (JSR). Document 32, filed February 16, 2023. https://fingfx.thomsonreuters.com/gfx/legaldocs/lbpgonqgmpq/frankel-SECvterra--SECmtdoppos.pdf

Lopatto, Elizabeth. "How the Anchor Protocol Helped Sink Terra." *The Verge*, May 20, 2022. https://www.theverge.com/2022/5/20/23131647/terra-luna-do-kwon-stablecoin-anchor.

Sun, Zhiyuan. "Terra Injects $450M UST into Anchor Reserve Days Before Protocol Depletion." *Cointelegraph*, February 18, 2022. https://cointelegraph.com/news/terra-injects-450m-ust-in-to-anchor-reserve-days-before-protocol-depletion.

Shen, Muyao. "DeFi App Anchor Protocol Promising 20% Interest on Stablecoin." *Bloomberg*, March 23, 2022. https://www.bloomberg.com/news/articles/2022-03-23/terra-s-promise-of-20-defi-return-raises-sustainability-concern?leadSource=uverify%20wall.

Braun, Helene. "Foundation Focused on UST Stablecoin Raises $1B in LUNA Sale." *CoinDesk*, February 22, 2022. https://www.coindesk.com/markets/2022/02/22/foundation-focused-on-ust-stablecoin-raises-1b-in-luna-sale/#:~:text=Foundation%20Focused%20on%20UST%20Stablecoin%20Raises%20%241B%20in%20LUNA%20Sale.

Dantes, Damanick, and Chen, Angelique. "Market Wrap: Bitcoin

Rallies as Crypto Holders Accumulate." *CoinDesk*, March 28, 2022. https://www.coindesk.com/markets/2022/03/28/market-wrap-bitcoin-rallies-as-crypto-holders-accumulate/.

Bourgi, Sam. "Luna Foundation Guard Purchases Additional 37,863 BTC as Part of Reserve Strategy." *Cointelegraph*, May 5, 2022, https://cointelegraph.com/news/luna-foundation-guard-purchases-additional-37-863-btc-as-part-of-reserve-strategy.

Stablecorp. "The Collapse of Terra Classic." Medium. August 31, 2022. https://medium.com/stablecorp/the-collapse-of-ust-classic-52db50e73a92.

Kelly, Liam J. "We Need to Talk about Terra's Anchor." *Decrypt*, April 23, 2022. https://decrypt.co/98482/we-need-to-talk-about-terras-anchor.

Yasmin, Mehnaz, and Nishant, Niket. "JPMorgan Amasses Deposits as Customers Move Money to Largest U.S. Bank." *Reuters*, April 14, 2023. https://www.reuters.com/business/finance/jpmorgan-amasses-deposits-customers-move-money-largest-us-bank-2023-04-14/.

Luna Foundation Guard. "LFG — Technical Audit Report." Medium. November 16, 2022. https://medium.com/terra-money/lfg-technical-audit-report-ddaf3f51e7d.

Kelly, Liam J. "How Terra's UST and LUNA Imploded." *Decrypt*, May 14, 2022. https://decrypt.co/100402/how-terra-ust-luna-imploded-crypto-crash.

@stablekwon. "Getting close ... stay strong, lunatics." X, May 11, 2022. https://X.com/stablekwon/status/1524164780189126657.

Liang, Annabelle. "Do Kwon: Fugitive 'Cryptocrash' Boss Arrested in Montenegro." *BBC News*, March 23, 2023. https://www.bbc.com/news/technology-65058533.

u/ CryptographerTop8162. "My Ex-Colleague Attempted Suicide." *Reddit*, 2022. https://www.reddit.com/r/terraLuna/comments/un40h4/my_excolleague_attempted_suicide/.

Park, Danny. "From Billionaire to Montenegro Jail: The Rapid

Rise and Fall of Terra Chief Do Kwon." *Forkast*, April 21, 2023. https://forkast.news/do-kwon-terra-Luna-what-happened-montenegro/.

Park, Danny. "Terra's Do Kwon, Wanted in South Korea, Left Singapore, Flew to Dubai." *Forkast*, October 20, 2022. https://forkast.news/headlines/terra-ceo-do-kwon-south-korea-singapore-dubai/.

@stablekwon. "1/ Terra is more than $UST." X, May 17, 2022. https://X.com/stablekwon/status/1526258273820651520.

Park, Danny. "Montenegro to Hold Terra-Luna Fugitive Do Kwon for 30 Days." *Forkast*, March 28, 2023. https://forkast.news/headlines/montenegro-terra-Luna-do-kwon/.

Park, Danny. "Prosecutor Says Terra's Do Kwon Should Face Trial in South Korea: WSJ." *Forkast*, May 8, 2023. https://forkast.news/terra-Luna-fugitive-do-kwon-south-korea/.

Davies, Pascale. "Terra CEO Do Kwon: 'I Alone Am Responsible for Any Weaknesses.'" *Euronews*, August 15, 2022. https://www.euronews.com/next/2022/08/15/terra-luna-crash-i-alone-am-responsible-says-ceo-do-kwon-in-first-interview-since-collapse

Mogilevski, Arthur. "Terra Luna Peg Loss Increases Rates of Mental Health and Suicidal Ideation." Inneractions IOP. May 11, 2022. https://inneractions.net/what-happened-to-terra-Luna/.

JS Held. "Analysis – Terraform Labs' and Luna Foundation Guard's Defense of the UST Price Peg. November 9, 2022. https://lfg.org/audit/LFG-Audit-2022-11-14.pdf

Chapter 9: How to Go from $26 Billion to $0: The Downfall of Sam Bankman-Fried and FTX

Chung, Frank. "Polyamorous Group behind Crypto Collapse." *News.com*, November 15, 2022. https://www.news.com.au/finance/money/investing/collapsed-crypto-trading-firm-ceo-was-28yearold-harry-potter-obsessed-polycule-member/news-story/2cd59da72e73216aefdec8a0862254eb.

Welham, Ben. "This Crypto Billionaire Sleeps on a Beanbag and Wants to Donate His $20 Billion Fortune." *Supercar Blondie*, April 11, 2022. https://supercarblondie.com/crypto-billionaire-sleeps-on-beanbag-wants-donate-20-billion-fortune/

Nguyen, Britney. "Sam Bankman-Fried was once caught playing the video game 'League of Legends' during a pitch meeting for FTX." *Business Insider*, November 11, 2022. https://www.businessinsider.com/ftx-sam-bankman-fried-league-of-legends-investor-pitch-meeting-2022-11

Rooney, Kate. "FTX Grew Revenue 1,000% during the Crypto Craze, Leaked Financials Show." *CNBC*, August 20, 2022. https://www.cnbc.com/2022/08/20/ftx-grew-revenue-1000percent-during-the-crypto-craze-leaked-financials.html.

Pavlovic McAteer, Ksenija. "Kevin O'Leary Interview: The Dagger That Finished Sam Bankman-Fried Off." *The Pavlovic Today*, December 19, 2022. https://thepavlovictoday.com/kevin-oleary-interview-the-dagger-that-finished-sam-bankman-fried-off/.

Quarmby, Brian. "FTX Founder Sam Bankman-Fried Urges Court to Dismiss Charges." *Cointelegraph*, May 9, 2023. https://cointelegraph.com/news/ftx-founder-sam-bankman-fried-urges-court-to-dismiss-charges.

Parloff, Roger. "Portrait of a 29-Year-Old Billionaire: Can Sam Bankman-Fried Make His Risky Crypto Business Work?" *Yahoo Finance*, August 12, 2021. https://finance.yahoo.com/news/ftx-ceo-sam-bankman-fried-profile-085444366.html.

Wallace, Benjamin. "The Mysterious Cryptocurrency Magnate Who Became One of Biden's Biggest Donors." *Intelligencer*, February 2, 2021. https://nymag.com/intelligencer/2021/02/sam-bankman-fried-biden-donor.html.

"Introduction to Effective Altruism." Effective Altrism, 2022. https://www.effectivealtruism.org/articles/introduction-to-effective-altruism.

Pincus-Roth, Zachary. "The Rise of the Rational Do-Gooders." *The

Washington Post Magazine, September 23, 2020. https://www.
washingtonpost.com/magazine/2020/09/23/effective-altru-
ism-charity/.

Hoffower, Hillary. "Sam Bankman-Fried Was an Effective Altruism Evangelist, Pledging to Give Away Most of His $26
Billion Fortune—It Might Have Ultimately Caused His
Downfall." *Yahoo Finance*, November 15, 2022. https://
finance.yahoo.com/news/sam-bankman-fried-effective-al-
truism-120000847.html#:~:text=Sam%20Bankman%2D-
Fried%20was%20an.

Faux, Zeke. "Sam Bankman-Fried: FTX's Crypto Billionaire Who
Wants to Give His Fortune Away." *Bloomberg*, April 3, 2022.
https://www.bloomberg.com/news/features/2022-04-03/
sam-bankman-fried-ftx-s-crypto-billionaire-who-wants-to-
give-his-fortune-away#xj4y7vzkg.

Morrow, Allison. "Crypto's White Knight Lost 94% of His Wealth
in a Single Day." *CNN*, November 9, 2022. https://edition.
cnn.com/2022/11/09/business/sam-bankman-fried-wealth-
ftx-ctrp.

Ešnerová, Daniela. "What Is Alameda Research? Sam Bankman-Fried's Secretive Proprietary Trading Firm Is Major
DeFi Investor." Capital.com. December 29, 2022. https://
capital.com/alameda-research-what-is-sam-bankman-fried-
trading-firm.

Deka, Chayanika. "Binance-FTX Botched Acquisition: A Timeline
of High-Profile Bailout That Never Happened." Crypto-
Potato. November 10, 2022. https://cryptopotato.com/
binance-ftx-botched-acquisition-a-timeline-of-high-profile-
bailout-that-never-happened.

McCarthy, Adam. "'Manipulative' SBF Led Alameda's Co-Founder to Quit in 2018 — Who Is Tara MacAulay?" *DL News*,
October 10, 2023. https://www.dlnews.com/articles/peo-
ple-culture/who-is-alameda-co-founder-and-sbf-critic-tara-
mac-aulay/.

Hart, Jordan. "Caroline Ellison Said She Took a 'Blind Leap' to Join Fast-Paced FTX." *Business Insider*, November 20, 2022. https://www.businessinsider.com/caroline-ellison-took-blind-leap-join-fast-paced-ftx-2022-11.

Yaffe-Bellany, David, Kelley, Lora, and Metz, Cade. "She Was a Little-Known Crypto Trader. Then FTX Collapsed." *The New York Times*, November 23, 2022. https://www.nytimes.com/2022/11/23/business/ftx-caroline-ellison-sbf.html.

Miller, Hannah. "Alameda Research Co-CEO Sam Trabucco Resigns from Crypto Market Maker." *Bloomberg*, August 24, 2022. https://www.bloomberg.com/news/articles/2022-08-24/alameda-co-ceo-trabucco-steps-down-from-crypto-trading-firm.

Lim, Michelle. "How FTX Crypto Exchange Won over 1 Million Investors and Grew 25-Fold." *Forkast*, May 13, 2021. https://forkast.news/video-audio/ftx-crypto-exchange-innovation-regulation/.

"Binance Announces Strategic Investment in Cryptocurrency Derivatives Exchange FTX." Binance (blog), December 20, 2019. https://www.binance.com/en/blog/all/binance-announces-strategic-investment-in-cryptocurrency-derivatives-exchange-ftx-414610870200725504.

Beer, Jeff. "How FTX Led Crypto's Takeover of Sports in Less Than a Year." Fast Company. July 2, 2022. https://www.fastcompany.com/90717799/how-ftx-led-cryptos-takeover-of-sports-in-less-than-a-year.

De Avila, Joseph. "Goodbye FTX Arena: Miami Heat Stadium Ditches Crypto Sponsor." *Wall Street Journal*, January 11, 2023. https://www.wsj.com/articles/goodbye-ftx-arena-miami-heat-stadium-ditches-crypto-sponsor-11673462807.

Gentrup, Abigail. "FTX Accused of Illegally Financing Super Bowl Ad." *Front Office Sports*, December 19, 2022. https://frontofficesports.com/ftx-accused-of-illegally-financing-super-bowl-ad/.

Loh, Matthew. "SBF Played 'League of Legends' so Much He Was Gaming during a Pitch Meeting. Now His Lawyers Say There'll Be No More Online Games for the Crypto King." *Business Insider*, March 29, 2023. https://www.businessinsider.in/cryptocurrency/news/sbf-played-league-of-legends-so-much-he-was-gaming-during-pitch-meetings-now-his-lawyers-say-therell-be-no-more-online-games-for-the-crypto-king-/articleshow/99082355.cms.

@AOC. "My Small Quarantine Accomplishment: Made it to Silver III." X, July 14, 2020. https://X.com/AOC/status/1282873451267661826.

Berwick, Angus, and Wilson, Tom. "Exclusive: Behind FTX's Fall, Battling Billionaires and a Failed Bid to Save Crypto." *Reuters*, November 10, 2022. https://www.reuters.com/technology/exclusive-behind-ftxs-fall-battling-billionaires-failed-bid-save-crypto-2022-11-10/.

Irwin, Kate. "CZ Says Sam Bankman-Fried Was 'Badmouthing' Binance in DC—but They Weren't in a 'Battle.'" *Decrypt*, November 17, 2022. https://decrypt.co/114974/cz-says-sam-bankman-fried-was-badmouthing-binance-in-dc-but-they-werent-in-a-battle.

@alexvalaitis. "However, CZ is not going down without a fight…" X, November 8, 2022. https://X.com/alex_valaitis/status/1589711051901538304.

Lopatto, Elizabeth. "Sam Bankman-Fried Oversaw FTX's Meltdown, and the Fallout Is Reaching DC." *The Verge*, November 15, 2022. https://www.theverge.com/2022/11/15/23459268/sam-bankman-fried-ftx-bankruptcy-crypto-lobbying-washington.

Young, Martin. "FTX CEO Sam Bankman-Fried under Fire over Proposed Centralized Industry Standards." BeInCrypto. October 20, 2022. https://beincrypto.com/crypto-community-slams-ftx-ceo-proposed-centralized-industry-standards/.

Shamsian, Jacob, and Sundar, Sindhu. "SBF Funneled $100M

for 'Woke Shit', Republicans: Indictment." *Business Insider*, February 23, 2023. https://www.businessinsider.com/sbf-political-donations-2-executives-republicans-democrats-woke-prosecutors-2023-2.

Pearson, Jordan. "Sam Bankman-Fried Funded 'Woke Shit for Transactional Purposes,' Prosecutors Allege." *VICE*, February 23, 2023. https://www.vice.com/en/article/5d3nwk/sam-bankman-fried-funded-woke-shit-for-transactional-purposes-prosecutors-allege.

Popli, Nik. "Sam Bankman-Fried's Political Donations: What We Know." *Time*, December 14, 2022. https://time.com/6241262/sam-bankman-fried-political-donations/

Chow, Andrew R. "'More *Veep* than *West Wing*.' Inside Sam Bankman-Fried's attempted conquest of Washington," *Time*, August 6, 2024, https://time.com/7006739/sam-bankman-fried-cryptomania-excerpt/

Francis, Theo. "It's a Close Race for CEO Support, Too." *Wall Street Journal*, October 28, 2020. https://www.wsj.com/articles/its-a-close-race-for-ceo-support-too-11603913772.

@carolinecapital. "nothing like regular amphetamine use…." X, April 5, 2021. https://x.com/carolinecapital/status/1379036346300305408.

@SBF_FTX. "a) stimulants when you wake up, sleeping pills.." X, September 16, 2019. https://x.com/SBF_FTX/status/1173351344159117312.

@AutismCapital. "Andrew says "It sounds like this is a bunch.,,,," X, December 1, 2022. https://X.com/AutismCapital/status/1598087959311716367.

Delouya, Samantha. "SBF Denies Rampant Drugs at FTX: 'Totally On-Label Use of Medication.'" *Business Insider*, December 1, 2022. https://www.businessinsider.com/sam-bankman-fried-drug-use-ftx-alameda-caroline-ellison-amphetamines-2022-11.

Jones, Wayne. "Sam Bankman-Fried Allegedly Used Anti-Psychotic Medications at FTX." Crypto.news. December 15, 2022. https://crypto.news/sam-bankman-fried-allegedly-used-anti-psychotic-medications-at-ftx/.

Tal Murphy, Heather. "Sam Bankman-Fried Confirmed He Wears an Emsam Patch. What's an Emsam Patch?" *Slate*, December 14, 2022. https://slate.com/technology/2022/12/sam-bankman-fried-ftx-emsam-patch-testimony-arrested.html.

Milk Road. "SBF on the Run." Milkroad. November 12, 2022. https://milkroad.com/daily/sbf-on-the-run-%ef%b8%8f/.

Barrabi, Thomas. "FTX's Sam Bankman-Fried Fumed over Media Spotlight on Polyamorous Sex Life: Report." *New York Post*, November 30, 2022. https://nypost.com/2022/11/30/ftxs-sam-bankman-fried-fumed-over-media-spotlight-on-polya-morous-sex-life/.

Khoo, Yong Li, Leow, Sandra, Polk, Niclas, and Chia, Douglas. "Blockchain Analysis: The Collapse of Alameda and FTX." Nansen. November 12, 2022. https://www.nansen.ai/research/blockchain-analysis-the-collapse-of-alameda-and-ftx.

Oliver, Joshua. "How Bankman-Fried Blurred Lines between FTX and Alameda." *Australian Financial Review*, December 5, 2022. https://www.afr.com/wealth/investing/how-bankman-fried-blurred-lines-between-ftx-and-alameda-20221205-p5c3nn.

Zahn, Max. "A Timeline of Cryptocurrency Exchange FTX's Historic Collapse." *ABC News*, December 13, 2022. https://abcnews.go.com/Business/timeline-cryptocurrency-ex-change-ftxs-historic-collapse/story?id=93337035.

@cz_binance. "As part of Binance's exit…." X, November 7, 2022. https://X.com/cz_binance/status/1589283421704290306.

@cz_binance. "Liquidating our FTT is just post-exit risk manage-ment…." X, November 7, 2022. https://x.com/cz_binance/status/1589374530413215744.

@carolinecapital. "@cz_binance if you're looking to mini-mize the market impact on your FTT sales, Alameda will happily buy it all from you today at $22!" X, November 7, 2022. https://X.com/carolinecapital/status/1589287457975304193

Irwin, Kate. "FTX's Sam Bankman-Fried Was a 'Master Manipulator,' Says Binance CEO CZ." *Decrypt*, December 6, 2022. https://decrypt.co/116548/ftxs-sam-bankman-fried-was-a-master-manipulator-says-binance-ceo-cz.

Lopatto, Elizabeth. "Binance Won't Bail out FTX, Cites Reports of 'Mishandled Customer Funds.'" *The Verge*, November 9, 2022. https://www.theverge.com/2022/11/9/23450044/binance-ftx-acquisition-abandoned-alameda-crypto-contagion.

@SBF_FTX. "4) A *huge* thank you to CZ, Binance, and all of our supporters…." X, November 9, 2022. https://X.com/SBF_FTX/status/1590012129876512769.

Hern, Alex. "Binance to Buy FTX in Major Cryptocurrency Exchange Merger." *The Guardian*, November 8, 2022. https://www.theguardian.com/technology/2022/nov/08/binance-to-buy-ftx-in-major-cryptocurrency-exchange-merger.

@Binance. "In the beginning, our hope was to be able to support FTX's customers to provide liquidity, but the issues are beyond our control or ability to help." X, November 10, 2022. https://x.com/binance/status/1590449164932243456.

@sequoia. "Here is the note we sent to our LPs in GGFIII regarding FTX…." X, November 10, 2022. https://X.com/sequoia/status/1590522718650499073.

Nguyen, Britney. "Chamath Palihapitiya Said Sam Bankman-Fried Once Pitched Him, but after the Investor Suggested Changes like Forming a Board, FTX Told Him to Get Lost." *Business Insider*, November 16, 2022. https://www.businessinsider.com/ftx-told-chamath-palihapitiya-social-capital-go-fuck-yourself-recommendations-2022-11.

@SBF_FTX. "1) I'm sorry. That's the biggest thing…" X, November 11, 2022. https://X.com/SBF_FTX/status/1590709166515310593.

Commodity Futures Trading Commission. "Release Number 8638-22: CFTC Charges Sam Bankman-Fried, FTX Trading and Alameda with Fraud and Material Misrepresentations." Press release, December 13, 2022. https://www.cftc.gov/Press-Room/PressReleases/8638-22.

Schulz, Bailey. "FTX Founder Arrested in Bahamas: How Sam Bankman-Fried's Alleged Scheme Unraveled." *USA Today*, December 13, 2023. https://www.usatoday.com/story/tech/2022/12/13/ftx-founder-sam-bankman-fried-arrest-indictment/10888749002/.

Schwartz, Dan, and Mangan, Brian. "FTX Founder Sam Bankman-Fried Hit with Four New Criminal Charges." *CNBC*, February 23, 2023. https://www.cnbc.com/2023/02/23/ftx-founder-sam-bankman-fried-hit-with-new-criminal-charges.html.

Stieb, Matt. "Stanford's Larry Kramer, Andreas Paepck Bailed out SBF." *Intelligencer*, February 15, 2023. https://nymag.com/intelligencer/2023/02/stanfords-larry-kramer-andreas-paepck-bailed-out-sbf.html.

@jconorgrogan. "Some of the things that SBF/Alameda bought…" X, January 31, 2023. https://X.com/jconorgrogan/status/1620439556750462976.

@mutCarolineDAO. "X profile." X, Accessed August 20, 2024. https://X.com/mutcarolinedao?lang=en.

Bekiempis, Victoria, and Anguiano, Dani. "Caroline Ellison says she felt 'relief not to have to lie any more' after FTX collapse." *The Guardian*, October 12, 2023. https://www.theguardian.com/business/2023/oct/11/caroline-ellison-testimony-sam-bankman-fried-trial

Cole, Samantha. "Simps Are Organizing to Worship Women with Their Crypto." *Vice*, January 20, 2022. https://www.vice.com/en/article/m7v34p/simp-daos-irenedao-belledaophine-elondao-pokidao.

Jenkinson, Gareth. "Alameda Had 'Unfair' Trading Advantage,

Special Access to FTX Funds: CFTC Filing." *Cointelegraph*, December 14, 2022. https://cointelegraph.com/news/alameda-had-unfair-trading-advantage-special-access-to-ftx-funds-cftc-filing.

De, Nikhilesh, and Nelson, Danny. "Binance Founder Changpeng Zhao Gets 4 Months in Prison." *CoinDesk*, April 30, 2024. https://www.coindesk.com/policy/2024/04/30/binance-founder-changpeng-zhao-to-appear-in-court-today-for-sentencing/.

United States District Court for the Southern District of New York. Superseding Indictment against Samuel Bankman-Fried. Case No. 1:22-cr-00673-LAK. Filed June 27, 2023. https://casetext.com/case/united-states-v-bankman-fried-20.

Elliott, Stacy. "Alameda Allegedly Traded These 18 Tokens on Insider Info through FTX." *Decrypt*, November 15, 2022. https://decrypt.co/114708/alameda-research-18-tokens-insider-info-ftx.

Rice, Jon. "Did CZ Really Have Any Intention of Buying FTX?" Blockworks. November 10, 2022. https://blockworks.co/news/did-cz-really-have-any-intention-of-buying-ftx.

@cz_binance. "5. "SBF vs CZ: The Epic Showdown….." X, December 6, 2022. https://X.com/cz_binance/status/1600083626179207168.

Chapter 10: $6.4 billion of free magic internet money: Uniswap and the airdrop revolution

Fitriansyah, Yudhisitra. "The History of Defi Summer - Minority Programmers". Medium. June 1, 2021. https://medium.com/minority-programmers/the-history-of-defi-summer-92b6ef6736bd.

Florant, Aria, Julien, J.P., Stewart, Shelley, Yancy, Nina, and Wright, Jason. "The Case for Accelerating Financial Inclusion in Black Communities" McKinsey. February 25, 2020. https://www.mckinsey.com/industries/social-sector/our-insights/

the-case-for-accelerating-financial-inclusion-in-black-communities.

Herrera, Edmond. "What Was 'DeFi Summer'?" Blockzeit. November 2, 2022. https://blockzeit.com/what-was-defi-summer/.

Surz, Ron. "Money Printing and Inflation: COVID, Cryptocurrencies and More." *Nasdaq*, November 16, 2021. https://www.nasdaq.com/articles/money-printing-and-inflation%3A-covid-cryptocurrencies-and-more.

Nassr, Iota. "From 'DeFi Summer' to 'Crypto Winter': Leverage, Liquidations and Policy Implications." On the Level. January 31, 2022. https://www.oecd.org/en/blogs/2022/01/from-defi-summer-to-crypto-winter-leverage-liquidations-and-policy-implications.html.

@OpanyRichard. "Thanks u, I used the coins to buy myself a goat during this Easter". X, April 1, 2024. https://x.com/OpanyRichard/status/1775899022324342854

@OpanyRichard. "Actually I have the goat house…". X, April 5, 2024. https://x.com/OpanyRichard/status/1774741973389148252

@open4profit. "JUP airdrop was so unfair….". X, February 3, 2024. https://x.com/OpanyRichard/status/1775899022324342854

"Introducing UNI." 2020. Uniswap Protocol (blog) September 16, 2020. https://blog.uniswap.org/uni.

Jhackworth. "The Uniswap Airdrop – Lessons for the Industry". Dune. November 23, 2022. https://dune.com/blog/uni-airdrop-analysis

Case, Michael. "Auroracoin Already Third-Biggest Cryptocoin—And It's Not Even Out Yet." *Wall Street Journal*, March 5, 2014. https://www.wsj.com/articles/BL-MBB-17512

ENDNOTES

Chapter 1: The Rise of Shitcoins

1   https://www.reddit.com/r/SatoshiStreetBets/comments/o4fimb/the_safemoonsqueeze_has_begun/

Chapter 2: The Million Dollar Photo of a Rock: NFTs

2   https://allquantor.at/blockchainbib/pdf/rosenfeld-2012overview.pdf

3   https://www.vice.com/en/article/someone-sold-a-dollar1m-clipart-rock-nft-for-under-a-penny-by-mistake/

4   https://dappgambl.com/nfts/dead-nfts/

Chapter 3: The $450 Million Dollar Lost Password

5   https://www.coindesk.com/consensus-magazine/2023/06/09/where-the-mt-gox-money-went-new-details-in-the-btc-e-exchange-case/

6   https://www.nytimes.com/2021/01/12/technology/bitcoin-passwords-wallets-fortunes.html

7   https://vanguard-x.com/blockchain/lost-millions-in-bitcoin/

8   https://www.reddit.com/r/Bitcoin/comments/36vnmr/heres_what_satoshi_wrote_to_the_man_responsible/

9   https://www.pwc.com/gx/en/financial-services/pdf/el-salvadors-law-a-meaningful-test-for-bitcoin.pdf

Chapter 4: How a Dog Meme Became Worth More Than the GDP of Sri Lanka

10   https://99bitcoins.com/bitcoin-obituaries/

11   https://www.businessofapps.com/data/binance-statistics/
12   https://www.cointree.com/learn/what-is-dogecoin/
13   https://junkee.com/an-interview-with-the-inventor-of-doge-coin-the-internets-favourite-new-currency/27411
14   https://www.businessinsider.com/what-is-dogecoin-2013-12
15   https://www.coindesk.com/markets/2015/04/24/doge-coin-founder-exits-crypto-community-citing-toxic-culture/
16   https://decrypt.co/97015/elon-musk-dogecoin-bitcoin-tweets-crypto-twitter-timeline
17   https://triple-a.io/crypto-ownership-data/
18   https://thesocialshepherd.com/blog/twitter-statistics#
19   https://www.nytimes.com/2022/04/16/business/elon-musk-politics-twitter.html
20   https://www.reuters.com/article/crypto-currency-bit-coin-musk-idCNL1N2N027X
21   https://www.coinbase.com/price/dogecoin
22   https://www.reddit.com/r/dogecoin/comments/mrsx8e/hey_guys_i_just_became_a_dogecoin_millionaire/
23   https://www.reddit.com/r/dogecoin/comments/mrsx8e/hey_guys_i_just_became_a_dogecoin_millionaire/
24   https://finbold.com/there-are-now-over-1000-doge-made-millionaires-after-dogecoin-price-skyrockets/
25   https://www.coinbase.com/price/dogecoin
26   https://www.axios.com/2022/04/15/elon-musk-asperg-ers-syndrome#
27   https://www.cnbc.com/2022/01/14/dogecoin-jumps-after-elon-musk-says-its-can-be-used-buy-tesla-merch.html
28   https://www.newsweek.com/dogecoin-millionaire-crypto-currency-price-crash-bitcoin-17174
29   https://www.reuters.com/markets/us/elon-musk-258-bil-lion-dogecoin-lawsuit-expands-2022-09-07/
30   https://www.binance.com/en/feed/post/385461
31   https://www.binance.com/en/feed/post/385461
32   https://www.analyticsinsight.net/dogecoin-killer-shiba-inu-

has-failed-here-is-why-dogeliens-can-take-its-place-in-2023/

33 https://docs.shibatoken.com/shibaswap/shibaswap-functionality/swap

34 https://www.forbes.com/advisor/in/investing/cryptocurrency/what-is-floki-inu/#

35 Tesla Owners Silicon Valley (@teslaownersSV), "Dogecoin was invented as a joke and yet fate loves irony," Twitter (now X), April 5, 2023, https://twitter.com/teslaownersSV/status/1643339912866045952.

Chapter 5: The $65-Billion-dollar Question: Who is Satoshi Nakamoto?

36 https://en.wikipedia.org/wiki/Satoshi_Nakamoto

37 https://bitcoin.org/bitcoin.pdf

38 https://en.wikipedia.org/wiki/Satoshi_Nakamoto

39 https://www.banklesstimes.com/how-many-bitcoins-does-satoshi-nakamoto-have/

40 https://blog.bitmex.com/satoshis-1-million-bitcoin/

41 https://www.forbes.com/billionaires/

42 https://bitcoin.org/bitcoin.pdf

43 https://www.pbs.org/newshour/economy/bank-to-pay-31m-for-avoiding-mortgages-to-minorities-largest-such-settlement-in-u-s-history

44 https://www.worldbank.org/en/news/feature/2022/07/21/covid-19-boosted-the-adoption-of-digital-financial-services

45 https://fintechmagazine.com/articles/crypto-regulations-and-building-financial-inclusion

46 https://www.mail-archive.com/cryptography@metzdowd.com/msg10152.html

47 https://bitcointalk.org/index.php?action=profile;u=3

48 https://bitcointalk.org/index.php?action=profile;u=3;sa=showPosts

49 https://plan99.net/~mike/satoshi-emails/thread5.html

50 https://bitcointalk.org/index.php?topic=175996.ms-

g1832533#msg1832533

51   https://blog.bitmex.com/satoshis-1-million-bitcoin/

52   https://www.newyorker.com/magazine/2011/10/10/
      the-crypto-currency

53   Amir Taaki (@Narodism), "Here's an interview with @jgar-
      zik who was an early core Bitcoin dev. He's an expert who
      came from writing Linux kernel code. He explains what I'm
      saying above. We both deduced this ourselves. My person-
      al hunch is that Satoshi spent a long time thinking about
      Bitcoin. Then he," October 12, 2024, https://x.com/Naro-
      dism/status/1844774934326772026

54   https://www.newsweek.com/2014/03/14/face-behind-bit-
      coin-247957.html

55   https://www.newsweek.com/2014/03/14/face-behind-bit-
      coin-247957.html

56   https://www.newsweek.com/2014/03/14/face-behind-bit-
      coin-247957.html

57   https://www.newsweek.com/2014/03/14/face-behind-bit-
      coin-247957.html

58   https://web.archive.org/web/20140319123716/http://
      www.forbes.com/sites/matthewherper/2014/03/10/data-
      analysis-says-newsweek-named-the-wrong-man-as-bitcoins-
      creator/

59   https://web.archive.org/web/20140319123716/http://
      www.forbes.com/sites/matthewherper/2014/03/10/data-
      analysis-says-newsweek-named-the-wrong-man-as-bitcoins-
      creator/

60   https://web.archive.org/web/20140319123716/http://
      www.forbes.com/sites/matthewherper/2014/03/10/data-
      analysis-says-newsweek-named-the-wrong-man-as-bitcoins-
      creator/

61   https://www.coindesk.com/markets/2021/08/31/rare-
      pepe-steeped-in-bitcoin-history-fetches-500k-on-nft-market-
      opensea/

62   http://www.hit.bme.hu/~buttyan/courses/BMEVI-HIM219/2009/Chaum.BlindSigForPayment.1982.PDF

63   https://www.wired.com/2014/08/hal-finney/

64   https://www.investopedia.com/terms/s/satoshi-nakamoto.asp

65   Documenting Bitcoin (@Documenting BTC), "The #bitcoin whitepaper appears to be hidden in every Apple Mac computer running macOS Catalina or newer," April 6, 2023, https://twitter.com/DocumentingBTC/status/1643760765814358018

66   https://bitkan.com/learn/what-is-satoshi-last-message-to-the-world-9415#

67   https://en.wikipedia.org/wiki/Nick_Szabo#cite_note-21

68   https://www.coindesk.com/markets/2014/04/16/linguistic-researchers-name-nick-szabo-as-author-of-bitcoin-whitepaper/

69   https://www.wired.com/2015/12/bitcoins-creator-satoshi-nakamoto-is-probably-this-unknown-australian-genius/

70   https://www.coindesk.com/policy/2024/03/14/craig-wright-not-satoshi-didnt-author-bitcoin-whitepaper-judge-rules/

71   https://news.bitcoin.com/the-many-facts-pointing-to-cypherpunk-len-sassaman-being-satoshi-nakamoto/

Chapter 6: How a Group of Internet Strangers Nearly Bought the US Constitution – the Story of DAOs

72   https://softwareengineeringdaily.com/2018/03/23/dao-reflections-and-slock-it-with-christoph-jentzsch/

73   https://www.cnbc.com/2016/05/17/automated-company-raises-equivalent-of-120-million-in-digital-currency.html

74   https://superrare.com/magazine/2021/11/17/the-history-of-the-dao/

75   https://www.economist.com/finance-and-economics/2016/05/19/the-dao-of-accrue

76   https://softwareengineeringdaily.com/2018/03/23/dao-re-flections-and-slock-it-with-christoph-jentzsch/

77   https://cointelegraph.com/magazine/griff-green-doge-loving-hippy-hacker-steals-crypto-before-bad-guys-can/

78   https://decrypt.co/93547/crypto-ceo-denies-11-billion-ethereum-dao-hack

79   https://www.nytimes.com/2016/06/18/business/dealbook/hacker-may-have-removed-more-than-50-million-from-experimental-cybercurrency-project.html

80   SE Daily, "DAO Reflections and Slock.it with Christoph Jentzsch," Software Engineering Daily podcast, March 23, 2018, 41 min, https://softwareengineeringdaily.com/2018/03/23/dao-reflections-and-slock-it-with-christoph-jentzsch/

81   https://moneymade.io/learn/article/best-dao-projects

82   Graham Novak, personal interview with the author, January 3, 2024.

83   https://edition.cnn.com/style/article/us-constitution-sothebys-sale/index.html

84   https://www.theverge.com/22820563/constitution-meme-47-million-crypto-crowdfunding-blockchain-ethereum-constitution

85   Graham Novak, personal interview with the author, January 3, 2024.

86   https://en.wikipedia.org/wiki/Martin_Shkreli

87   https://en.wikipedia.org/wiki/Edward_Snowden

88   https://iq.wiki/wiki/pleasrdao

89   https://finance.yahoo.com/news/dao-trying-buy-us-constitution-201444374.html

90   https://unumdao.org/

Chapter 7: How One web3 Game was Played by 2% of the Philippines for a Living

91   Assumptions here. Adult population of the Philippines is 68.43M. Peak MAU was 2.8M. Assume 50% from the Philip-

pines.

92   https://www.dexerto.com/world-of-warcraft/how-many-people-play-world-of-warcraft-wow-player-count-population-tracker-1842964/

93   https://www.bbc.com/news/technology-42237162

94   https://playercounter.com/axie-infinity/

95   https://www.youtube.com/watch?v=Yo-BrASMHU4&ab_channel=PLAY-TO-EARN

96   https://www.youtube.com/watch?v=Yo-BrASMHU4&ab_channel=PLAY-TO-EARN

97   https://www.youtube.com/watch?v=Yo-BrASMHU4&ab_channel=PLAY-TO-EARN

98   https://therecord.media/more-than-30-million-seized-from-north-korean-hackers-involved-in-axie-crypto-theft

99   https://www.coindesk.com/layer2/2022/04/07/how-the-play-to-earn-industry-can-rebuild-better-after-the-ronin-attack/

Chapter 8: How a $40 Billion Cryptocurrency Went to Zero in 72 Hours: The Collapse of Luna

100   https://koreajoongangdaily.joins.com/2022/05/20/business/finance/korea-terraform-labs-Luna/20220520144215830.html

101   https://www.youtube.com/watch?v=5g9ycHS0xtU&ab_channel=Coinage

102   https://icodrops.com/terra/

103   https://icodrops.com/terra/

104   https://u.today/terra-Luna-collapse-predicted-4-years-ago-check-out-this-visionary-statement

105   https://www.youtube.com/watch?v=5g9ycHS0xtU&ab_channel=Coinage

106   https://www.theverge.com/2022/5/20/23131647/terra-Luna-do-kwon-stablecoin-anchor

107   https://cointelegraph.com/news/terra-injects-450m-ust-in-

to-anchor-reserve-days-before-protocol-depletion

108   https://www.coindesk.com/markets/2022/03/28/mar-ket-wrap-bitcoin-rallies-as-crypto-holders-accumulate/

109   https://cointelegraph.com/news/Luna-foundation-guard-purchases-additional-37-863-btc-as-part-of-reserve-strategy

110   https://cointelegraph.com/news/Luna-foundation-guard-purchases-additional-37-863-btc-as-part-of-reserve-strategy

111   https://www.coinbase.com/price/terra-Luna

112   https://www.sec.gov/litigation/complaints/2023/comp-pr2023-32.pdf

113   https://www.sec.gov/litigation/complaints/2023/comp-pr2023-32.pdf

114   https://decrypt.co/98482/we-need-to-talk-about-terras-anchor

115   https://www.forbes.com/sites/qai/2022/09/20/what-really-happened-to-Luna-crypto/?sh=10eb9ef24ff1

116   https://www.tradingview.com/symbols/LUNAUSD/history-timeline/#dark-side-of-the-moon-2022-05-10

117   https://t.co/P3g2WbLh4h

118   https://www.tradingview.com/symbols/LUNAUSD/history-timeline/#a-terrable-end-2022-05-13

119   https://inneractions.net/what-happened-to-terra-Luna/

120   https://www.reddit.com/r/terraLuna/comments/un40h4/my_excolleague_attempted_suicide/

121   https://forkast.news/do-kwon-terra-Luna-what-happened-montenegro/

122   https://www.taiwannews.com.tw/en/news/4551502

123   https://forkast.news/do-kwon-terra-Luna-what-happened-montenegro/

124   https://twitter.com/stablekwon/status/1526258273820651520

125   https://www.euronews.com/next/2022/08/15/terra-Luna-crash-i-alone-am-responsible-says-ceo-do-kwon-in-first-interview-since-collapse

126 https://forkast.news/do-kwon-terra-Luna-what-hap-
pened-montenegro/

127 https://www.bbc.com/news/technology-65058533

128 https://www.bbc.com/news/technology-65058533

Chapter 9: How to Go from $26 Billion to $0: The Downfall of Sam Bankman-Fried and FTX

129 https://thepavlovictoday.com/kevin-oleary-interview-the-
dagger-that-finished-sam-bankman-fried-off/

130 https://www.businessinsider.com/sam-bankman-fried-sbf-
bahamas-mansion-penthouse-condo-photos-2023-10#

131 https://www.dlnews.com/articles/people-culture/who-is-al-
ameda-co-founder-and-sbf-critic-tara-mac-aulay/

132 https://www.businessinsider.com/caroline-ellison-took-
blind-leap-join-fast-paced-ftx-2022-11

133 https://www.cnbc.com/2022/08/20/ftx-grew-revenue-
1000percent-during-the-crypto-craze-leaked-financials.html

134 https://www.businessinsider.com/ftx-sam-bankman-fried-
league-of-legends-investor-pitch-meeting-2022-11

135 Alex Valaitis (@alex_valaitis), "However, CZ is not going
down without a fight. And he recently got the opening he
needed to strike back," Twitter (now X), November 8, 2022,
https://twitter.com/alex_valaitis/status/1589711051901538
304?lang=en

136 Alex Valaitis (@alex_valaitis), "However, CZ is not going
down without a fight. And he recently got the opening he
needed to strike back," Twitter (now X), November 8, 2022,
https://twitter.com/alex_valaitis/status/1589711051901538
304?lang=en

137 https://time.com/7006739/sam-bankman-fried-cryptoma-
nia-excerpt/

138 https://www.businessinsider.com/sam-bankman-fried-
drug-use-ftx-alameda-caroline-ellison-amphetamines-2022-
11#https://crypto.news/sam-bankman-fried-alleged-
ly-used-antipsychotic-medications-at-ftx/

139   https://slate.com/technology/2022/12/sam-bank-man-fried-ftx-emsam-patch-testimony-arrested.html

140   https://nypost.com/2022/11/30/ftxs-sam-bankman-fried-fumed-over-media-spotlight-on-polyamorous-sex-life/

141   https://www.nansen.ai/research/blockchain-analysis-the-collapse-of-alameda-and-ftx

142   https://coinmarketcap.com/currencies/ftx-token/

143   https://coinmarketcap.com/currencies/ftx-token/

144   https://www.afr.com/wealth/investing/how-bankman-fried-blurred-lines-between-ftx-and-alameda-20221205-p5c3nn

145   https://abcnews.go.com/Business/timeline-cryptocurrency-exchange-ftxs-historic-collapse/story?id=93337035

146   https://www.theguardian.com/technology/2022/nov/08/binance-to-buy-ftx-in-major-cryptocurrency-exchange-merger

147   Sequoia Capital (@sequoia), "Here is the note we sent to our LPs in GGFIII regarding FTX," Twitter (now X), November 10, 2022, https://twitter.com/sequoia/status/1590522718650499073

148   https://www.businessinsider.com/ftx-told-chamath-palihapitiya-social-capital-go-fuck-yourself-recommendations-2022-11

149   https://www.businessinsider.com/ftx-told-chamath-palihapitiya-social-capital-go-fuck-yourself-recommendations-2022-11

150   https://www.businessinsider.com/ftx-told-chamath-palihapitiya-social-capital-go-fuck-yourself-recommendations-2022-11

151   https://www.businessinsider.com/ftx-told-chamath-palihapitiya-social-capital-go-fuck-yourself-recommendations-2022-11

152   https://www.usatoday.com/story/tech/2022/12/13/ftx-founder-sam-bankman-fried-arrest-indictment/10888749002/

153   https://storage.courtlistener.com/recap/gov.uscourts.
      nysd.590940/gov.uscourts.nysd.590940.80.0.pdf
154   https://www.cnbc.com/2023/02/23/ftx-founder-sam-bank-
      man-fried-hit-with-new-criminal-charges.html
155   https://www.documentcloud.org/documents/23310507-ftx-
      bankruptcy-filing-john-j-ray-iii
156   https://www.cumrocket.io/
157   https://blockchain.news/wiki/what-is-tendies-tend
158   https://twitter.com/mutcarolinedao?lang=en
159   https://edition.cnn.com/2021/02/19/health/what-is-simp-
      teen-slang-wellness/index.html#
160   https://www.vice.com/en/article/m7v34p/simp-daos-ire-
      nedao-belledaophine-elondao-pokidao
161   https://www.theguardian.com/business/2023/oct/11/caro-
      line-ellison-testimony-sam-bankman-fried-trial
162   https://cointelegraph.com/news/sam-bankman-fried-main-
      tains-innocence-trades-jail-rice-awaiting-appeal
163   https://blockworks.co/news/did-cz-really-have-any-inten-
      tion-of-buying-ftx
164   https://www.coindesk.com/policy/2024/04/30/binance-
      founder-changpeng-zhao-to-appear-in-court-today-for-sen-
      tencing/

Chapter 10: $6.4 Billion of Free Magic Money: Uniswap and the Airdrop Revolution

165   https://www.mckinsey.com/industries/public-and-so-
      cial-sector/our-insights/the-case-for-accelerating-finan-
      cial-inclusion-in-black-communities